Beyond the Broken Gate

AN ORDINARY MAN'S EXTRAORDINARY
JOURNEY IN LEARNING WHO WE ARE,
WHY WE LIVE, AND WHERE WE'RE GOING

Serenity Hill
Press

CHARLES
GRAYBAR

Beyond the Broken Gate

ISBN: 0-9740265-2-2

First Edition, Second Printing 2003

Published by: Serenity Hill Press, Inc.

P.O. Box 8130
Rolling Meadows, IL 60008

E-Mail: info@serenityhillpress.com
Web: www.serenityhillpress.com

Book design & production: Weblinx, Inc.
Cover graphics: Weblinx, Inc.

ACKNOWLEDGEMENTS

No work of this kind can ever make it into final form without the support and encouragement of many people. In that spirit, my undying appreciation, gratitude and love go out to: Susan W. for never – ever allowing me to quit. To Catherine and David who pushed, pulled and thankfully, dragged me across the finish line with their ceaseless encouragement and kind words.

For Harribear, who, through the shining of his spirit and the relentless pursuit of his dreams has shown me that anything we truly focus on and hold in our hearts can be accomplished.

To Jessie, Jenny, Jake, Schuster, Annabelle and Emily who selflessly relinquished their time so that I could write and share the wisdom of Kalista with those that wanted to hear it.

For Mom & in memory of Dad who took in an orphan and had the kindness, wisdom, patience and love to let me pursue my own path in this life leading to wherever it did.

To Jojo, whose love never ceases, whose support never wanes and whose eyes shine that much brighter every day as she helps all others that she reaches out to. No better partner could be found. No higher honesty, from anyone, could be wanted. No greater love – in this world – could be conceived of.

In loving memory of Buddy the Bear, who kept my feet warm and my soul aglow as I wrote.

THE JOURNEY BEGINS...

In August 1993, I had reached a crucial point of frustration in my life. I had progressed as far as I ever cared to in the corporate world. At age forty, I was a corporate officer in a Fortune 100 company and sat on several corporate boards of directors. I had already acquired most of the material things that I could want, and was in a place where they no longer did anything for me. I gave up my attachment to them. Life, though, seemed inordinately empty. Hollow. Close to purposeless.

This wasn't routine mid-life crisis blues. I wasn't particularly concerned or focused on my mortality. My frustration had everything to do with a certainty within me, that I had yet to even vaguely grasp the reasons that I even made the effort to exist every day. I recall driving to work one day thinking, "It can't possibly be for this; it can't be just to have a great car, a nice house, eat, sleep and be merry... can't be." I spent one day sitting by the ocean watching the waves roll in and reflecting on the irrefutable fact that, no matter what we do in this life, when we're done, when we leave here, we depart with the sum total of our actions and our learning. And only that. All the rest; they are simply props in the play. Leased for a period not to exceed your lifetime.

I also pondered the naysayers who proclaim that when we leave here we simply depart into timeless oblivion. That thought was even more depressing and, something inside of me just knew that was wrong.

If there was a purpose, I couldn't see it, which carried with it a profound emptiness. This didn't seem to bother others at all, which completely mystified me. Worse, it felt as though many of those

1

around me knew something that I was struggling, but failing, to learn. It felt as though others had found some hidden key to fulfillment in life. They were tolerating it, if not actually experiencing happiness and contentment and meaning. At that time in my life, I had come to the depressing conclusion that there was little, if any, real deep purpose in life or, if there was, that I wasn't going to find out what it was. Ever.

A few weeks later, my contemplations led me to a state of mind where I began passively empathizing with those who choose to leave this world voluntarily. I reasoned they believed they could only find answers elsewhere, and that the pain of feeling as though one is without meaningful purpose is simply too great to tolerate. The prospect of a meaningless life followed by a meaningless eternity drove me to search for some answers. I had become determined. Focused.

Starting at the age of fourteen, I had voraciously consumed every book, article and other source of information dealing with the spiritual realm that I could get my hands on. I didn't know what drove me back then. Later on, I endeavored to leave no stone unturned and, starting sometime in my early thirties, I resorted to immersing myself in audio tapes while driving from one place to the other, listening to every topic imaginable, from Taoism to Buddhism to Past Life Regression. I even went through a period where I had almost convinced myself that the answers had been discovered long ago and since forgotten, so I began exploring everything from the Jaines to the Toltecs. In a near desperate effort to find even a semblance of true meaning, I went through a phase where I even toyed with true "fringe" material – Atlantis and even further out than that. Stuff that probably should carry a warning not to listen to, or even think about, while operating a motor vehicle. Looking back, it had become absolutely clear to me at about that point that I was supposed to be doing "something," to recollect some mission directives or execute some plan of action with my life. I had no specific frame of reference as to what it was I was trying to recall. None. The more I read, the further away I actually felt from attaining my objective, which I could only loosely define as "enlightenment." Worse yet, I felt as though I was absolutely alone in my quest. I had in some panicked portion of my mind that virtually everyone else in the world either already knew their "assignment" or, as with some that I had come across it in my travels, they simply didn't care. As the summer of 1993 came to an end, I had never felt more alone in my life.

I began asking friends whom I believed to be more or less spiritually open-minded, if not very well informed, about their insights and their understanding of our purpose here in this world. "Why do we live?," I would blurt out after barely getting past hello. "What the hell are we doing here?" "For god's sake, tell me what you think... even if it's wrong!"My theory was that if I asked enough intelligent, spiritually inquisitive people the essential questions that had been gnawing at me for more than two decades, then sooner or later I could assemble a composite view of the essential issues. I idealized that I might even come across a few answers. Instead, I ended up aggregating an ever-growing list of questions, as it became clearer to me that, pretty much everyone is mystified by these essential questions. Those that say they aren't are just in denial.

A few of the well-read people that I had questioned mentioned that there was some fascinating work being done in the area of deep regression hypnosis, including Past Life Regression therapy/investigation. This, for want of a more accurate description, involves temporarily altering a person's basic awareness state by inducing a hypnotic-like process. This affords the subject access to a deeper focus on information that is already there within the existing subconscious memory, even going back into previous lifetimes. The work of Dr. Brian Weiss and others in the field provided me portions of the essential, basic first steps for the journey that I was about to embark upon.

Based on the description of the regression processes being used by Dr. Weiss and others in the fields of regression and meditation, I began experimenting with a meditative process. I placed myself into a state of deep relaxation and acute awareness that had many similarities – but also dissimilarities – to regression states. Over the course of time, through trial and experimentation, I refined the process further until I finally attained a state where I ostensibly suspended myself at the extreme outer edges of consciousness. In this state I was still able to maintain contact with my normal state of awareness. I had no expectations when I began the practice, just to attain deep states of relaxation that would approximate, or potentially exceed, those achieved in meditation, something I had already practiced for several years.

In mid October 1993, while in a state of self-induced deep meditation, I had an experience that, in normal conscious terminology, would have been characterized as an exchange of "dialogue" with what I could only construe at the time was some form of spiritual entity. It wasn't God and it wasn't Jesus Christ. My belief system at the time would not have allowed for those possibilities. After regaining my bearings from this meditative state, I jotted down brief notes and dismissed the entire event as being an unusual dream state, irrespective of how interesting and insightful the content of that exchange might have been.

As curiosity gnawed away at me, I engineered a similar meditative state and discovered, over time, that I was able to reengineer this "connection" with some degree of consistency. I learned, over the course of time, that the spiritual being with whom I was communicating was a deeply advanced soul with significantly greater states of learning than most had achieved thus far – a spirit guide or a form of ascended master. I learned that this spirit guide also served as a formal advisor on my "soul counsel." This is a learned body comprised mostly of disincarnate souls that provides guidance and advice to us at various stages in our existence continuum, including that time when we are between lives and in the process of planning our next lifetime.

It also became clear over the course of my interactions that any of us can communicate – if we open ourselves to the connection – with these advanced souls in our current state of incarnation. There is no doubt in my mind that every person or soul on Earth also has a soul counsel that guides and provides insights to them between lifetimes. And that they too can communicate with their soul advisors in this life, if they choose.

The meditative state that I access to achieve this connection is just that and not a "trance" per se. While there have been other spiritual investigators that claim to have attained distantly similar states using psychotropic substances, I have opted not to use any drug to achieve this state. This was the only choice for me to assure that the communication was valid in every respect and not in any way attributable to outside influences or substances.

At the very earliest stages of these experiences, I thought for a long time about how likely it was that the information that was flowing to me was "real" and not, as one friend stated, "the product of a man on a mission to find answers." The trouble with this theory was that the "answers" and insights I was getting didn't correlate with my own thinking. Neither were they very reflective of any single or even composite of the belief systems I had already studied. The insights that were flowing to me were far too original, creative and simply made sense in the grand scheme of things for me to have assembled them, even subconsciously. The underlying view that was shared with me illustrated the prevailing conditions of our existence as conscious beings. Other stunning realities of the universe that were shared described an image of reality that was permeated with an incredibly purified form of compassion and depth of love that I had not been fortunate enough to have learned, much less contemplated, at that point in my life.

There was real cogency to the message that was coming through to me. The fabric being described included the nature of existence, why we live, and where we're going when we leave this Earth. Also, many more of the questions that we seek answers to were being revealed in a way that described a tapestry that only a true master could possibly conceive of, much less actually weave. What was shared with me was a deeper understanding of the work of the Source/God and those responsible for maintaining the mechanism of the universe than I had ever even vaguely contemplated.

It also became clear early on in my interactions that I was only seeing the next level, or possibly two, of detail. There was more that was not disclosed yet. Simply put, the insights that were being shared with me were far beyond my knowledge and abilities to construct and, in some cases, even to comprehend the first time or two they were explained to me.

The first advanced soul that communicated with me calls herself Kalista. This is as close to writing her name as I can come. In the actual experience of communication, when she expresses her name, it is

more the imparting of a thought/idea than it is "speaking" information. Thus, "Kalista" is barely an approximation of the impression that
I receive of her "name." I also communicated with – although with far
less frequency – two other advanced discarnate souls. Geradl, a male
personality and, based upon my observations, a genuine superior
ascended master with knowledge above and beyond Kalista's. The
other advanced soul, Tresden, is seemingly a female personality, but
quite androgynous in both appearance and conduct most of the time.
I am given to understand that Tresden is more or less an understudy
to Kalista, although still an advanced soul him/herself.

As I have come to understand, both Geradl (pronounced: Ger ah'
dull) and Tresden (pronounced: Trez' din) are also a part of my soul
counsel, although they have made it clear to me that Kalista is pri-
marily responsible for helping to guide me. When I am able to attain
the proper meditative state, my initial communication is always with
Kalista. Tresden comes only when Kalista needs him/her. Geradl
appears very rarely, although I often have the impression that he is
sometimes "watching" from just beyond my scope of perception. He
arrives and departs when he chooses. Both Kalista and Tresden are
extremely respectful (but clearly not fearful) of Geradl.

All three, as I have come to understand by way of observation and
interaction over the last ten years, have clear and well-defined personalities that I discuss in greater detail in the following chapters. All
three of these advanced souls have spent lifetimes on Earth at one period or another in recent history. Of particular interest to me was the
fact that Kalista, Tresden and Geradl all claim to have had fairly basic,
uneventful and low profile existences while last incarnated on Earth.
None of them ever laid claim to being anyone worthy of significance
in history.

As to the form and substance of the communication that I experience with Kalista, Geradl and Tresden, it is both accurate and inaccurate to say that I have "conversations" with them. There is an
exchange of communication. But, due to the unusual hybrid form of
communication used in this state of perception, I do not experience
the exchange as routine dialogue. In many cases, I experience it similarly and, after giving the matter great thought, have chosen written

dialogue to share some of the insights that they have conveyed to me.

In very rare instances, I have asked for something to be explained in some other way, as I was unable to comprehend the explanation the first time in the manner it was given. In those cases though, it was not the communication that failed, but my ability to comprehend some advanced concept that was being shared with me. It is a form of absolute and immutably concise communication that was completely foreign to me at the outset of my interactions in this realm yet never once created any obstacle to our communication. I simply "know" what has been "said" in my communications with these three advanced souls with the same degree of confidence that you know that you are reading these words.

Upon coming out of a deep meditative state, I usually attempt to immediately write notes so that I can endeavor to reconstruct the "conversation" as best as I can. I have found it equally beneficial to draw diagrams or crude illustrations that serve as prompts for me to later reconstruct the essence of what was communicated in a session. The substance of those notes and drawings accumulated over the years were consolidated into a notebook in mid-1999. This notebook has served as my primary reference material for this book.

On a few occasions, I have been unable to convert the substance of an exchange with Kalista into reasonably cogent thoughts. Those specific experiences were of such overwhelming impact and dynamics, that they defied my ability to come up with words, drawings or even notions that might describe the experience. Still, in those instances, I am usually able to recollect the conceptual thrust of what was conveyed and am careful to describe only the essence of what was experienced without embellishment. Over the course of ten years of these experiences, I have come to accept that I either know what was conveyed, or surrender to the reality that I do not know or that the experience can not be adequately described. Certain things can only be experienced and simply defy anything but elliptical articulation.

This book includes some of the major insights that were shared with me dating from October 1993 with respect to some of the earliest spiritually-related questions that had been plaguing me then and, to a significantly lesser degree, since.

Some friends have told me that I have an obligation to share what I have learned with those that might have an interest in this material. Others have said that the insights were given privately and are probably intended to stay that way. My internal debate about whether I should even write this material down went on for almost 10 years before I finally decided to share what I had learned. I never had any illusions about this material changing or saving the world. At best, I believed that some readers might take the insights shared here and integrate them into their own belief system with the hope of gaining, to some degree, what I got from them: an unending, ever-expanding sense of inner peace, tranquility and happiness. The security of knowing that there is a reason for all things and all events in life, even if we cannot comprehend those reasons immediately. No matter where one starts – or how deeply in a pit one happens to be at any particular moment in life – there is a way out along a pathway to almost unimaginable happiness and well-being. And far, far more than that.

Whether those seeking answers to many of life's most essential questions will find solace in the bottomless wisdom shared by Kalista, Tresden and Geradl will be determined only in the fullness of time. Clearly that is my greatest desire. At a minimum, my hope is that what I have learned might serve as a springboard for other thinking of your own on these subjects. Such an outcome would be an end well worth the effort of writing all of this down.

To those pursuing the greatest mystery and highest mission of all – the search for the true meaning and purpose of this life while walking the pathway that leads to a deeper understanding of our eternal purpose as souls – I wish for you a peaceful, loving, miraculous and enlightening journey.

CHARLES GRAYBAR

CHAPTER ONE

This is not the end,
this is not the beginning.
This is not the beginning of the end.
It is, the end of the beginning.

- Anon.

If we're fortunate to live long enough, I mused in the laziness that often accompanies hazy summer afternoons, the things we really seek will eventually become more clear to us. This was foremost on my mind as I tried aimlessly to concentrate on a new form of meditation I had been experimenting with. Sooner or later, even a dolt like me must be able to sort it all out if I just hang in there. The way things were working out recently, the few spiritual insights that I *thought* I'd had were actually making things a little *less* clear. The harder I tried to understand things, the blurrier they got. Almost in an attempt to provide comfort for my failings, I thought, the mysteries of why we live and what we really are were taken on by the likes of Plato and Einstein and they didn't exactly come away with "the answers" either. Maybe my inability to make headway wasn't so mysterious after all.

Some of the thoughts I had echoing within my mind that afternoon as I strained to get more comfortable and started to sharpen my focus on regressing into a deeper state of calm included:

What is life; is this all a dream; a nightmare? Why do all these terrible things happen in the world all the time?

Why does our mission – our very purpose for living – have to be such a mystery to us? Where is the manual that tells us how to live?

Does God, whatever we might perceive that to be, really have a plan for how and why things are, no matter how disorganized and unfair the world seems to be at times?

Why are happiness and peace of mind always just one step beyond our reach?

Why does everything in life have to be so difficult all the time?

Why do children die?

I could have gone on endlessly, as I often do at night when I'm trying to fall asleep. My version of counting sheep was a self-induced exercise in futility where I traverse my failure to get any traction on the meaning of life and the ways of the world above and beyond the profit and loss mentality that seemed to be the focus of pretty much everyone else. I was disgusted that, after twenty years of seeking answers to such questions, that I didn't know more. The pattern was all too familiar to me; whatever truth I thought I might have seen in some "answer," upon closer examination became just another unanswered question. "If God even exists and is really paying attention, then why did she let Hitler run amok?"

My determination remained steadfast. I'd recently been reading everything that came out about work being done in something called past life regression hypnosis. I was determined to explore and develop a meditation hybrid of my own using parts of that technique. With these questions as my last fully conscious thoughts then, I gradually entered that mysterious state between waking and another reality of the non-ordinary sort. The place where, for a very brief period, it feels as though we are neither here nor there, wherever "there" is. I had read that, under the right circumstances, both the conscious and subconscious mind function fully and are broadly accessible in such a state.

I had hoped that somewhere in the mix of the various consciousness states there was some kind of natural fissure in both realities where we can – if we attain just the right meditative balance – somehow exist at least momentarily, suspended in both states of awareness.

And neither. No one had written anything about that. I wasn't even sure what I might find in such a state. Maybe a few minutes of shelter from the blaring noise that was the daily world. A harbor of sorts in which I could rest in a kind of absolute peace, without surrendering my sensibilities.

But on that particular afternoon, as I gently and gradually slipped further into a deeper and subtler meditative state. I suddenly became aware that I was now perched on a precarious precipice of completely unfamiliar mental acuity. A reality that softly slides our daily world completely out of focus and is temporarily replaced by a totally unfamiliar reality. Yet at the same time, our daily world somehow still echoes vaguely off in the distance. As though it were a dream yet at the same time closer than a dream. And farther. And this other place, shifted into sharper focus from my state of perception. As I fought through the haze of this unfamiliar, deep meditative state, I retained barely enough awareness to recognize what it was. At that very moment I had begun a journey that I was to learn over the next few years had come about only after many, many lifetimes of learning.

✥

From my perspective, the journey began in earnest that afternoon in October, 1993 when I achieved a not so subtle mental awareness that I had succeeded in shifting into a highly unusual state of meditative acuity. This state was overwhelmingly peaceful – on the extreme side of placid – particularly when compared to my usual moderately relaxed meditative state. There was a sharpness to the state I had managed to attain while at the same time, in ways that I couldn't quite understand, the normal day-to-day world somehow remained almost part of the imagery but lost somewhere off in the upper left hand corner of my perception.

I'd been practicing meditation for years, but up until that day, I had never succeeded in reaching such a mysteriously deep, hazy yet acutely conscious place like this. I had been determined to try out some variations on the process of a regression technique called imagery targeting that most of those writing about past life regression were suggesting was among the most effective methods.

At the outset of my efforts, I had been very cautious and modified only to very slight degrees the methods that had been broadly documented in various books and tapes on the topic. As I experimented more aggressively with the techniques, I began to insert some of my own methodology. I moved further and further away from the outlined practices and more aggressively in the direction of a true hybrid of the practice formats that the leading-edge practitioners of regression therapy were using.

To accomplish this objective, I had integrated one part of the standardized imagery targeting regression techniques being used with one part non-focused and one part focused meditation. As such, I was not using mantras as the point of non-concentration. This was particularly difficult since the regression practice that was becoming so well documented in various books was being performed on other people. No one had written about how to regress oneself, much less how to do so while integrating two different types of meditation. I was in deeply uncharted territory and there were no meditative life jackets to carry along the journey.

With practice and intense concentration, I had been able, over the course of several weeks, to attain progressively deeper and deeper states of physical and mental relaxation. This resulted in an almost surrealistic feeling of inner quiet that was of a nature unlike I had been attaining over the years with generalized meditation techniques. More importantly, even at the peak of the deeply relaxed states that I was attaining, I felt as though my conscious faculties were still available to me. Some of the variations I tried allowed me to achieve a level of conscious awareness that felt as though my mental acuity was far higher than my normal state of awareness. Some that I'd read about had used various forms of hallucinogenic compounds such as LSD to boost or attempt this type of process. My commitment was to attain whatever state I might end up using only hybrid meditation.

This particular day, I knew almost immediately that I had reached a state that I had been hoping for. This was because I became aware, subtly at first, that I was able to experience the image that I had been concentrating on in my mind as opposed to imagine that I was in the image. It was as though I had actually entered and become a participant in the scene that I had been envisioning, but without relinquishing the essential control over my conscious awareness. I was able to think and rationalize quite clearly in spite of being in an extremely deep meditative state. From my perspective, one moment I was in a state of tremendous concentration, trying to meditate, and the next, I found myself sitting exactly on the razor-sharp edge of non-ordinary reality that I had sought to achieve. "Now what happens?" I asked myself.

The absolute vividness of the state that I had entered was so acute that my first impression was that I had drifted into a unprecedented, deep dream state. At first I experienced a sense that I was surrounded by – and then drifting within – a near boundless void. Its dimensions were so vast that I felt as though I was tumbling endlessly within an eternity. I found myself trying to define the outer edges of the void with the softer parts of my perception. I vaguely recollect that this void somehow conveyed an eerie sense of non-ordinary reality and that it completely encompassed the image that I had been using as a focus for part of my meditative process.

As this thought entered my consciousness, I had the sharply distinct impression that I heard someone say in a very gentle, almost wispy voice, "It's not a dream but you're not awake, either." I wasn't scared; however, I'm not prone to hearing voices and never had been. Still, I was interested enough to wonder what the source of the voice was and thought at that moment to try to look for it. I attempted to scan the area that I was in with my senses. Nothing. It was only then that I realized that in whatever form of meditative state I had reached, my normally acute senses of sight and sound appeared to be completely useless to me.

My state of awareness was that different from anything that I had ever experienced before. I knew that it wasn't even vaguely any meditative state that I was familiar with. It wasn't a dream-state either. At least none that I had any experience with. Maybe I was having a heart attack or stroke.

I'd read Raymond Moody's and Kenneth Ring's books on near-death experiences and was entertaining the notion that somehow I'd just skipped – or possibly had been unaware of – a few of the early steps in my dying process. I was now about to enter the later stages of the death event. I actually remember scanning the edges of the images, hoping I was able to mentally identify some sign of a tunnel with brilliant light in it. I still retained that level of cognitive awareness. If I could find that, I thought, I would at least know where to go. After what I perceived to be a moderately brief period, I was somehow able to convince myself that I had not died. I was acutely aware that I was having an experience that was not death, but I was also cognizant that the experience was not even vaguely a life experience that I was accustomed to feeling.

"No silly, you're not dead," I heard the voice say, almost lilting. It was an odd dream. How often in a dream do we hear someone tell us that we're not dead and we're not dreaming? I have to admit that I have fallen asleep while meditating. Anyone that meditates will tell you that this happens every now and then no matter how practiced or efficient they have become at meditation. But this did not have the feel of a dream. Nor did it resemble anything that would equate to a hallucination. As I said, I don't do drugs. Then the rest of the surrounding imagery began a gentle yet definitive shift into sharper focus.

My sense of "it" was that the presence that was in proximity to my general area was female in nature. This couldn't be determined from the tonal quality of the voice nor any indications from the still, somewhat nondescript image of a body that was forming in front of me. It was solely that the experience, as it began to unfold in the area around me, afforded a fairly indisputable impression of being a female persona. More significantly though, there was an absolute and overwhelming sense of complete peace and absolute inner security that came over me as the image continued to gather deeper resolution. I had never experienced an inner peace of such an absolute nature in my life and I knew, to a certainty, that it was the being and not the place that was the source of this feeling.

What had been not much more than a poorly defined blur a few moments before now began to resolve itself as a woman. She wore a simple yet elegant soft yellow chiffon dress that flowed to the ground.

She had long, flowing, chestnut colored hair that fell past her shoulders. In my state of perception, the woman appeared to me to be possibly mid thirties and of medium height. There was a single strand of pearls around her delicate neck and a bracelet constructed of some sort of soft metal with a brushed surface, I'd guessed it to be platinum, with a single dark blue or possibly even purple stone partially inset. The gem gave the appearance of emitting a definite, yet subtle glow. I had never seen any similar gem or optical effect quite like it.

The only other remarkable thing that I noted at the time was that I had great difficulty focusing with any consistency on this woman's eyes. They were a greenish hue, close to jade green, but had an endless depth to them. The color was remarkably richer than anything I'd ever seen. Her eyes also had a refractive quality that was, in a word, mystical. Every attempt that I made at focusing directly on her eyes had failed.

Overall, she conveyed the impression of a simple, yet stunning appearance without being what one would think of as fashion model beautiful. She exuded in every sense of the word absolute competence and confidence.

In an attempt to get some perspective, I shifted my attention from the woman to the surroundings. We were in a kind of garden, but the variety, depth and rich color of the foliage was more abundant and unique than my imagination could withstand. Although the lush garden was the image that I had been concentrating on as I entered into meditation, the detail was far greater; much more ornate and beautiful than I could ever imagine. The rich garden was set on a small island in the middle of a small body of water – it was very difficult for me to discern where.

The color of the water, whether it was river or a lake, was the most stunning, vivid shade of aquamarine blue. It wasn't the color as much as a brilliance from the water that made defining it with accuracy impossible. The water seemed to be highlighted with sharp, silver wisps of a magical nature wherever the water happened to be breaking. The sheer intensity and color of the water, as well as everything that surrounded it, far exceeded anything that I had experienced in my life.

The garden surrounding this area was immaculately planted and maintained with more varieties of flora than I could count and several that I had never seen, even in the more exotic tropical zones of the world I had traveled in. There was a fountain made of some unusual type of marble that gave the impression of bearing a pale green hue. The color was vaguely similar to the woman's eyes but without the strange glow. It almost felt magnetic. Meticulously crafted into an arch that spanned the width of the fountain was another carved material, even deeper still in tint – a basket handle with birds, wrens maybe, that sat along the rim. The detail was so immaculate that it seemed artisans might have worked on it for hundreds of years or more. Spraying gently straight up out of the fountain was an endless perfect stream of the silver-blue water that appeared to be flowing from the larger body. The effect was other-worldly mystical. I stood there totally hypnotized, mesmerized by the magic of the scene.

The woman sat on a bench with her hands gently folded. Her posture was almost as if she was posing for a picture. At the same time though, she conveyed the impression of someone totally at ease. The bench was made of simple oak and sat just underneath a very large and majestic-looking weeping willow tree. Behind her and just off to her right was a lattice structure woven out of interlacing thin slats of wood, painted in an subtle shade of off-white. The lattice had been antiqued with delicate touches of gold that were almost imperceptible, but skillful highlighting had apparently been worked in.

From the lattice hung the most meticulously crafted, outrageous baskets of flowers, perhaps petunias. Whoever attended these baskets simply had to be some sort of miracle gardener. Flowers seemed to pour out over every side of the baskets from vines more than six feet long. There were several hundred very vibrant blooms of so many colors in each basket that it defied my ability to count them. The most striking of the colors, though, was a rich deep purple. The color almost seemed boosted by some kind of electrical effect. Off to the left of the oak bench was a pathway set in a soft white marble. Abundantly planted on both sides of the pathway were roses of every imaginable variety, color and design. They, too, were perfectly manicured and, as with the hanging baskets, teemed with what seemed to be an unreal number of perfectly formed and near iridescent uniquely colored blooms.

I wasn't scared but I was cautiously curious. Where was I? What was this experience that I was having? What was this voice that I was hearing – and now perceiving in other ways? As these questions formed, other thoughts and answers began flowing into my consciousness, like water pouring gently over a small spillway. The audibility of what I "heard" was so gentle that it was barely distinguishable. What came to me was not in the form of an audible voice as I had thought before. Instead of hearing streams of words normally equated with language, it felt as though my mind was receiving concepts directly implanted. The purity of the communication I was receiving was conveyed with unequivocal clarity to my conciseness. It was a softness uniquely unlike any human voice. There was no question that that the source of the communication was this woman sitting casually but attentively on the bench.

"You seemed quite confused about some things, so I thought I'd stop by and try to help you sort them out," I received from her.

The words came across to me as though they were blended with the sound of water gently trickling over stones. Maybe it was the gentle spraying sound of the fountain in the background. I'm a rational person, not prone to panic or delusions. Still, there's a time and a place for everything, and I was beginning to think that panic might be pretty much justified at this juncture. Without wanting to sound challenging, I tentatively started off, "O.K., I know I must be dreaming, but why does it feel so different from any other dream I've ever had? Who are you?"

The woman gave me the impression that she was smiling. She replied, "You are where you have always been but, for this exact moment, let's just say that your perception has been boosted and you're seeing things a bit more clearly right now. As to who I am, my name is Kalista. Is that what you really wanted to know, though, 'who' – or did you mean *what* am I?"

I'm unsure whether it was the content of the response or that there was a response at all that jolted me so sharply. If I had known how, I'd probably have run out of there as fast as I could. While I did not in any way feel that I was in danger or restrained in any way, I also did not feel as though I had the facilities to leave. Besides, I didn't know how to based upon the state of perception and awareness that I was in. Beyond that was the form of communication being used; this was something that was very unsettling, irrespective of the clarity that it obviously afforded. It was as though words were completely passé and that the only effective manner in which to communicate was the wholesale exchange of entire sentences and paragraphs in one brief burst. These thoughts, though, clearly came across as entire cogent ideas. I was uncertain as to whether I was still accessing normal language to communicate or, if in the state of acuity I had temporarily attained, whether I, too, was communicating conceptually. I decided to engage in a calmer, more conversational manner, hoping that I could gain some insight on how to get the hell out of here... wherever "here" was.

"O.K., you said your name was Kalista," I said tentatively.

There in no way to accurately represent the thought impression that I had received from the woman when she conveyed what I took to be her "name." Kalista is, at best, only a vague approximation of the impression she had inferred as to what she was to be called. In reality, I cannot come close to duplicating, in any form of writing, the thought concept that was meant to reflect her "name," although it is absolutely clear to me and I have no trouble communicating it back to her.

With the impression of a gentle smile, she responded, "Okay, the name is close enough."

I could not have been more shocked than if I'd gone to the zoo and had a giraffe ask me where to get a cup of coffee. Even though I had the clear impression that the communication was emanating from what I perceived to be this woman, I somehow had not really prepared myself fully that this was actually happening. Nevertheless, I continued. "No. No... if I'm mispronouncing it, I'd like to get it right."

"Don't be silly. You did just fine," she said.

"Thanks. You're right of course. What I really want to know is what are you? What is this place? I assume I'm having some form of dream – delusion?" I was nervous.

"Good question: Let's just say for now that, we are students in the same school. Think of me then as someone that has finished three or maybe four more grades than you have so far. And, you're not dreaming or delusional, at least any more than usual," she said.

"O.K., I can deal with that. So, I know I'm not dreaming but... "

"Relax, Chuck. Breathe in, breathe out. Remember? Tell me, how do you know when you are dreaming?" she asked.

I got the sense that she genuinely wanted to help me – and would if I listened to her. So I decided that until I could figure out how to leave, I'd let her be the guide. Looking back, of course, I really had no choice in the matter. "Well, dreams have a certain quality to them and, well, I don't know... you just know," I tried to respond.

"Let me try to explain it this way; where I come from, so to speak, the life you live from day-to-day; that form of existence to us is barely even a dream."

"I'm not sure I understand." I was stunned by her response.

"Oh, yes you do," she said confidently.

People who know me know that I don't swear much. I used to when I was much younger but I pretty much outgrew it and am happier for it. But as I thought about what she had just said, many of the words that you might blurt out when you hit your thumb with a hammer were running through my mind. This woman who called herself Kalista communicated in a way that simply left no possibility that what she was saying was inaccurate or untrue. She was very confident. Her presence made me think seriously about the possibilities of what she had said. Still a bit stunned, I took my best shot at proceeding in a nonchalant manner.

"So, are you some kind of teacher? Advanced soul? Ascended Master?"

"You really like putting labels on things, don't you? I am a soul, much like you, but as I said, I've moved through a few more stages than you have. If you concentrated a bit harder, you'd recall that we get together for a while between each life that you have with a few of your other advisors and look at where you just came from and, more or less lay out where it would be helpful for you to go next."

I didn't believe her but thought I'd play along for now. "And I'm not dreaming and I'm not delusional?"

"No, but I have a feeling if you don't stop beating your head against the wall you might end up that way," she said with a genuine laugh.

"Well, I've been struggling a bit recently; I'm feeling not too happy about my inability to find some of the answers that... "

"Yeah, I heard your call. That's why I'm here," with this, she stood up andin an over exaggerated manner, curtsied, beaming from ear to ear.

"And you'll help me?" I asked.

"Like always, I'll help you remember what you already know but might have forgotten. It's more obvious than usual that you have forgotten – again."

"Forgotten? What do you mean forgotten? If I knew it, I'd remember. I don't, so why not just tell me all the stuff I'm having trouble with?"

"You're kidding, right? I'm not running a summer lecture circuit here. I can help you recall what you know, but you have to ask direct questions. What's been bothering you the most?"

"Hmm, let, me think. Bothering me the most... hmm. Okay, can you tell me what happens when we die?" I asked.

"What?" She was incredulous.

"Well, you know; there are all these books now, people that have gone through near death experiences and things similar to it. They talk about traveling up through a tunnel, meeting a being of light and... "

"Oh, that," she said.

The way she said it made me feel completely inept. Embarrassed. It was as if I was asking what the color green looked like. She gave me the impression that answers to all of my questions – things that I had spent years pondering and reading about – were no further away than a few clicks of the mouse and that it was only a simple matter of learning how to use one. As I awaited her answer, I noticed that she was distracted by something in the foliage, although I was unable to tell what.

"Sorry, what was it you wanted to know?"

"What really happens?"

"In what sense?"

"I think its obvious; in *every* sense!" I was exasperated.

"I've told you, I'm not here to render a dissertation. If you want answers, you have to ask direct and cogent questions."

"Oh, sorry. First, what about the actual death experience itself; what's it like?"

"Well, it has been a while for me," she smiled. "As I recall, it feels a lot like you have been sitting in a hot air balloon on the ground spending time talking to friends and the ground crew. Then, at the moment of death, someone releases all of the weights that are holding you to the ground. From there, you just soar. No longer held down by the weight of the illusion of life. You just soar."

"So, its not scary? And the 'friends and ground crew' you mentioned, are those supposed to equate with the people we have met in life? Illusion – what illusion?"

"Whoa, hold on; one thing at a time. First, it's only scary for people who choose to forget what it feels like. Second, yes, good pick up: the ground crew are people that helped us with critical parts of our mission and learning while we were incarnated in human form. I'm impressed – you're smarter than you look. We can talk about the illusion another time."

"What? What do you mean people choose to forget? You keep saying that." I ignored the back-handed ribbing she was doling out.

"Well, almost everyone on earth has already lived and died at least several times before. They have within them the recollection of what it feels like to die as well as all of the information about the way the Universe is put together and works. If they would let go of the belief that they **don't** know it, they'd remember pretty much whatever they wanted to."

"Geez Kalista, I don't know. I know quite a few people that really want to know this stuff. If it was that simple, I think a lot of other folks would have figured it out by now, even if that only meant remembering," I said.

"Well, there are a few obstacles in the way."

"Always a catch, isn't there?"

"Relax, it's nothing that can't be overcome with a bit of work," she said, smiling.

"O.K., give it to me straight; what stops us from seeing all of this? What stops us from knowing what it feels like to die and having the insights into all of the rest of life's little mysteries?"

"Well, fear stands in the way to a large degree."

"Fear? I thought we were afraid of death itself?"

"That too, but people need to fully understand and accept that what you call life is little more than a place for you to take in certain forms of learning. That it is only a perceptional state," she said sadly. "A lot of the motivations that drive people on Earth would simply go away if they accepted this. Just as people are driven into behaving in certain fairly predictable ways when they are told from a young age that something is a "sin" and if they do thus then they'll 'go to hell.' In a similar fashion, if they knew that the world is mostly illusory and that the effects beyond that of learning certain lessons are hollow, they wouldn't get the full impact of all of the lessons."

"You're saying the world we live in isn't much more than a classroom of wayward souls?"

"Well, it's a classroom, I'm not sure about the last part," she laughed.

"So, people only pay attention 'in class' if there's the threat of being sent to the principal's office... in essence, going to hell?"

"Well, that's one way to put it. Let's just say that, unless people believe, and very deeply, that the freight train bearing down on them is a real train, they might not be very motivated to move off the tracks. So, the world has to appear to be very real to you or you wouldn't end up learning what you were sent there for."

I thought about that. What if Kalista was right? What if what we call life was not much more than a state of mind and that the main reason we experience life was just another form of schooling? This only brought up more questions.

"Boy, Kalista, I don't know about that. I mean, it seems pretty real to me for just a state of mind – perception, I think is what you said."

"Have you ever had a dream?"

"Are we changing subjects?"

"No."

"Oh. Well sure, I have dreams all the time. I can't remember some of them, though."

"When you're dreaming Chuck, does it seem real to you?"

"Actually, come to think of it, it does seem pretty real most of the time. So what you're saying is that life is more or less like that?"

"Only if you're actually going to make me say it but, you're not are you?"

"But we're not actually dreaming when we're experiencing life. I mean, not really."

"That depends on how you're going to define dreaming doesn't it? From my perspective, believe me, you're all dreaming - or what may as well be dreaming."

This was becoming a bit of a problem for me. I remember pretty clearly that it was around this point in the conversation that I stopped to have a little meeting with myself. From my perspective, all of what was occurring seemed and felt very real. Too much so. I also had the thought that, no matter what I might *think* was going on, I had to be having this conversation with myself. For me to accept that I had somehow permeated some mystical cloud base and floated into a place where I could talk to a disincarnated spirit – advanced or not – was a bit too difficult for me to accept. Still, the insights, the examples she was using were definitely not coming from me. They weren't even close to the nature of my philosophy or my way of thinking at that time. I simply had no choice but to accept that, even if I eliminated the imagery of the garden and the woman as metaphors that my mind had somehow created, the underlying content of what was being said was coming from somewhere outside of me. But where? Thinking this, and assuming that I would never again be able to obtain this kind of contact, to find Kalista again – I was determined to press on and get at least some of the answers that I had been looking for.

"I'm not so sure that I understand the answer to that myself at this point. But, if life, or what we call life, is barely a dream, then what is real?" I asked.

"Real? I don't recall saying that life wasn't real. You already said yourself that when you were having a dream it seemed real enough at the time. It's only later, after the dream is over and you're in your 'waking state' that you realize that it was a dream."

That made me stop and think. For some reason, when she said it that way, it all came pouring down on me at once and it was as though a little light bulb did go off over my head. I began to not only think about an existence after this life, but also see it in reality. I don't know why, or where it came from, but out of the blue, the children's song began to echo in my head.

> *Row, row, row your boat*
> *gently down the stream*
> *merrily, merrily, merrily, merrily*
> *life is but a dream.*

"Oh, I think I'm beginning to get it."

"If I thought that was true, I'd dance an Irish jig right here."

"Very funny. Really though, what I think you're saying is that we really have to die in order to fully appreciate that what we called 'life' was actually no more than a dream."

At this point, Kalista stood up and broke into what looked like some overly-exaggerated ancient Irish dance step, the kind where the hands are kept stiff at the sides of the body. It would have been comical save for the fact that something told me it was probably executed better than the players of "Riverdance" could possibly do it. Still, the image of an advanced soul dancing in this idyllic garden was more than I could stand, taking into account all the other assaults that had been flooding my senses that afternoon. Sensing I was about to lose it, Kalista ceased the dancing but was beaming from ear to ear as she stopped.

"Whew! That'll get your heart pumping."

"Very funny. Is what I said before it though, about **having** to die to realize... "

"Well, yeah. That's pretty much it. Except, the having to die part."

"What?"

"Sorry."

"What do you mean?"

"Look around you. Right now, do you think you need to die to realize what I've told you about life in your world, dying and all the rest?"

"Oh, I see what you mean. But, I'll probably forget it," getting her meaning.

"Ah ha!"

You'd have thought she'd just won Wimbelton or some other major sporting event. She actually seemed excited that I had come to this realization, or that she had brought me there, which I thought much more likely.

"Then, we do forget?"

"Well, yeah Chuck, you do. But, that doesn't mean it will always be that way. Let's come back to that part another time," she said with compassion.

"O.K., but, I'm still back to where I started in some ways, though. Why do we fear it so much then? I mean, it would be like being afraid to wake up after you've been asleep all night."

"Pretty silly huh? You have to remember; people don't remember that. To them, it would be as though someone in their dream came up to them and said, 'O.K. now Chuck, you're dream is going to be ending pretty soon now,' and not telling them what happens when the dream is over. It's the not knowing, and the not remembering, that creates the fear. And the fear, well, that paralyzes many people so much that they end up not doing near what they could in their lives."

"I'm not sure that I know what you mean."

"Remember when you were in the fourth grade and you went on that roller coaster at the amusement park?"

Recalling the experience in my mind and, feeling a bit unsettled that Kalista could possibly know about it. "Yeah, sure, I remember."

"The first time you went on it, you were scared to death."

"Was not. "

"Were too!" She was smiling and laughing at the same time, clearly not at me, but with me.

"Whatever."

"In any event, by the time the ride was over, you couldn't wait to get back on it, mostly because you weren't scared anymore. It was old hat for you before the ride was even over."

I thought about that and, oddly enough, it was true. The moment they strapped me into that thing, it was called the "Racer" because a second roller coaster ran on a parallel track to it and raced it to the end. The third time I rode the Racer that day, I was yawning as we went up the first hill. Pondering this, I asked myself 'What if we can impart our previous experience dying on what scares most people out of their minds in life?' Maybe the fear that death holds over us could be beaten back a little with knowledge. What could I accomplish with my life if the fear of death was truly removed?

Seeing I was getting the concept, Kalista said, "Well, the death experience is a lot like that. If you will only recollect what it felt like the last time, you won't find it very frightening at all. No more so than waking up in the morning."

"And after people die, and they're remembering the life they just came from, it's like they can't wait to get back on the ride again so they choose to be reborn in another lifetime?"

"If they want to, sure."

"But, they start out all over again from the same place; not remembering that it's only a dream of sorts and they go through the fear of dying all over again."

"Most people, but, they don't have to. Like everything else, it's a choice. Most people choose not to remember because they know if they did, the 'ride' might lose its sense of realism. Besides learning, people go there for the thrills. To feel what it's like to have physical sensation among other things."

"So people can come back without the fear... or with less fear?"

"Like I said, it's a choice. Some people choose not to."

"But not all people?"

"Do you think you'll ever be as afraid again?"

"Probably not," I considered, smiling.

All of this had the irrefutable ring of eternal truth to it. As I said, when Kalista said something, it just had a resonance of resolute soundness to it. I just knew that everything she was saying was true. With that in mind, I thought to learn all I could about death and the dying experience.

"So what is actually happening to the person experiencing the death process. How to they get from here to there, so to speak?"

"I don't think I understand the question. Are you suggesting that at death there is some physical pathway that is covered, as if people 'go' someplace?" she asked with a quizzical look.

"They don't?"

"Not really, no. At least, no place that they aren't already."

"I'm lost. Can't you just tell me what actually happens at the moment of death and skip over all the Kreskin stuff?" Now I was puzzled.

"Sure."

"So?"

"Release."

"Release? I don't understand."

"Sure you do. Just remember back... "

"To when I've died before?"

"Exactly!"

"But I can't."

"That's the spirit!" She smiled with a tinge of slight exasperation on her face. "You're capable, you just choose to believe that you can't, so you don't."

"But how do I remember?"

"The meditative state you're in now; go deeper without letting go all the way. From there, just focus completely on remembering back to the last time."

It must have been something that she did because, before I knew it, I saw myself exactly at the point of death in my most previous life. I had joined the experience precisely at the moment of release that Kalista had spoken of. I felt myself moving out and accelerating at the same time. I *felt* the experience, I saw that it was not in fact, a "rising" up as we would think of in terms gaining altitude. Heaven is not up, it's just... out. When I felt this experience from that particular perspective, I saw that what happens to us is not really a rising up out of our physical bodies. It is more a shifting out and away from the weight that is holding us in, not down in this case, from our human form. Many reports of near-death experiences talk about "rising up out of

29

the body up to the ceiling to look down upon one's body." This perspective appears true enough but in reality, since our "movement" is actually a shift only in perception at the moment we perceive "death," we could "look" at our bodies, or anything else that we wanted to, anywhere, at any moment we choose to, because we have just been unshackled from all the limits of our perception in this dimension.

As Kalista continued to move me through the experience, everything became abundantly clear to me; what actually changes at the moment of death is only our perception. And that perception has suffered a unique type of temporarily blindness as a condition of what we call "life." Death is Life and Life is virtually sleeping, I thought just then.

No longer tethered to a simple three-dimensional perspective or a belief system that we "are" defined by our bodies, I could begin to see things as they actually are in the universe of true reality. We don't need to rise up to heaven and experience all of the universe's limitless dimensions because we already span the limits of the universe just as we are.

Dying merely unchains us from the albatross of delusion that the human form temporarily tries to convince us to accept as "reality." And it happens that the perception of reality the human form and our ego attempts to limit us to is wrong. The immutable truth is that the universe is a reality where absolutely everything – without exception – is, by its very structure and nature, linked together and boundless. At that moment, I realized that the human form through the trickery of the ego – our silly belief that we "are" the name that we've been given for 60 or 70 years – is absolute pure illusion. Evacuated from existence in a matter of a lightning bolt. That very illusion that we call "life," is actually an aberrational state of perception for us to be in. And temporary.

Our true state is one of a perfect and purified spiritual nature where we not only span the universe, but also, in fact, are the universe. Being in human form is merely a kind of bizarre vacation of perception from what we really are although, for better or for worse, we *do* learn here. This thing that we call life that we mistake for defining who and what we "are" is actually no more than a temporary classroom. The bodies we occupy, our class uniform for that period that we are here to learn specific lessons. From whatever state that Kalista had allowed me to view all of this, it was so obvious that it was all undeniable. Brilliant. Glorious.

"I see it! I can really see it Kalista!"

"I know Chuck. I know." A gentle, compassionate, almost all-knowing smile formed at the edges of her mouth.

"So, what's next? Tell me about... "

"I think you've had enough for one day, don't you?"

I felt as if someone had let all the air out of my tires and then told me that my dog was going to die. I knew that the experience I was having was life changing – soul changing, for that matter – and one that I had waited all my life to come about. My fear was that I would never again get this kind of access. Be in a position to get all my questions answered about the purpose for living and things of that nature. It was a fluke, I knew, that I had found my way to the garden and to Kalista. Now my fear was that I would never again be able to find my way back.

"Whoa, whoa, whoa, whoa... wait! Hold on wait a minute. I'm not in any hurry if you're not."

"It's O.K. Chuck, really it is. Now that you know your way here, all you have to do if you want to find me is come here, to the garden. Just hold me in the image and I'll be here before you know it."

"But, but what if I can't do it?"

It was too late. Before I could say another word, she had gotten up and walked across the bridge that connected the small garden island to the shore. I walked after her, but as I got to the near side of the bridge, I noticed that she was nowhere to be seen. Another mystery for the day.

I started to think about how to get out of where I was. I began thinking about the details of my study, the color of the carpet, the picture of the Caribbean sunset over Tobago on the wall and, before I could make it through some of the lesser details of the room in my mind's eye, I found myself sitting on the floor of my study. The dog was barking at some children playing in the yard across the street. I heard the sprinkler splashing water against the downspout as it swept across my other neighbor's backyard. The sun had pretty much set. I looked at the clock on my desk and was stunned. I had been gone for almost six hours.

CHAPTER TWO

*...and if you listen very hard
the tune will come to you at last
when all are one and one is all
to be a rock
and not to roll*

- From, Stairway to Heaven, by Led Zeppelin

As I gained my bearings, the part of me that had set out to be a scientist instead of a corporate officer had the sense to reach for a pad of paper and write a few notes before I lost the context of what I'd just experienced. For some reason, I opted to draw a picture of a hot air balloon. There were weights on the side that I labeled "death." I wrote a caption that said, "we are only just born, released at the moment of death, not the moment of birth." It was just the impression that I had from the experience that I had just come from that I was to learn later was not precisely on point. Just underneath it I jotted, "we know, but we forget." I also scrawled a note in the corner of the picture that read, "what flowers grow on vines six feet long? Petunias?" And, in the handwriting of a child across the top of the scrap of paper I wrote, "caw lees ta," coming as close at the time as I could to my understanding of the woman's name. I fed and walked the dog and then promptly fell asleep for almost thirteen hours. I usually sleep about five.

The next day, I went back to my study and stared for some time at the hastily-scrawled picture of the hot air balloon and the few brief notes I had written. They had lost some of the impact and context that they had held for me only the day before. For reasons that weren't clear to me, I just wasn't getting the same impression from the insights that Kalista had shared with me. It was a very frustrating experience. Determined to find out whether I had stumbled into a one time event, and possibly to convince myself that it was all a dream, I set out to find my way back to the garden and, hopefully, locate Kalista for some answers.

Half excited and half terrified, I positioned myself in the same place on the floor of my study as I had the day before. As I did so, my heart sank; for some reason I could not remember the specific steps of meditation, particularly the conceptual imagery focus that I had used to find my way to the bizarre location the previous day. I had the raw concept in mind but no specifics of the exact technique that had ultimately worked. A feeling of sheer panic came over me as I searched my memory desperately for some touchstones that would trigger something in me that might remind me of what I had done to find the way. Nothing. It was as though that entire section of my memory had been wiped clean.

Frantic, I thought back, trying as hard as I could to remember Kalista's words right before she had left. In a few seconds it came to me: "Now that you know your way here, all you have to do to find me is come here, to the garden." Those were her exact words before she walked across the bridge. But what exactly did that mean? It couldn't possibly be as simple as envisioning the garden and the surrounding scenery.

Then I remembered that the day before, as the image had coalesced into its sharpest focus, there had been a certain indisputable sense of absolute peace that came over me. It felt like I was covered with a warm blanket that had just come out of the dryer on a freezing winter day. Up until that point in my life, it was the most miraculous feeling I had ever experienced. Somehow – I didn't really know how at the time – it all just became clear to me. Only a moment before I was totally lost as to how to engineer the visit to the garden and then a second later, it was as clear as it could be. It was merely a matter of focusing at a place very deep inside of me, not in my conscious mind, but within the garden scene. I had to see myself *in* the scene and simultaneously recreate that warm blanket feeling at a very specific deep level of my awareness.

In what seemed like no more than a few moments, I was back. It was odd, too, that this time, the journey seemed virtually instantaneous. The previous day I felt as though I had spent hours wandering about aimlessly inside of whatever zone was between my world and the garden. Just what or where "there" was I had absolutely no notion at all. The only thing that was clear to me was that as I "remembered" the particulars of the warm blanket feeling and focused intently on many of the specifics of the general image of the pathway, and specifically the roses, a moment later I found that I was simply *in* the garden. There was only one problem: no Kalista.

I started to look around slowly and very carefully. Taking into account that Kalista had shown me only the previous day that she had a highly developed sense of humor, I considered the possibility that she might be hiding. Probably watching me right at this moment laughing herself silly, waiting to jump out of the bushes and scare me half to death, I thought. No such luck. Not knowing what else to do I decided to take a closer look at some of the flowers that had so completely overwhelmed me when I had seen them the day before.

I made my way over to the hanging baskets and began to study them carefully. I knew very little about flowers at that time, but I knew that someone had to know horticulture and apply great care to make a simple plant like this grow so dramatically. It wasn't just the length of the vines that was so astonishing. I noted upon closer inspection that the vines were actually closer to seven feet in length. What was so overwhelming was that each basket easily had at least a thousand blooms or more. And the colors! The hues ranged across the entire rainbow as well as many colors outside of the spectrum of the rainbow. They somehow gave the impression of being near iridescent in brightness. Almost as though there was a small neon bulb in each bloom. Each bloom was seemingly that alive and bursting with energy. Just as I took one of the vines in my left hand to examine it more closely, I heard Kalista say, "Petunias... yup, I think you would call those petunias for sure."

Trying to be nonchalant has never been my strong suit. Particularly when I've been surprised like that. Still, I wanted Kalista to have the impression that I wasn't in any way startled and answered her in what I hoped was a cool and collected tone. I didn't even turn around to look at her but instead continued to study the other-worldly hanging flower baskets.

"Really? Gee I don't know Kalista, they look more like daffodils to me."

"Oh, really? You might be right," she giggled.

I have to admit that, at the time, I wouldn't have known a daffodil from a petunia if they both had labels on them with lettering two inches high. It simply wasn't anything that had ever interested me up until that point in my life.

"What makes them grow like this?" I asked

"Oh, I'm pretty careful about how I water them," she said, then flashed a wry smile.

I knew that wasn't it but I was determined to play along. "Really? C'mon. I know I've killed more house ferns than any other man alive but, I'm not gullible enough to believe that you can make a flower look like this just because you water them correctly."

"Well, I do a few other things to them too."

At the time, I was so impressed with the brilliant radiance and range of colors of the flowers that I had completely forgotten that I was in more a perceptional state than an ordinary one. By the way the discussion was going, you'd have thought I was down the street at a neighbor's backyard, asking them how much MiracleGro® plant food they used.

"Really? Like what?"

"Are you actually interested?"

"Yes. I am. I want to learn this."

Kalista walked over to where I was and began very carefully and quite artfully pruning the basket of flowers by hand. As she progressed through the process, she explained in great detail to me how she was "teasing" the energy of the plant into not only growing more, but also creating more blooms. Her explanation was quite intricate.

"So, do you understand now?"

"That's it?"

"Well, that would be a pretty good start for you, don't you think? I have an idea. Let's have you take care this one for now. Whenever you come here, you take care of this one and we'll see how you do. I'll keep them watered when you're not here."

With that, she showed me one of the hanging baskets that I would take responsibility for. We went on to prune it together. In spite of several stumbles on my part, she was very patient with me. When I made a mistake, she took great care to show me not just how to do it correctly, but *why* certain things worked, or didn't work. She detailed for me how we were in essence manipulating the energy that comprised the flowers. This was a concept that I had never even vaguely entertained up until that day. To me, a flower was simply a flower, no matter how beautiful it might have been. As we were finishing up working on the basket, it was Kalista who picked up our conversation from the previous day.

"You were asking about death and what happens... "

"Yes, from what you were saying it sounds like the experience of death itself doesn't have to be that traumatic. Frightening. What happens after that? Most of what I have read talks about a kind of life review process? They talk about the images of one's life passing before their eyes."

"Well... "

"Oh c'mon, you can't whet my appetite like that and then close the theatre with no notice."

"Can't?" She was smiling again but it was difficult to read whether it was contempt or sheer amusement.

At that moment, it occurred to me that I still didn't know very much about the experience that I was having or, who and what Kalista really was. I also had the vague notion of thinking how unwise it probably was to agitate a soul with far greater learning than I had attained. Thinking this, I immediately lowered both the pitch and the content of my approach.

"Well, what I meant to say was, I hope this isn't going to end. I have so much more that I need to learn."

She laughed gently and then showed me the most gentle smile I have ever seen. "It's O.K. Chuck, you and I have been through this quite a few times already over the eons we have known each other, what's another time or two? Sooner or later I'm figuring you're going to get it, and remember it."

"You make me sound like the class idiot of the Universe."

"Oh Chuck, not at all. Actually, you've come along quite nicely. Keep this up and you'll be getting that promotion any ole lifetime now."

With that, she took a few steps back, and appeared to half-close her eyes. She was concentrating on something, although I couldn't even guess at what. What I saw next in front of me was the impression of a holographic image. The clarity and detail that was conveyed by the imagery defied any experience I'd ever had or any technology that I could imagine. The images and feelings that derived from the projections overwhelmed any attempts at description.

The experience itself had so many different components and qualities that I could never detail all of them beyond saying that it was far more vivid than any experience one might have in real life. Above and well beyond the imagery was the unprecedented feature of the projections. Within the experience, you could "see and feel" the emotions and thoughts of every participant in the scene. I joked to myself that if the guys in Hollywood could ever duplicate this experience, they'd have everyone's money.

The particular imagery that Kalista had selected was a scene from when I was ten or eleven years old. My best friend and I had somehow come into possession of a BB gun and we were having a field day shooting out our neighbor's picture window. We were in some way certain that the neighbors were gone on vacation and were sure that we would never get caught. As it turned out the neighbors were home and at that very moment hunkering down in the dining room trying not to get hit by the shards of glass flying off of each hit we scored on the picture window.

The ability to feel every person's emotion from their perspective was, sobering, painful. As each BB hit the window and sent glass flying, I felt the absolute fear, anger, resentment and pain in our neighbor's essence. The experience had a feature where the entire scene could be stopped, slowed down, rewound or to add any effect of that nature you could imagine. This would allow the viewer the ability to take in the full impact of the scenario playing out. It also afforded the experiencing of the events to be all the more instructive of specific parts of the events being projected.

"Wow, it's a good thing I don't have to experience that for an entire lifetime. That might be really uncomfortable."

Kalista remained stonefaced.

"No. Really, I don't think I'd want to endure that. I mean..."

"Really? Why not?" A mischievous grin crept up around her mouth to the edges of her eyes.

"Is that what its like? I mean, does one have to go through that for his entire life's experience?" I asked.

"What do you think of it as a teaching tool?" she asked, cleverly avoiding my question with one of her own.

"Somehow I had envisioned that God was not the vindictive sort. That the concept of retribution and rubbing our faces in past mistakes was pretty much just a human thing."

"Dream on."

"WHAT?????"

She rolled on the ground almost choking with laughter. Tears rolled down her cheeks.

"That's not funny."

"Sorry. I couldn't resist. What did you think of being able to actually feel what other people around you – people that you directly affected – felt?"

"I didn't like it."

"Didn't like the feature or the experience?"

"Oh, no. Not that. The gizmos are definitely first rate. Kudos to the guys that do your technical work. I just didn't like how it made me feel."

"Will it make you think before you take a BB gun to a neighbor's window again?"

"Absolutely!"

"Really? Are you certain?"

"Sure, why not?"

39

"Well, unfortunately, not everyone absorbs their lessons the first time through."

She had a deeply ingrained half-frown on her face that made me feel the disappointment that she felt for all of the needless suffering that goes on in the world because people aren't either better – or faster – learners about their own actions and outcomes.

"Is that it? I mean, is that the entire experience that people go through?"

"Not exactly. You have to bear in mind that running scene after scene after scene of a person's life with that degree of detail – where you can feel all of the consequences of what you did and didn't do – requires the assistance of a genuinely compassionate guide. So, we monitor and assist in the process of life review, as well as act as spiritual coaches to assist souls through this process."

"How do the more advanced souls assist them?"

"The purpose of the process is not to rub your face in your mistakes and actions where you could have done better. Human nature being what it is, each person usually does a better job of that for themselves than anyone else could. The purpose of this process is to reaffirm for the soul that their core essence is that of pure compassion and a form of purified, unconditional love that few, if any, while still on Earth ever get in touch with. Although they could if they wanted to. Guides are there to show souls the way – at various times and junctures in a given lifetime – that they might have better availed themselves of that innate nature. How they could have used compassion and love instead of fear, greed, anger and hatred as a pathway. That, as souls, they have a choice between those two approaches in how they will accomplish their mission and their learning. How, in a given situation, if they shifted their basic intent to that of compassion and love instead of retribution, revenge, fear, retaliation and things like that, their lives might have resulted in much happier and better outcomes."

"Does it work? I mean, do people undergo a dramatic change after going through this process?"

"You tell me. Do you think just from experiencing that one scene that you might be inclined to change your approach in any way?"

As she asked me that, I felt as though a bolt of electricity went through me. I re-experienced at that instant the entire sequence of events and results of my behavior that she had run me through just moments before. I felt the effect and feelings that my actions had directly imparted on others. What struck me most acutely at that moment was how completely unaware I was at that point in my life, of how my actions had direct effect on how others felt. That others took actions because of what I had said or done. And did so in ways that far exceeded what I had ever contemplated.

I had not seen before that very moment that my actions are inexorably linked to the feelings and actions of those in my direct proximity and in turn, theirs are linked to those around them and so on, indefinitely. Like the butterfly that flaps its wings in Hawaii and ultimately, due to the chain of resultant events, it results in a windstorm in New York. But with the extensive range of human interactions taking place on our planet, the outcomes and results of our actions, inaction and behaviors are far more complex. The simple and indisputable truth is that we deeply and directly affect people around us through everything we do and say. And they, in turn, affect others around them and so on. It travels everywhere. Our being unaware of the extent to which this is true in no way makes it any less so. I had been viewing the world in terms of what was done to me and not very much from the perspective of the feelings of others.

My thoughts tumbled down then through an awareness where I became conscious that this is far more than a universal concept. It is a universal reality. The effect that we have on others is not solely from a negative perspective but potentially, a positive one as well. At least, it can be. I closed my eyes and "saw" that any action that we affect – no matter how small and insignificant it may seem – not only has the *prospect* to trigger broad-ranging events that affect large numbers of people in turn but, in fact, does so. We just don't see it. Not at the time.

The window that we'd shot out with the BB gun was replaceable. But the relationship between my parents and the neighbors would never be quite the same. For that matter, the relationship with my parents and me suffered for quite a while as well. I know they were both disappointed and hurt that their son would do such a thing. The trickle-down effects of my actions just went on and on. But at the time I was shooting out the window, I had no concept at all of the potential reach and broad consequences of my actions. I was solely focused on how cool it felt to shoot out a window.

Initially, as I stood there with Kalista in her garden, I thought, well, kids will be kids. How spiritually advanced are we expected to be when we're ten? But as I thought it through, I saw that Kalista had actually been quite compassionate that day. Had she opted to show me some of the scenes in my life from my twenties, or even early thirties – when my behaviors had less than optimal effects on certain people when I should have known better, although no windows were broken, other people's feelings had been. I had seen at that moment, with painful clarity, that my own thoughtlessness and insensitivity had real effect on others that I had known. Those negative effects were passed along to other people in those person's lives. And I had responsibility for what I had created all the way down the path.

Every day since Kalista played that scene for me I have endeavored to do better and better in that regard. I rarely take any action that might affect another person anymore without giving at least some thought to the consequences and effects that it may hold for others. More than once I have been very grateful for having found this self-censoring mechanism. I have also wondered how the world might change if everyone remembered that there is, in fact, a day when all of our actions and the affects those actions had on others will be reviewed in this unique and impactful way. If only they could experience what I just had, I thought, the world would change overnight. Thinking that, Kalista jolted me back into reality.

"I was asking if you think the experience will have a real effect on you?"

"Yes, I believe it will," I said.

"That's the goal of the process then. Not to impart punishment, as there is no permanent effect of any sort like that from the review process, but hopefully to help people gain a true understanding of the effects their actions and intentions had upon others. At the core of it, people should come away from that process and ask if their actions were compassionate and loving or, something else. That is how they learn."

"Why?" I asked.

"For one word, that's a pretty complicated question."

"Sorry, I have the time if you do."

"The essence of it has more to do with gem polishing than anything else."

"I'm sorry, did we change topics again?" I was dumbfounded.

"Nope," she said with a straight face.

"Gem polishing?" I asked.

"Well, it's sort of self-explanatory if you picture that the construction material of all souls is like the most perfect form of unique diamonds anywhere in the universe."

"I feel a metaphor coming," I said. Although Kalista smiled, I could tell that she was serious about her point.

"Imagine that as each soul is formed from the Source it is pure, perfect and unblemished in any way. Perfect is only a concept to you but an absolute reality in every sense of the word in this regard."

"Sounds good so far. Ah, and you mentioned 'Source?'"

"In your terms, you might think of God as being the Source, but we'll talk about that some other time. Along the pathway as this soul makes the choice to take on incarnations and, begins to carry the weight of its actions – Karma you like to call it – the soul starts to accumulate a little dust here, a spot of soot there and so forth, by virtue of their actions. Before too long what had started out when it was originally spun-off from the Source as this perfect, unique diamond is pretty well covered with stuff that, well, isn't something you'd want to track into a palace of white carpets."

"Oh, I get it, I get it; so the idea is to get all of the dirt off before you can get back into the club more or less."

"Hmm, that's pretty rough around the edges but, I guess we could say that more or less you have the general idea," she said.

"And, this process of reviewing the life scenarios through this comprehensive experience process, that is what helps remove the dirt. Cool!"

"Unfortunately, no. What it can do though is allow the soul to see what actions it has taken that tend to result in acquiring 'soot' along the way. It also helps in planning for the next lifetime they take on and opens up likely scenarios in that next lifetime that will allow them to learn more effectively what they didn't do too well on in the last lifetime. Through learning, a soul can remove some of what you call dirt."

"So, shooting out the window wasn't such a great idea?"

"Think of it this way, the process of shooting out the window itself got you dirty – that specific action you took. But, being completely unaware of the fact, the basic concept, that your actions had consequences on others, got you twice as much. Before you can get to a developmental state where you start to clean off the diamond, you need to arrive at the place where you stop taking on any meaningful new soot."

"How do you do that?" I asked.

"By experiencing lifetime after lifetime of making mistakes, reviewing them and, becoming aware on your own accord, with the help of guides, of the immutable truth that your actions have consequences on others. You also need to fully absorb and actualize the reality that conducting your life from a platform of loving as opposed to hating and fearing facilitates your spiritual objectives. That and learning how to use the ultimate gem cleaner, compassion. You can't gain admission without mastering and having doled out some pretty heavy doses of compassion," she said.

"But why does it take so long to get it? I mean, trust me, I'll never shoot out another window no matter how many times I live," I assured her.

"Yes, you will," she said with a smile.

"Why?"

"The simple truth is that in human form we tend to forget. There are human emotions that drive you and, in the basic process of interaction with other people it sometimes ends up putting you in a place where you do things – take actions or fail to take actions – that you might know otherwise that you shouldn't. No matter how advanced you might be, the rude driver on the road just simply gets to you sometimes."

"Then why can't we just remember what we felt when we were

looking at the last lifetime, the pain that we caused others? How discompassionate we were?" I asked.

"You can, but until the message is recalled at your deepest levels, you don't."

"So, we keep coming back lifetime after lifetime because we can't remember? That's pretty screwed up. This is depressing," I said.

"Don't be too upset," she said laughing gently. "It takes most souls lifetime after lifetime after lifetime to even start asking these questions much less finding some of the answers. But while they're doing that, they have amazing experiences. They get to experience love and, if they are fortunate, to be loved. They get to watch the sunrise and set over the ocean and watch their children take their first steps. It's not all bad."

"Sounds like you miss the place. You know, you could always come back and... "

"No way – and take a chance on ending up in a place like Los Angeles or Mexico City? All that traffic, ugh!" she giggled.

"Well, it was just a thought. Oh, by the way, a while ago you mentioned 'dirt points.' How many are you allowed to have? How many do I have? What can you... "

"It was figurative, Chuck. There are no points, although, at a management meeting last week, you'll be happy to know that we considered a point system but decided to just stay with the one that we have." She laughed and then winked at me.

Knowing that she was teasing me now, I said, "So, eventually, we get all this soot off of us and... "

"You're missing the point, Chuck. And it is the most crucial point."

"Which is?"

"In the end, no matter what happens, no matter how much dirt and grease and soot or anything else that you acquire the diamond is still there. I mean, the essence of what's underneath it – no matter how much crud might be covering it up – is still the unique diamond that was spun off from the original Source. It will always be there, in everyone that you meet. All of them. Always. Forever."

"And that part can't ever change? You can bury the diamond in 10 tons of cow manure and it will always be the diamond. And still be perfect?"

"Beyond perfect really but, if you have to think in terms of words then, yes, perfect is an O.K. place to start for that."

"Everyone?" I asked.

"Everyone," she said.

"But, there are some pretty horrible people out there. I mean Hitler, a good portion of the lawyers in the world... "

"Yes," she sighed, then frowning said, "but, some have chosen to virtually swim in soot lifetime after lifetime. And even worse than that in some cases I'm afraid."

"But I don't understand. Why would someone choose to do that?" I asked.

"You might not like the answer," she warned.

"No, really. It's okay. I want to know this," I insisted.

"Those people that you see acting in such reprehensible ways; blatantly disregarding the needs and feelings of others, greedily defrauding the masses, murdering, raping everything from the person down the street to whole parts of society, they do so because they have convinced themselves that they are actually evil. That they have moved so far away from the Source – and the essence of what that represents – that they believe that they are, in some way, unredeemable. They're wrong, of course. But still, they begin to hate themselves so greatly for having moved far away from the Source that the negative energy they are manifesting simply has to go somewhere. If they directed it inward, they would ostensibly self-destruct, as some do.

Many though, choose to direct that energy outwardly in very, very unconstructive, non-productive and overtly destructive ways. The results... well, the results you know about – read about in history books and in the newspapers every day. Campaigns of 'ethnic cleansing,' 'holy wars,' the strong victimizing the weak and the wealthy exploiting those with far less resources. All those acts, and other behaviors that are so violently against the brotherhood of souls, they are all committed by souls that have invested deeply in self-hatred. They believe themselves completely unworthy. Unredeemable. And while many of their actions are beyond reproach, the reality is that those souls – no matter how despicable their behaviors – can never be separate from the Source. They have simply just forgotten that."

I was quite shocked. Somehow, in all my thinking about what made people do such horrific, often unspeakable things to other people and even other living beings, I'd never considered the possibility that their problem was that they hated **themselves**. I had calculated that they just hated everyone else. What Kalista was saying made sense; if there was that level of intense, unabated of self-hatred going on, that energy certainly had to go somewhere. It reminded me of a conversation I had one day on a flight from L.A. to New York with a psychologist that was sitting next to me. He had explained to me that anger turned inward eventually results most often in depression. Until he'd said that, I had simply never thought of it in that way. Kalista's explanation of evil-acting people resonated similarly with me. It still left some blank spots that I decided to try to clarify.

"But it can't be that they get off scot-free. There have to be repercussions for acting like that. I mean Hitler, that horrible guy in Serbia... what's his name? – oh, Milosovich, murderers, rapists, animal abusers, child molesters... "

"Do you remember what I just showed you? The BB gun, the window, the neighbors?" she asked.

"Yeah, so what?"

"How would you like to be Hitler re-experiencing the feelings – EVERY FEELING – that he caused in EVERY person that he affected? And, the feelings that others ended up feeling because of what those that he directly affected ended up feeling?"

"Hmmm, good point." I thought about that. It's very difficult for me to convey how overwhelmingly acute and powerful the feelings experienced in life review really are. I felt such sorrow and guilt as each BB hit the neighbor's window and scared the neighbors senseless. And continued to feel that discomfort as they relived the experience over the ensuing days. It really was as though I was feeling exactly what they must have felt for the entire span of the event, and even weeks later as the residual effects took their time to wear off.

Thinking this, I thought about what an Adolf Hitler must have experienced at his life review, assuming that it wasn't still going on even now. What a rapist must feel. What someone that abuses or murders a child must feel. I began to see the absolute perfection of a system that worked in this way. There was no escaping for these people, I thought, with some glib satisfaction. And then I remembered that, although not even remotely in this class of offender, I had not been particularly sensitive to a few people in my life, either. At that moment I heard a voice in my head echoing that famous line, "Ask not for whom the bell tolls, it tolls for thee." It was tremendously sobering. Kalista's voice, thankfully, shook me out of my thinking.

"So, you see, all in all, the mechanisms work pretty well."

"That's it? I mean, you take a Hitler, run him through the life review mill and straighten his butt right out?" I asked.

"Unfortunately, no. Not really," she said.

"Aha! I knew it; there IS a Hell. And if the review process doesn't get 'em... "

"Relax cowboy. There is no Hell. Well, there is a Hell actually, but it's a place that we create for ourselves. A place where there is a total absence of love and compassion that we choose to inflict on ourselves when we think we deserve that. No one, besides the souls themselves, can sentence a soul to hell."

"Let me get this straight; no Hell? I mean, no real Hell? No fire and brimstone, burning skin, monsters imparting endless torture, suffering eternities and... "

"Nope," she interrupted.

"I can think of many, many members of Congress that will be very happy to hear that."

"Ever hear the expression, 'Judge not lest ye be judged'?" she giggled.

"Oops. Sorry," I said.

"No problem."

"So, if the life review doesn't work, and there is no Hell, what can possibly get people to change?" I asked.

"You tell me. What would be the best possible lesson for say, a persecutor or a bigot? What mechanism might be employed to help a rapist truly understand the full range of consequences of their act?"

I took some time trying to sort this out.

Tapping her foot and smiling almost wickedly, "Take your time, take your time."

"I think I have it. In a perfect world, a bigot would come back as the oppressed. The southern plantation owner who had black slaves, that he beat and abused; he'd be sent back as an oppressed black slave himself." I was excited by my discovery.

"Pretty close," she said.

"What do you mean close? It was **brilliant**!"

"Parts of it were," she said.

"Where did I go wrong?"

"I don't know. Where did you go wrong?"

I thought about it for a while and, to me, it seemed a pretty solid idea. If there was a major hole in the concept I wasn't seeing it. Then something occurred to me; if the plantation slave owner came back as an oppressed slave, he'd need a new plantation owner to persecute **him**. As I thought it through, in a system like that, you'd create cycle after seemingly endless cycle of persecutor/persecuted, victim/victimizer. If the participant players didn't make some real progress in the process of life review it could go on, well, endlessly. Lifetime after lifetime after lifetime.

"Well, I guess if it worked that way you could have a little problem with, well, sort of creating endless cycles. The rapist returning as the rape victim and then returning again as the rapist. Victim/victimizer/victim ad infinitum. If people didn't learn to break the chain, on their own it could continue, well, I guess it could continue virtually forever."

"Really?" she was smug. "You might end up with what would look like a pretty messed up world then, huh? A place where vendettas carry forward, generation to generation. Violence on almost a wholesale basis – geographic, religious, ethnic. Things like that?"

"Very funny. So, that's the problem with what I said."

"No, it isn't funny."

"But what about the endless cycle problem?"

"What about it?"

"Well heck Kalista, if the world worked like that you'd... "

And then it occurred to me. It was as if my head rang like it had been hit with a sledgehammer. The world we live in, the horrible things we see and read about every day, what if it was just victim and victimizer playing out cycle after cycle after cycle of previous roles that they had had in previous lives? Somehow – I don't know how – I managed a flashing moment of total clarity. I saw that, if a person was say, murdered and felt as though the murderer got away with it, and could not find the wisdom within them to let it go, they might come back and try to repay their killer in kind. Murder them.

And then I saw something else. What if, in trying to kill the original offender, their aim was less than perfect and they ended up accidentally shooting someone else. Killed – or even just permanently maimed – a completely innocent person? A completely new thread of karma was then created. Now that debt had to be repaid. That cycle had to be resolved. In this brief, fleeting moment of true insight – probably enhanced by Kalista in some way – I saw the world, at that moment, exactly as I complained about it every day. It was a madhouse with people acting almost routinely in what seemed like completely senseless ways such as road rage, holy wars and persecution based upon everything from gender to race to ethnic origin. Indifference. And everything in between and beyond.

The only difference was, with the insight into what the "motivations" of the players are, at least there were the semblance of some understanding, some basis to explain why some of the seemingly insane things were happening in the world. Still, the absolute senselessness of it all. If you took full measure of the endless cycles that were being played out, the stupidity of it seemed both monumental and obvious. Kalista, as I learned only much later, had the ability to – and had been – reading my thoughts.

"A little more clear now is it?" she asked.

"Yeah, a little bit. How can we be so stupid?" I was saddened by what I was learning.

"I'm not sure that stupid is the right word," she said.

"So that's it. That's how it works?"

"Almost."

"Please tell me it doesn't get worse than that," I begged.

"Not really. You just missed a couple of the finer points."

50

"Such as?"

"Well, before, when you were suggesting how it all worked; you said something about 'sending the plantation owner back as a slave.'

"Yeah, and?"

"Well, I don't know exactly how to say this but... "

"Just give it up Kalista. I can't take much more, I'm exhausted."

"Okay, here it is: no one gets sent back," she said.

"What? No reincarnation? No one... "

"Oh no.Reincarnation is absolutely true enough. It's just that no one sends you."

"You're losing me."

"You decide," she said.

"Stop being cute. I decide what?"

"No silly. I mean the soul decides on its own. To go back, and the circumstances under which it **will** go back." She giggled again, but I knew she was serious.

"I don't believe you."

"What?"

"I said, I don't believe you. Who the hell would decide to go back as a murder victim?"

"Who indeed?"

I was beginning to think that maybe I didn't see the big picture after all. I thought, who would really volunteer to come back and be a murder victim? Even a murderer – hell, particularly a murderer – wouldn't do it. Who better to know how much pain and suffering such an act causes. But, what if that was the only way back out of it so to speak? What if, once committed, an act like that could only be made right with the Universe by being a victim to the same act? It occurred to me right then that having this information – this insight – was indeed life changing, as I made a solemn promise to myself right then and there to be very, very careful of what I did going forward. Who in their right minds would want to keep coming back and play the victim of what we ourselves have done to someone else?

"I'm stuck, Kalista. I can see where, if it was the only way to repay your debt, you might have no choice but to come back as a murder victim. Is that it? There's no choice so you have to come back and get killed?" I asked.

"No. You always have a choice," she said.

"Then, I have to say that I can't imagine volunteering to come back."

"Think. You're giving up way too easily."

"I'm sorry. I just can't see it," I protested.

"Let me give you a head start. What if, and this is purely hypothetical, what if your choice was to stay in the disincarnate world for oh, say, 1,000 years or so to think, completely alone in a room about the impact and effects of what you had done or... "

I jumped in, "or, you could go back and experience it directly. And by experiencing it, you truly own it as opposed to just pondering it? Just thinking about it limits what you can learn from that. And, if you actually experience the receiving end of what you did, the lesson is forever deeply implanted in you because you've experienced both parts, including the remorse the first time you felt the impact of what you did in the life review." I was catching on.

Smiling, appreciating that I had made some progress as a student, she said, "Yeah, maybe that's how it should work."

"So that's it?" I wanted her reassurance.

"I hate to frustrate you, but only sort of," she said.

"Why? What am I missing now?"

"Do you think Hitler was remorseful?" she asked.

"Oh. Damn. Maybe not. What do you do then?" I felt like I was back where I started.

"Well, how about just letting the soul think about it," she suggested.

"For how long?" I asked.

"What do you think?"

"As long as it takes?"

"Ding, ding, ding... and what do we have for our winner, Johnny?" She was laughing now.

"Do you enjoy taunting me? I mean, is it part of your job?" I asked.

"Actually, it's more like a perk. Sorry, I'm just proud of you. Takes some people quite a while until they see this," she said.

"Not very fair though. I mean, kill six million people and you have to go sit in the corner for a while." I could not fathom it.

"Do I have to remind you again what the life review felt like?" she asked.

"No, but what happens after they've thought about it for a while?" I asked.

"What do you think? What would be in the best interests of perfecting the understanding of a soul that had done such a thing... of cleaning off that much soot?"

"A very big vacuum cleaner?"

"That's actually pretty funny. C'mon, think."

"How about having to live six million lives where he is victimized in some terrible way?" I added.

"If he so chooses, sure."

As she was talking, something else occurred to me. I had always been troubled by accounts in the news about people that had been the victims of terrible crimes, particularly violent crimes. Then I considered, what if this is the way the system works – that you have the option to come back and really learn the compassionate way that you could have acted? In essence, learn your lesson by being a victim of your previous act. Wouldn't we need a certain number of victims to play those roles? As horrible as many of these things are, the reality is that terrible things have been going on for a long time in our world. In fact, human history is riddled with such accounts, literally from the outset of recorded time. Sad.

But if we haven't been smart enough yet to break through some of these cycles, the fact is, there will be plenty of roles for victim and victimizer alike for a very long time to come. And much like the Energizer Bunny®, it keeps going, and going and going. Until we stop it. Until we, as individuals collect the insight and the courage to say, 'no more; I'm not doing this any more.' And put an end to the cycles by absorbing the wrongs with our intellects and with the strength of our souls once and for all. My mind was flooding with thoughts. If all of this was true, if this was really the way it worked, there was so much that we could learn, so much potential gain to be had from applying this knowledge.

"May I shift gears for a minute?" I asked.

"Sure."

"If all of this is true, couldn't you then look at someone's current life and infer an awful lot about where they came from in their previous life? I mean, if a woman is say, the victim of an abusive husband, couldn't you suggest that she was the abuser in her previous life?"

"Ah. That's a good question. Unfortunately, it's not always a straight line. There's not always a connection where it's necessarily that apparent. Usually, but not always."

"I'm lost then. Why would someone volunteer to be the victim of anything if it wasn't to make up for what they did?" I asked.

"Often it is because they think they've failed in other ways. Sometimes, it's to try to compensate for what they feel they did in some earlier lifetime that hasn't been resolved yet in their mind. Hasn't been learned and absorbed fully quite yet." she said somberly.

"When you say, 'think they've failed,' what do you mean?" I asked.

"Listen. This is important. One of the reasons people take on lives with lots of problems is because they think that by getting soot on them in the first place that this in some way, by itself, makes them bad, or evil, or whatever. They believe, because they have a little dirt on them that God will not want them back. But a mother doesn't care about the dirt on a child's face. They actually expect them to get a little dirty when they are at play or at school or at work. Still, some people get it in their minds that they need to be punished because they did things that got a little dirt on them and they end up writing themselves into life scripts where they are punished. Before you know it, they become entangled in one more victim/victimizer script or relationship or another and create *new* reasons that they need to come back to sort all that new stuff out. And it goes on and on. It can turn into quite a mess, really, and it's all completely unnecessary."

"But if they keep coming back and not seeing that it's them and their actions, and solely their own actions, that are the very causes for them having to keep coming back." I paused.

"It could go on for a long time," she said.

"How long?" I asked.

"Fortunately, the Universe is a patient master. The Universe has an eternity for us to sort all of this out. Because in the end, you will learn that time is a very limited form of dimension and because of this fact, it doesn't matter how long it takes to sort these matters out."

"But based on our discussion, it doesn't have to take much time. We could change all of it if we would only break the cycles that we create and perpetuate on our own. If we'd refuse to play either victim or victimizer in any of our relationships, we'd wind it down in no time."

"Well, a lot less time than it would the way things are going," she replied.

"Why don't the spirit guides help us then?" I asked.

"We do. Probably more than you know. But, of the very few 'laws' that there actually are in the Universe, one of them is that a soul cannot directly intercede in the pathway of another soul's primary mission. You can give them information. You can provide encouragement and support for them. But much like the emergence of a small hatchling from the egg, in the end, the hatchling – the soul – has to make its own way out and back."

"Back? Back where?"

"Home, of course. Our true mission, our very purpose, is to make it back home."

It must have been the incredible weight of what Kalista said. Maybe it was the way she said it. I was completely overwhelmed with emotion at that moment. I felt as though I were an orphan that had just been told it was all a mistake – some bureaucratic mixup of sorts – and that my real parents were on their way over to pick me up. Momentarily. That, no matter what happens to us today, tomorrow or in the next lifetime or fifty lifetimes from now, if we will only persist and improve ourselves – to be more and even more compassionate – that we do have a mission, that the real parent is waiting for us with open arms. And that parent holds the reality of absolute and genuine unconditional love and compassion for us. Forever. When Kalista said "home," she had somehow allowed me to feel, even if for only a moment, what that love and absolute, boundless compassion feels like. It was so complete, so comprehensive and all-encompassing, that it shocked me out of the state I had been in. Completely.

I regained my normal senses again, on the floor of my study. I was sobbing from the absolute elation that flowed into my heart. This, even though what I had just felt had lasted only for a brief second or two. The only session note I wrote – or needed to write for that day – was "home, we're all going home."

CHAPTER THREE

May I be a protector to those without protection,
A leader for those who journey,
And a boat, a bridge, a passage
For those desiring the further shore.

- Shantideva, 14th Buddhist Saint

The insights Kalista had shared with me created two problems that I had to deal with at this juncture: First, the next day was Monday. Somehow, I needed to find a way to strap on one of those designer business suits in my closet, something that I'd foolishly thought at some point in my life actually meant something. Then it was off to work fulfilling my role as a Fortune 100 senior vice-president. Competent. And of a "take no prisoners" mentality distinctly unlike the one Kalista had spoken about.

I also needed to find a way to behave outwardly as though nothing had happened. In corporate America, once you make it to vice-president, you don't talk to your colleagues at the water cooler about conversations with disincarnated souls, unless you're thinking about taking early retirement on a forced psychiatric pension. The reality in the corporate world is simple: if you tell someone something like this, you may as well write a mass distribution memo about it. Suddenly, everyone has his or her eye on your office and your job. Every slip-up is not only noticed, but immediately pounced upon and exploited. No matter how brilliant Kalista's insights were, I wasn't ready to throw it all away, not just yet. I did the only thing I could do at the time: I told no one.

Next, I had to figure out a way to sort through and make some sense of what I'd experienced. What did it mean? What were the experiences? Delusion? Inspired dream? Was I finally, as some of my closer friends had predicted was inevitable, cracking up for good? If I was truly onto something, I needed to figure out just what it was and, what I was going to do with it.

Many of the things that Kalista had said to me continued to reverberate in my mind. No matter how much effort I applied to setting those ideas aside, Kalista's words kept rising to the forefront of my consciousness. Day after day, I'd zone out at crucial meetings. I'd ponder ideas like how simple it would be to change the world for the better if only people could only understand that their sadness and suffering is purely of their own design. That when the world feels as though it might be collapsing around them, that ultimately it was *they* who were the architects and engineers of the disaster. Most importantly, no matter how bad things might seem, that it could change.

We need only recognize that we, on our own, write these painful scripts because we are perpetuating various age-old cycles. Some as time-worn as the feud between the Hatfields and McCoys, where no one even remembers what the original offense was. But our ego forces us to respond. To retaliate. And in turn become targets for retaliation. We choose to suffer because we believe we deserve to, or need to – to compensate for what we did to someone else. It shocked me that I'd not considered it before. Sadly, I reminded myself, it also all rang so true with basic human nature; you hit me and I'll hit you back twice as hard. Of course, no one in that cycle bothers to think about what happens on the fifth or sixth blow when someone may get killed. I thought about how it had only been going on this way for the last five or six thousand years. Maybe we'd change. Then again, maybe we'd just end up eradicating each other at the rate we were going.

It occurred to me that there were some problems with this perspective. In order to make sense of it all, I had to be able to take into account the more painful cases that troubled the world. How could we tell a starving child in Africa or the woman that had just been raped in Pakistan because her brother went out with the wrong woman that whatever their suffering, it was for some greater soul purpose; to serve some longer-term perfection of their soul? Or possibly that it was in response to suffering that they had caused at some point in their previous incarnations. That they had agreed to live this life with all of its weight and pain – as well as all of the opportunities for joy and love – in a form of "soul contract" that they had scripted out long ago; that there was tremendous learning to be done. There was limited benefit to such insights, I thought, if they had conditional practical applications like these.

I went through a period of several months where I engaged in a silent yet broiling self-debate over what to do about this dilemma. I also began to question the validity of the entire experience. More than once it occurred to me that I might not have the whole picture. That I had either missed, or possibly misunderstood, some of what Kalista had said to me. It was only after months of thinking about it that I thought to seek out Kalista again, hoping that she could shed some light on my quandary. To fill in some of the gaps where what she had said did not make complete sense to me.

In the frigid iciness that so often defines mid-February in New Jersey, I again retired to my study, determined to learn more and to ascertain with finality, whether the insights that had flowed to me were delusional or an inevitable twist of fate. Ones that were leading me to the answers that I had sought for so long. As I had on previous occasions, I meticulously went through the procedures that allowed me to enter the unique meditative state that led me to Kalista's garden. I had learned that the more careful I was in envisioning some of the finer details of the garden, the more expeditious the journey became. I was also mindful this time to immerse myself even more deeply in the warm blanket feeling that had turned out to be the missing element the last time I had attempted to make the connection.

I was grateful to learn that the passage of time had not compromised my ability to accurately recollect the pathway into the experience. In what seemed like moments, I saw and then felt the garden taking form all around me. Kalista was standing by the hanging baskets, pruning away, pretty much where I had recalled leaving her the last time I had visited. As my perception became more acute and I focused on the details of what Kalista was doing, I felt a sharp, sinking feeling run through my midsection. All of the hanging baskets were doing brilliantly, as they had been when I had last visited save for one; the one Kalista had assigned to me, which looked mostly dead. I was shocked. I quickly made my way to Kalista – marched over in a huff, really – and stared at her defiantly.

"What? What the hell happened to my basket?"

"I don't know. What happened to it?" She responded with a straight face.

"This isn't funny Kalista. I take responsibilities very seriously. I'm a... "

"Really? Did you think it would take care of itself while you were away?"

"What? While I was... what are you talking about?"

"I said I'd water it for you. That was it. Did you forget what I told you about them? That they need care too."

"Well I... "

She looked down the pathway surrounded by roses. "Just a second. I have an idea. Tresden, hey Tresden."

"You have a dog named Tresden?"

"Ah, well... no. Not really," she giggled.

"Hey Kalista, look, I just wanted... " I felt edgy.

"It's O.K., really. I just thought we could get some special help on your basket issue. Maybe a few other things too. There's someone I wanted you to meet anyway," she said.

With that, I clearly heard – and then saw – a person walking down the rose garden pathway toward us. I've no idea what was so amazing about that to me. Possibly I thought that a delusion with three people in it was a very complicated affair and well beyond my ability to handle. In any event, I found the entry of a third person into whatever perceptional state I was in to be a bit circus-like. Clearly, I was not in control of these events. Recognizing and accepting this, I again surrendered to the momentum of the circumstances, fascinated to see what could possibly happen next.

The person that had made their way down the pathway was, unusual looking. Androgynous either by design or by nature, I couldn't really tell which. At the time, I was quite embarrassed that I was having such great difficulty ascertaining the gender of this person, even as he/she came within a few feet of me. Every time I would convince myself that the being was a female, some subtlety would make me consider just the opposite. After much consternation and changing my opinion several times, I concluded that the person was most likely a female but I remained quite guarded on that determination. I made a conscious note not to comment out loud on any gender issues until I was certain. I felt ridiculous.

She was slightly taller than Kalista, I would have guessed possibly 5'8", maybe a bit more. Her hair was jet black and cropped short and quite straight. Her eyes were set rather wide apart, with faintly defined eyebrows. The effect was to over-emphasize her very large, striking eyes that gave the impression of being of a light purple shading. I had never seen eyes of this color in my life. Much like Kalista, I found it quite difficult to really focus on her eyes for more than a second or two.

There was an unusual, yet haunting, glow to her eyes that defied any attempt at my really looking deeply into them. It was more than a bit disconcerting. I also noticed immediately that she had perfect skin. More than that really. It was as though it had been polished with a smooth cloth for many years. It had a velvet quality to it that gave the impression that it was close to being opaque. She was quite thin – it was almost as though I was looking at a ruler. I'd guessed her age as early forties.

She was dressed in what appeared to be ordinary green denim jeans and a simple off-white, short-sleeved tee shirt. Over this, she had on a gardening smock that was shaded in a distinctly unusual tint of green, not unlike the color of the material that the fountain was made of. In her left hand she was holding a pair of gardening shears with bright red colored handles. On her right wrist was a simple silver bracelet with a light blue, possibly teal-colored, stone in it. She was a light-skinned black as nearly as I could tell. Had I been in the Caribbean, I might have thought she was Jamaican or possibly Bermudan. In any case, she was very attractive for a woman. A little less so if this was a man.

"Chuck, this is Tresden. Tresden, Chuck."

"Hi... uh, is it Trez dine?" I badly misinterpreted the impression that Kalista had conveyed when she introduced her.

"Good day. Well, actually, it would be more like **Tresden**. But I shouldn't fret about it."

When she reinforced the impression of her name, I understood it much better. In an identical manner to Kalista, Tresden obviously had the ability to communicate in concepts and by directly imparting those impressions to me without the obstacle of language as we know it.

"Oh, sorry," I said.

"Don't be ridiculous. You did perfectly. So, you called Kalista? Did you need something?" she asked.

"Yup. Chuck's having some problems with... "

"I'm not having any problems."

"Really?" Kalista gave me a gentle smile.

"Well, nothing major. I just... it's just that I can't make sense out of some of what you told me."

"You sound surprised. Did you think you'd learn all that you needed to about the Universe in a couple of short conversations?"

"I guess not," I admitted.

"So, where are you stuck?"

"I'm still a bit lost on what life really is? I mean what we call life where I come from... what you said you call a dream," I said.

"Hmm, you really don't like to take on the easy questions do you? Tresden has always had a pretty interesting way of explaining that. Care to give it a shot, Tresden?"

"I'm happy to try. O.K., First off, I know that Kalista must have explained to you that we are all spun off from Source. And that as such, no matter what happens to us – no matter where we go and what we do or don't do – we can never be separated from Source. Have you grasped the full impact of that yet?"

"I don't think so. Source? Source... what is Source?" I asked.

"Kalista, you haven't gone over that?" Tresden feigned surprise.

"I was saving that for... well, another time and, let's say a more powerful presenter."

A sly and knowing smile creeping up around the edges of Tresden's lips, "Oh. Quite right, actually. Excellent. O.K. then, for now, let's just leave it that Source would roughly equate in your terms with God. But don't become too attached to that concept yet."

"The old man with the white beard in robes?" I asked.

At that, both Tresden and Kalista burst out laughing almost uncontrollably, yet still well within the limitation of what would be considered good-natured. I would not learn until somewhat later why they had this odd response. After a few moments, they regained their composure and continued.

"Let's just say for now that, the popular concept of God as an old man in white robes has been... well, it has been over-interpreted quite a bit over the years," Tresden said.

"Yes. I know. And, it's getting worse all the time. Look. This is a simple straightforward question: Is there a God, yes or no?" I asked.

"It's funny how you think the most simple and direct questions are actually the most complex ones," Kalista said.

"Kalista, why can't you just answer the question?"

"O.K.; yes, there is a God and, no, there isn't," she said.

"Screw you!" I shouted.

"Oh my, I shouldn't think that was the best approach with Kalista," Tresden said.

"I'm sorry, did I hear one of your colorful metaphors slip out?" Kalista chided me. I couldn't tell if Kalista was really offended or not. The look on her face was completely flat, and the timber of her delivery had not changed at all.

It was at this point that I'd also realized that Tresden's thought imprints had a very unique quality to them. While I did not experience, or "hear" a voice, when Kalista or Tresden communicated, I was now aware that both of them had a uniquely distinct impression or style that they used when they accessed this form of communication. What triggered this awareness in me was an observation I had that Tresden's communication seemed to have almost a British quality to both the content and intonation when she "spoke." As I was pondering and about to comment on this, I decided that I should just apologize to Kalista for my remarks and deal with the communications

63

dynamics later. "I apologize Kalista, but this is very frustrating for me."

"Never mind all that. I understand your frustration; really I do. Go on Chuck."

"Wait, just a sec. When you say spun out, are you saying that we, in essence, are a piece of "Source?" I asked.

"In a manner of speaking, absolutely! You have to think of it as you might think of a hologram. Even though we are spun off from Source we also constantly contain the whole of the Source. Understand?" Tresden asked.

"No, not really. I'm completely lost," I said.

"Let me try, Tresden. Even though, as an individual soul, you are spun off and have the 'appearance' of being separate… a distinct soul unto yourself – you are always not only completely connected, but you also completely contain everything that Source is. Always. Forever." Kalista said.

"But that would mean that everyone, everywhere was completely connected. All in essence one thing," I said.

"Brilliant!" Kalista applauded.

"Brilliant what? I'm still lost," I said.

Tresden moved a bit so as to be able to address me directly. "Possibly it will help you to think of it in this way. Imagine that the Source of all energies of all life is an ocean. Simply put, an inconceivably enormous mass of pure, pristine pulsating, flowing and perfect light energy. Over-saturated with compassion and unconditional love, far beyond your – or anyone's – ability to conceive. All life, all sentience, exists in all forms within and flows from, and only from, this Source. Some of the water is closer to the shore and some is more in the middle of the ocean. No matter where the water is though, it is still part of the same ocean. The water off the coast of Africa is the same water as that touching New England. Imagine then that wherever there is sea shore is a place that incarnations can take place. And, that when the water crashes up on the beach, that it is the same as a life taking shape, an incarnation being created."

"But Tresden, a wave crashes up on the beach for only a few seconds and then sort of just seeps back into the ocean."

"Yes Chuck," Tresden smiled. "It does. How long do you think a life is in the grand scheme of Universal existence?"

"Oh, I... "

"And when the wave does return back... "

"It's still part of the ocean," I chimed in. "Still connected to the ocean. It's still water."

"Chuck, was it ever not water? Even while the wave crashed up on to the beach, wasn't it still just water, no matter what container it happened to be walking around in for a few years?" Tresden asked.

"So, are you saying that no matter what form of incarnation we might take at any given time, we're still part of the Source? Is that what I should consider?"

"No need to do so. You just did. You're right Kalista, he's much smarter than he looks." Tresden was smiling from ear to ear as she said this. There was nothing at all demeaning about what she said, or the way she said it. It was simply understood, without communicating any further, that my having grasped this concept in fairly short order was very much appreciated by both Kalista and Tresden.

"I'm still lost a bit. It can't be that a life taking shape is as random a thing as whether the water happens to crash up onto the shore, can it?"

"She didn't say that. Besides, it's a metaphor and, no matter how beautiful or how brilliant, metaphors will never be as perfect as the Universe itself," Kalista said.

"So Kalista, is it the case that, much like waves that come to shore and seep back out again, that, since that particular water is still nearby the shoreline that it is more likely to come ashore again? In essence, for the soul to reincarnate in this world again sooner as opposed to later?"

Tresden grinned. "Wow Kalista, he is on the way. Yes, Chuck but, it is not necessarily so. As Kalista has told you, it depends on what the soul – as guided by consultation with their counsel – has decided. Obviously though, it's a bit easier to effect an incarnation if you happen to be near the shore as opposed to the middle of the ocean."

"Interesting. Now that you mention it though, what's it like in the middle of the ocean?"

"Kalista?"

"I don't think so, Tresden. Not yet."

"What's with the secret code?" I asked.

"Kalista doesn't think you're ready to know that yet. Don't take it personally."

"What do you mean?"

"The fact is, we learn things when we are ready to learn them. You'd have little frame of reference for that particular explanation or that experience. It would be like teaching you calculus before learning algebra. Although in that example, it would be more like trying to teach you calculus before you learned how to walk. No matter though. In this case, before you go sailing off to the middle of the ocean, your soul counsel wants to make sure that you understand a bit more about navigation."

"And weather," Tresden added.

"Right! Weather," Kalista giggled.

Much like my conversations with Kalista, Tresden had a special ability to impart knowledge well beyond the limitations of just her words – her "concept transfers," as I had begun to call them. All at once, a view of life that I had never before pondered began to cascade into my thoughts. The analogy that Tresden had used triggered images in my mind of my recent visit to the beach only a few months before. I had watched with fascination as waves lapped up onto the shore only to ease back out into the water. And then, the same water would seemingly wash back on shore again only a few moments later.

What if our lives were just like that? And those around us were neighboring waves. Would it not make sense that, since they are so close to us that they would more or less come "ashore" at the same times and in the same places as we did? Why did so many of the people that I came across in my life seem so familiar to me? I reflected back on all that I had read about groups of souls incarnating pretty much at the same time, in the same place. It all made sense. It was like listening to the tumblers of a lock fall into place. Still, there were other aspects of what they had said that left some holes in the explanation for me to fill.

"Actually, that helps me quite a bit, but I'm still unsure about what life actually is." I said.

"Oh, that," Tresden said.

"Yeah, that!"

"What would you like to know?"

"Is it real?" I asked.

"Real?"

"By the way, Tresden, Chuck's got a genuine blockage on that word," Kalista said.

"Real. Let me think about that. Real. Hmm, from the point of view of those that are living it at the time, sure, I suppose it's real."

"What kind of answer is that?" I asked.

"You didn't like that one?" Tresden asked.

"No. It was very clever, actually. It just doesn't tell me anything."

"Real, huh? Well, let's say that, if it didn't have the impression of reality, it would be useless."

"You're going the wrong direction, Tresden. That's even less clear than the last answer."

"Just tell 'em, Tresden. He'll have to deal with it like we all did," Kalista said.

"All right. You asked for it. Life is quite unreal for the period when it isn't being experienced."

"What the hell does that mean?" I snapped.

"Think about it for a while," Kalista giggled.

I did. It made less sense the more I thought about it. If the point was that it was "real" from certain perspectives, why didn't they just say so? "Kalista, are we going back to what you told me about dreams; that they only seem real at the time but, once you wake up and examine them from the perspective of being fully awakened that it's clear at that point that they were not real? In essence that the degree that something is "real" depends upon the unique perspective of who's asking the question; the person that is experiencing the "real life" or that same person after they ostensibly "wake up."

"Oh golly Kalista, he _is_ a bright one, isn't he? Excellent."

"Is that a yes?" I asked.

"Pretty much," Kalista said.

"So, if I was trying to explain this to someone else, what would I say?"

"Good question. What would you say?" Kalista was encouraging me with her eyes – to follow through.

"I guess I'd say that what we call 'life' is real while you're experiencing it, but that afterward, when you're in the... ah, is it... would you say the 'natural state'?"

"True State will do," Kalista said.

"O.K., O.K. I can do this; when you're in the True State you see it as non-real."

"Relative to your True State," Tresden chimed in.

"What?"

"Don't let go now. You're just about there."

"Relative to?"

"Think back. When you go to sleep at night, you 'know,' well, you believe actually, that your Waking State is what you call your 'normal' state. When you fall asleep and have a dream, for that period of time, you forget about your 'normal state' and believe, if even for the few brief moments that the dream lasts, that the dream state is your 'real' state. To you, at the time, that dream feels like all there is. From your limited perspective at the moment that dream is ongoing that **is** all there is. It feels real to you. Then, when you awaken, you immediately realize that it was not real at all, although you might well be sweating bullets from the villain that you believed was chasing you in the dream," Kalista summed it all up.

"I think I get it," I was beaming with comprehension.

"Kalista, he does appear to have the look as though he's got it," Tresden said.

"So, what we call life just **feels** real to us?" I asked.

"That's close. We already covered this, though," Kalista pointed out.

"Wait. I'll get it. It has to feel real to us," I said.

"Why?" Kalista asked.

"I don't remember."

"Have you ever learned anything – had any insights – from a dream that you had?" she pushed.

"Well, sometimes. Sure," I said hesitantly.

"Think about it, people expend all sorts of energy trying to figure out their dreams. They talk to friends about it. Spend fortunes talking to psychiatrists about it. They search for endlessly for meaning in them. So, I'll ask again. Can you learn anything from what has happened in a dream?"

"You mean what we *think* has happened."

"Brilliant! There you go."

"So, if 'life' didn't *feel* real to us, we wouldn't absorb the lessons that it has?" I asked.

"It's worse than that really. No matter how real the Universe manages to make life feel real and no matter how perfect an illusion the Universe sets up to convince everyone experiencing what they are calling life at the time that it *is* real, there are plenty of people that make the trip into life and still don't learn the lessons." Tresden said.

"And what happens to them?"

"Your memory can't be that bad," Kalista chided.

"Oh. Right. They go back over and over again until they do learn."

"If... " she prodded.

"If they choose to learn that way."

"And if they don't?" Tresden asked.

"Solitary confinement."

"WHAT ?" Kalista was appalled.

"You said... "

"I said what?" she challenged me.

"You said they get sent off to think about it for a thousand years or so."

"Did I?"

"Didn't you?" I asked confused.

"Oh brother. Chuck, if I were you...," Tresden attempted to intervene.

"It's okay, Tresden, let him dig his own pit even deeper. He's really good at it."

"What did I do?"

"Listen, it's your life and all but, as someone that's been learning from Kalista for a couple thousand years, I can tell you that she's going to respond much better if you don't misquote her," Tresden said.

"I thought that's what she said."

"Care to shoot for best two out of three?" Kalista asked.

Maybe it's better if I just ask you to tell me again. Maybe in a different way so that my dense brain has a chance to grasp it."

"I was just about to say self-deprecation doesn't work on Kalista but... "

Kalista chimed in, "It's O.K., his heart is in the right place. Listen. This is one of the essential lessons. A soul counsel will only intervene and 'direct' the soul on a path after first giving that soul many, many, many chances to see the most beneficial pathway on their own. Remember what I said: you decide. It is the soul themselves that decides whether to go off and think about it for a year or ten thousand or, to go back and take on an incarnation that will help them learn what they need. You're never really forced to do anything. It is very, very rare for us to ever have to do more than hint at what might be the most beneficial pathway for a given soul to take. Remember, too, the Universe has an eternity for you to learn what you have to. Literally."

"But you **can** intervene. I mean, if you need to."

"Wrong focus. You're seeing it as though the more advanced souls are some sort of disciplinary body. The Universe doesn't work, or need to work, in that way. As souls, as individual spun-off parts of Source, we have forever plus one day for everyone to learn what they have to in any way that they think will help them learn best. If they need to take five hundred lifetimes to work out their issues with other souls, if they need five thousand lifetimes to somehow convince themselves that they are not evil or bad or to clear up whatever other delusions they might have convinced themselves of, they have it. No questions asked," Kalista explained.

"So people just convince themselves that they're bad? They're actually not evil, no matter what they've done?" I asked.

"Of course they're not," Tresden said. "Because we're all spun off from Source at the outset. In essence, we're already perfect even if..."

"Even if we get a little soot and dust on us along the way. Even a lot of soot and dust," Kalista added.

"So, you're saying that our essential nature sort of keeps us programmed along some path of reasonability," I asked.

"Reasonability?" Kalista asked, raising her eyebrows for emphasis.

"Well, that we're basically programmed in such a way that, say, if we get 'dirty' to a certain extent that we know to go back and do a few lives to get the soot off before we try to come back into the palace with the white carpets," I recited.

"Bollocks Kalista, just when you thought he was close."

"What? What did I say?"

"You're suggesting, even indirectly, that there's some 'palace,' some 'heaven' to return to when you get all the dirt off," Tresden said.

"There isn't? No heaven?" I asked.

"Not in the way you're thinking about it," Kalista said.

"Where did I fall off track?"

Kalista sharpened her approach, "I told you. Everyone – no exceptions – was spun off from Source. Can't change that. It is not only our essential nature, it IS what we ARE. You can't *return* to the palace because... "

"We're already there?" I jumped in.

"As long as you don't think of 'there' as being a 'place'," Tresden said.

"I'm not sure I... "

"Remember what Tresden said about the ocean?"

"Yeah but... "

"Is the wave, no matter whether it's on the shore or washing back out to sea or whatever... is it ever separate from the ocean? Is it ever not water? Is its essence ever anything *other* than water?"

"No, it isn't."

"No, it isn't," added Tresden.

"No, it isn't," Kalista said.

"So, what stops us from *feeling* like we're part of that ocean while we're experiencing what we call life?"

"Dirt. Soot. Debris. Our completely misguided belief that we're less than perfect," Tresden responded.

"Which causes temporary blindness," Kalista added.

"And, to rid ourselves of all that dirt?" I asked.

"Compassion. Love. Recollection that, we not only came from Source but, that we are Source at our essence. Remember, a diamond is a diamond, even if it's buried in the ground. It's not going to turn back into coal no matter how much it might 'think' that it can."

"And once we're pretty much cleaned off... I mean, do we come back here, do we continue to take on lives – incarnations – even then?"

"There are other lessons. Other venues. Different pathways. Deeper and more colorful parts of the ocean to swim in. More significant pathways to walk along," Kalista said.

"But, you could if you wanted to. Dirty place though. You never know if you might get some on you and kick off an entirely new cycle of karma all over again," Tresden said wryly.

"You could see a few Broadway shows, get some star's autographs. I always wanted to drive a Maserati." Though straightfaced, I knew Kalista was joking.

They looked at each other and burst out laughing. Having made their point, they clearly didn't want me to get mired in the heaviness of the subject matter. It had shaken me to my bones, though. Life, what I had thought of as life before today, was turned on its head, and in reality turned out to be not much more than an illusion. I'd read Richard Bach's "Illusions" years ago. It had made a certain amount of sense when I'd read it the first time. But more in theory. Kalista and Tresden were talking about it as though it needed to be taken almost literally.

If life was a dream state designed as a way for us to learn certain things, without doing any real damage to what we actually are, a piece of the original Source, it made me ponder certain dreams that I had. Did I learn anything from them? Did I have any lasting insights from them? Yes, I did. No matter how much my heart might have been pumping in sheer terror when I woke up from some of those dreams, I wasn't really hurt. That spear thrown by the angry native didn't really puncture my lung. I thought it did as it was happening, but there was no real damage.

The concept of life as an advanced form of classroom started to make sense to me. The soul could perfect – re-perfect – without really risking any true damage. The dragon only felt real to us, I thought. We can choose to believe that life is real as much as we want. In the end though, the diamond, our souls, were unscratched. As Kalista had pointed out, it actually can't be scratched. Whoever thought all this up, I remember saying to myself, really did their homework. As with before, though, the ideas Kalista was speaking of evoked a few more questions.

"Yeah, very funny guys. Listen, I'm still confused on a few things. If we have a choice to live an incarnated life or, say, just hang out in the disincarnated spirit world where, I assume there's no disease, taxes or any of life's other little joys; if that's our choice, why bother to live at all?"

"Why bother to go to school? Is that the question?" Tresden asked.

"What?"

"We've told you; life is a school where certain lessons are learned with much greater efficiency than you can learn anywhere else. And I guess that you want to just skip over the joy, occasional elation and the wide range of incredibly positive physical and emotional experiences that also come into lifetimes in the incarnate form? Love, sex, walking on the beach... "

"No, but that can't possibly be the reason for living, for taking a physical life on Earth," I protested.

"Maybe it's just compensation for all of the less attractive aspects and difficult challenges of incarnate life? A reward of sorts for putting up with the school. Consider it recess."

"Well said Tresden."

"Maybe, but, that still leaves a pretty large gap in the explanation. So why bother to incarnate? Why live what is no more than a fancy dressed up illusion?"

"Hmm, let's see; Kalista has tried to explain this to you a number of different ways over the years, none of which have worked. Let's try this: say that you want to learn to be a locksmith."

"I would never, **ever**, want to learn to be a locksmith. Not in a million years. Even if I was locked out of my house," I said.

"Ah but, you see, that's just it; eventually, there are a wide variety of core essential lessons that each soul simply has to fully absorb into their essence, whether it's a lesson that you recognize as being essential or not," Tresden said.

"And locksmithing is one of them?" I reminded myself silently that higher souls have a great deal of influence over a number of things that can make our lives miserable if they are agitated, but it was too late.

"I was just thinking it's about time for you to have a few lifetimes as a mosquito," Kalista said, with a sinister smile.

"Sorry. O.K., back to locksmith school. Actually, it's starting to sound like an interesting career."

Kalista smiled broadly at my vague attempt at humor and my weak effort to smooth over my marginally inappropriate remarks.

"All right. Let's say that you have a choice between having all of the locksmith course material sent to you where ever you are and, that with those materials in hand you can complete home study. Or as an alternative, you can take some initiative and actually go to the school where locksmithing is being taught. Now, some people would eventually learn everything they needed to just from studying the books at home. However, most people would learn much faster and far more effectively if they actually went to the school and experienced what it feels like to take a lock apart, watch an expert repair one and so forth," Kalista explained intently.

"So, you're saying that its purely a matter of learning efficiency? Hands-on experience, more or less?"

"That's one part of it. Remember, though, souls that have taken physical incarnations tend to generate some karma for themselves just by virtue of living. Unfortunately, that experience of living quite often results in some negative accumulation, particularly from the younger souls out on their early attempts at life. So they often need some lifetimes to work things out with other souls that have been built up over lifetimes of complicated relationships," Tresden said.

"So between the two things, learning and working out karma, we pretty much keep coming back."

"Wasn't it you that was thinking about how people themselves perpetuate their own cycles, by failing to break their own cycles?"

Kalista asked.

"Yeah, that was me," I pouted.

"Don't take it too hard, Chuck. This is a tricky business and some of the essential lessons that a soul has to master are pretty complicated. It all takes time, which is why we are granted an eternity to sort it all out," Tresden said.

"Why don't you help us? I mean, wouldn't it save a lot of wear and tear on people if you guys with all of the answers gave us a hand now and then?" I asked.

"We do. I shudder to think what shape your world might be in if the disincarnated souls didn't drop hints and give people a few gentle nudges in the right direction now and then," Kalista said.

"You forgot something Kalista," Tresden interjected.

"Did I?"

"Yes. He said, 'you guys with all the answers'."

"I assumed he was kidding."

"Didn't seem like it."

"You were joking right?"

"Well, I... "

"Oh good gracious sakes! I told you this; we're in the same school. Tresden and I are just a few grades ahead of you."

"Right. But, you'll probably meet someone with pretty much all of the answers one of these days," Tresden assured me.

They once again looked at each other and one more time, at my expense, began a subtle burst of giggling. I had no idea at all what they meant. It had the air of mystery to it, though. But I opted to leave it alone and press on with the subject at hand.

"So, you're saying that you *do* help? That you do intervene?"

"Help, yes. Intervene, no," Tresden said.

"Boy, I don't know guys, that sounds like a pretty thin hair to split," I replied.

"But one that has to be split nevertheless," Kalista said.

"Why?"

"I told you this already. The nestling has to fight their way out of the egg on their own. We can put on our pom-poms and stand on the sidelines and cheer, exhort, encourage and provide all the spiritual support in the world. And we do. But in the end, it wouldn't mean anything if the soul didn't fight their way back on their own. Didn't master the lessons on their own. Didn't sort out and resolve all of their own karma, on their own."

"Why not?"

"I was just about to ask you the same question. Why not?"

"Kalista, I rarely ask questions if I already know the answer."

"Yes, you do. In fact, you do it all the time. You just aren't sure that you genuinely know the answer so you try to play it safe and see if you can get someone else to answer it for you. You're not getting your grade promotion until you learn to stand up and say what you do know, so may as well start now. I'll ask again, why does the soul need to scratch and claw its way back on its own?"

"Maybe because they wouldn't believe in themselves completely if someone else helped them. They'd think they were somehow less deserving to 'be in the club' because they had help," I replied.

"Would they be right?" Tresden asked me.

"I guess they might be."

"It wouldn't matter. To move on, you need the confidence that you can swim in the deep water on your own. The soot, the dirt; it weighs you down. You simply need to be able to make it without a lifeguard or you don't get to wander very far from shore. If you don't have that confidence, you might get lost someday," Kalista said.

"Lost? Lost where?" I asked.

"It was a figure of speech," Tresden replied.

"So, when you say things like, "fight their way out of the egg on their own," you're talking about a soul making it back home. Returning in some other way to the Source since, as you've already said, we're completely and permanently connected to the Source as it is."

"See. I told you. You know more than you think," Kalista said.

"Before we go there though, I still don't understand why it takes us so long to get it. I mean, people – souls that is – have been incarnating on the Earth for a long time. Are we really that dense that it takes us thousands of years to get all this?"

"Oh my. You're not going to like the answer she has for that one,"

Tresden said.

"It's worse than you think; souls were incarnating on places other than Earth long before they came there."

"Other than Earth?" I asked, incredulous.

"Do all waves come ashore in Florida?" Kalista quizzed me.

"Oh. I never thought about that. So the bad news is, we're even dumber than it seems."

"I wouldn't say dumber at all. Remember, the Universe has done a pretty good job of making the world seem like a very real place. And, it's basic human nature to get into a mess now and then. If you add in the complicating factor that people create karma for themselves without even knowing it until they advance to a certain stage, it's even more complex. Takes time to sort all that out. Time, and patience," she reminded me.

"And... "

"Oh, right, Tresden. And, we make you drink the brew before you incarnate."

"Brew. What brew?" I asked skeptically.

"Ah, sorry. Well, one of the conditions of incarnation is that you have to accept a sort of temporary amnesia about your True State. We do that by making you take some stuff before you take off for a life. What's that drink called Tresden?"

"This is bull... "

"Ah, ah ah... careful. Kalista is still young and innocent," Tresden laughed.

"Sorry. What possible benefit could there be to making us endure amnesia?" I asked.

"I already told you. If you didn't believe fully in the illusion of the world you wouldn't take the lessons with the level of seriousness that they require in order to get the complete impact of the experience. But beyond the issues dealing with the experience itself, if you *knew* that the learning experience was mostly illusory you probably wouldn't absorb the lessons very well. You must believe that failure has consequences to some extent. Otherwise, people tend to act out basic delinquency scripts. They don't go to school. They don't learn. And because of this pattern, their ability to progress and become a contributing soul in the Universe is compromised until they do." Kalista explained.

"But... but," I was stymied.

"But what? Are you going to try to tell me that if you had the presence of mind while you were having a dream to really recognize it **as** a dream that you wouldn't rather wake-up in the place where you are comfortable and completely and forever safe and secure? If you knew it was that illusory are you telling me that you would still run away from the dragon that was chasing you in the dream?" Kalista asked almost breathlessly.

"Hmm, maybe not."

"Probably not," Tresden said.

"Definitely not," Kalista concurred.

We all looked at each other and burst out laughing. It was contagious. I noticed that my head was almost swimming with all of the insights Kalista and Tresden had shared with me. The view of the Universe they had explained to me had such incredibly broad and powerful implications on the meaning of our lives. Our purpose and our pathways here. The world, at least as I had been seeing it up until then, was a completely different place with different rules. I felt as though someone had whispered some major portion of a secret code in my ear and that many of the puzzles that had been confounding me all of my life would rapidly begin to sort themselves out. I also had the presence of mind to realize that I only had some portion of the secret code. There was much more that I needed to know. That I was desperate to learn.

Tresden took a few minutes to show me some particulars about maintenance of the hanging flower baskets. The instructions set my mind at ease about the disaster that had greeted me as I had arrived that morning. She also advised me that she'd look in on my basket now and then while I was away, as long as I didn't tell Kalista that she was helping me. I knew intuitively that there were no secrets between Kalista and Tresden, but I winked at her when she said this anyhow.

More importantly, I knew to an absolute certainty that the experience I was having with Kalista and Tresden – no matter **what** it actually was – was real and not delusional. Not a dream. Possibly it was because Tresden had illustrated for me that the concept of "real" wasn't all that substantial and firm after all. Maybe it was simply that what they were telling me just resonated as being undeniably "true" at some place in my being where I just know when things are true as differentiated from "correct."

From that day onward, I never again doubted the validity of the experience. And despite my usual curious nature, I found that I had no real interest in learning any deeper insight into what the experience actually was, nor to define it in any way. It didn't matter. Any doubt that I'd had about the viability or truth of the insights that were being shared with me simply left, and left completely. Never to return after this session.

Kalista managed to communicate to me that I'd had enough for one day and, as always, she made it abundantly clear that I was welcome back whenever I wanted to come. With that, Tresden smiled gently and then waved goodbye. The two of them went walking up the pathway that was bordered by the roses. They were gone in a matter of moments.

As I had done on previous occasions when I wanted to return to my home, I began to concentrate on the details of my study and, in what seemed like a few moments, I found myself back home, exhausted, elated and to some degree enlightened. At least more then when I had set out that day.

As nearly as I could tell, I had been gone almost four hours this time. I spent several minutes scrawling a number of notes to myself. I guess that I was far more depleted than I had gauged because as I attempted to get up off the floor and make it upstairs to my bedroom, I lost my initiative. My energy had become so depleted from this session with Kalista and Tresden that I decided to simply sit back down and then passed out on the floor of my study until the next day.

As I drifted off into a deep sleep, I remember thinking about the classroom that we all share here. Bullies. Lessons. Grading on the curve. Pass/fail. Recess. Graduation. I made a mental note that, before I was done with Kalista and Tresden, I would learn about the spiritual equivalent of all these things. As it turned out, before it was over, I would learn far more than just that.

CHAPTER FOUR

Take this kiss upon the brow!,
and in parting from you now,.
this much let me avow;
You are not wrong, who deem.
that my days have been a dream,
yet if hope has flown away
in a night or, or in a day,
in a vision, or in none,
All that we see or seem,
is but a dream within a dream.

- From A Dream Within A Dream, Edgar Allan Poe

By early spring 1994, I had begun to make subtle adjustments to my lifestyle in order to compensate for the dramatic effects that the spiritual insights shared at Kalista's garden were having on me. I had attained a true knowing somewhere deep inside of me that the exchanges were not dreams, delusions or simply the product of an overly active, vivid imagination. This gave me a much-needed foothold and the confidence required to support my next steps along this journey.

It took constant effort on my part to make sure that the overwhelming insights that I was gaining by virtue of my visits to Kalista and Tresden didn't outwardly affect my behavior in the business world. This was a substantial challenge and, to some extent, remains so to this day. The insights often invaded my daily world in ways that were difficult for me foresee much less control. In the middle of conversations dealing with topics like corporate strategy, I would sometimes drift off into my own little world. I'd ponder how the genuinely unscrupulous business dealings that I had just witnessed one businessperson impart on another might affect them when they got to the time and place where they would see, and feel, the playback of those events.

I came face to face several times a day with people where I worked, or folks who I conducted business with, who had no concept of the consequences of their actions. That their actions would someday come home to roost in ways that they never could imagine. If they only knew, I thought, the entire business world would turn on its ear overnight. Then again, maybe not. There is no shortage of people in the world that conduct their lives as though there was never a day when we face our actions. People actually believe that "this" is all there is. That the only consequences and lessons are those that arise within the limit of our 70 or 80 years here.

Having this unique perspective placed me in a decidedly unenviable disadvantage in the business world: I was playing by the "rules." The reality of consequences and lessons as explained to me by Kalista and Tresden. The trouble was, virtually no one else was. Not these rules at any rate.

This thread of thought gave rise to other issues that I felt compelled to explore with Kalista. The examples that she used; the incredibly thought-provoking illustrations that came across as metaphors that she and Tresden came up with seemingly out of thin air shook me to my essence. After the last session, I had assigned myself two days off and had taken a drive down to Atlantic City to watch the ocean's waves come ashore for a while. To think and to carefully ponder what Kalista and Tresden had taught me so far.

Early March is not exactly ideal beach weather in New Jersey. So I bundled up in two sweaters and sat by the window of my hotel room, watching wave after wave make their way onto the beach only to observe them slowly seeping their way back out. Thinking about what Tresden had told me about souls reincarnating more or less in that pattern.

In a moment of scientific fascination, I drove over to the convenience store and bought several large bottles of liquid food dye in as many colors as they had in stock. I stopped at a sporting goods store and bought a dozen ping-pong balls as well. I then took my packages back to my hotel room and began dyeing the ping pong balls in various color schemes which, in my planned experiment, were going to represent different souls that would be incarnating by coming ashore over and over again on the waves.

After allowing the dyed ping-pong balls to dry, I drove over to a small inlet where the waves were much smaller and coming ashore very gently. I took each ball out of the bag one at a time and tossed them as far out as I could – a fairly difficult task considering they weigh close to nothing and the wind was pretty much directly in my face.

As I flung each ball into the water, I envisioned; this one's Mom, here's Susan, this one's me and so forth. Over the course of an hour or so, I watched with riveted fascination as the ping-pong balls washed up on shore and then back out. Sometimes a ball would wash up on its own. But usually with one or several others of the original group or in different combinations. As the balls came ashore less and less often, I began to think about them washing ashore later that day, maybe a mile or two away or, in France or Africa weeks or months later.

Tresden's explanation made complete sense to me at that point. There were no doubts left in my mind about how we incarnate in groupings of souls. Most often, but not necessarily, with others that we know. Or we can, as Tresden said, "if we so choose." I recalled what the Dalai Lama had said when asked about reincarnation, "It is no more amazing to be born twice than it is to be born once."

This exercise served as fodder for even more thinking on this broad topic. More questions. Much deeper and intricate issues. I had become frustrated with the brilliantly insightful information Kalista and Tresden had shared. Most of it, to this point, felt more theoretical than practical. In the day-to-day reality that is life, there were real complications and situations were hard. And while everything that Tresden and Kalista said made complete sense to me, I was becoming frustrated as to how practical the information actually was. I had problems and issues that I needed to deal with. There were unreasonable people in my life every day. Personal relationships that were more "mystery" than spiritual exercise. Having the view from on high – an ascended master's perspective – was interesting. But it wasn't helping me deal with reality. My reality.

Above and beyond that was what I had come to call the "scalability issue." There are four billion people on the Earth, I thought. Unless Kalista was planning on expanding the garden to a great extent and, holding sessions around the clock, how much could the world really change for the better if only a few, or even a few thousand, people knew about these insights? And just knowing about them wasn't enough to affect outcomes; you had to do the work, right? Make the effort.

The last time I visited the garden I learned that if I could hold one or two key thoughts at the top of my mind as I entered the meditative state that I might be able to retain the essence of them as a starting point for a conversation. Holding two of the issues in my mind that were troubling me the most, I set out to find Kalista hoping that she could once again lead me down the pathway toward greater clarity. My journey to the garden on this occasion was uneventful, and I found Kalista smiling peacefully. She was sitting on the bench below the gigantic weeping willow tree and appeared to be waiting for me. As the details of the garden came into sharper focus, Kalista opened up the conversation as though I had never left.

"I know, I know. You're still confused about a few things. It's okay, really," she said.

"It's not that bad, Kalista. A lot of what you and Tresden explained last time really had a profound effect on me. I'm much better off than I was."

"Yeah. I told you. Tresden is a real master explainer," she smiled broadly at me.

"The trouble is though... "

"The trouble is that you have problems that bother you every day. What you call 'theory' isn't helping you with all that. Right?"

"Kalista, how do you know all that? That's not the first time you've known what I was thinking."

"It's no more than a basic spiritual sleight of hand. You'll pick it up before you know it. There are much better things for you to focus on at this juncture in the road though. Let's go back; tell me what is bothering you the most."

"If you already know, why bother to ask?" I inquired.

"I'd rather that you try to tell me in your own words. It will mean more to you that way," she said.

"There are so many things in life Kalista that seem unfair. Things out of control that catch us in the whirlwind. Innocent people every day that just... "

"Sorry, I got distracted for a moment. Did you say *innocent* people?"

"Sure. What's wrong with that?" I asked.

"It seems that you may have been asleep part of the time when we explained some concepts to you," she said.

"Why? What did I miss?"

"O.K., Look, let's take this slowly. When you suggest that things happen to innocent people, you're inferring that people can be *innocent* aren't you?"

"You're not going to tell me there's no such thing as innocence," I protested.

"Sorry. No there isn't. Not in the way that you're using it," she replied.

"That's a very, very hard concept for me to accept," I said.

"Possibly because you're looking at it in the wrong light? Assuming things that shouldn't be assumed?"

"What do you mean? How *should* I look at it?" I was astounded.

"First off, the most important thing for you to remember for this entire topic is that everyone – without exception – writes their own script in life. There are no exceptions. So, when something happens to someone – anything, from a heart attack to being overweight, to failing a math test – it can pretty much only occur because they agreed to it. More than that though, the likelihood is that they wrote the conceptual details of how it would happen overall. Either way, whatever is happening, that soul set it up as a learning device."

"Wait a minute Kalista. When I was in high school this seventeen-year-old guy named Curt was in a horrible traffic accident. He was in a body cast for a year. He felt unbelievable pain and he, his parents, family and friends suffered incredible stress. And what you're saying to me is that he **wanted** all that to happen? What are you – nuts?" I was incredulous.

"'Wanted' might be the wrong word, particularly the way you're thinking about it. Let's say that he knew it was coming and that he agreed to it," Kalista countered.

"I just can't believe that. I can't!" I said.

"And do you know why you can't?" she asked.

"I'm not sure."

"Because you've believed your whole lifetime, as most people have in many lifetimes, that when bad things happen, its either a quirk, a mystery or an 'accident.' Or because 'God was punishing the person for something that they did.' Because that's what you had always been told. Because most people would rather assume that bad things can only be attributed to external sources. It's the ultimate in avoiding personal responsibility; whatever happens, blame someone else. Whatever happens, I know that I wasn't responsible for it occurring. The trouble is, that assumption, that philosophy, is the exact opposite of what is true. Because, whatever is happening in your lifetime, you – and only you – brought it there. Believing anything else gets people into lifetimes of trouble and builds terrible spiritual habits," Kalista explained.

"I find that all pretty hard to believe, Kalista," I said.

"Really? What did *I* miss?"

I thought about what Kalista had said. Unfortunately, even though it went against my instincts, or actually, my programming, after thinking about it I had to agree with her. When something bad happened to someone, really bad, like terminal illness, murder, rape, whatever – my inclination was to be more mystified than anything else. A child ends up murdered by his mother and the last thing I'd ever think was that the child had somehow "agreed" to it in some complex "soul contract." But then I thought back to something that Tresden had said about karma and our actions creating a seemingly endless cycle of victim and victimizer candidates.

What if someone had killed a child in some previous life? If that person decided on their own, that the best way for them to learn the intricacies of just how terrible this felt they would, within the same act, find a pathway to otherwise resolve their karma. So they volunteer to be the victim this time. What other script could possibly work besides them stepping-up to be murdered as a child? I hated seeing things that way though. And the reason I hated it had more to do with having to accept this as an explanation for the way the world actually was, as opposed to holding out false hope that the madness in the world was attributable to something else. In a strange way I almost was rooting for some organized, evil forces to pin the woes of the world on. Needing answers that went far deeper I pressed on.

"I'm still unclear on something. What you're saying is that the only reason people agree to something horrible – even entire terrible lifetimes – is to make up for what they did previously? In some earlier life?"

"I never said that," she said.

"O.K., then why agree to a miserable and difficult life? Why would we agree to take on a life where there is so much pain, suffering and aggravation?" I asked.

"I don't know, why did you?" She had turned the question back on me.

"What did you say? WHAT?"

"You heard me. Why did you take on a life with so many problems? So much pain. Such incredible suffering. Such sadness."

"Gee, Kalista, I don't know about that, there are plenty of people in the world with a lot more difficulties in their life than I have." I was becoming confused.

"That's true but, let's think about your life for a while," she said.

That gave me cause to review the challenges that I had dealt with in this life. If what Kalista was saying was true, why would I have agreed to take on a life where I was orphaned at six months old? Placed in several foster homes where the abuse, beatings and torture were so bad that I had to be removed by the police multiple times. Diabetes at fifteen. All of the related challenges that go along with being a diabetic for twenty-five years and then a quintuple bypass at forty-eight. Failed relationships earlier in my life stacked up like air traffic over Chicago's O'Hare field. There were other issues and challenges, painful ones, that went on – mostly deep into my own dark pit. Still, Kalista was right, life hadn't been particularly easy for me. Tremendous physical and emotional pain sustained over most of my life, certainly. But everything in life is relative, I thought.

"Kalista, I find it very hard to believe that I would have agreed to all of that. That anyone would have," I said.

"To be honest, Chuck, at the time, we were a bit surprised as well," she answered.

"We?" I asked skeptically.

"Your soul counsel, your advisors. I told you, we get together in between lives and help you sort out what you did and didn't accomplish in the last life and other lives. We look at what you could have done better. Then, we help you do some planning for the next lifetime – show you several options – that will give you the best possible opportunities to learn what you need most to learn," she explained.

"Does everyone have a soul counsel?"

"Of course."

"So, you all sit around and say, 'Gee, Chuck really screwed up in his last life, let's put him someplace where they'll beat the hell out of him as a child and just for added measure, let's saddle him with a terrible disease that will last his entire life.' Is that what this counsel does?" I asked angrily.

"Is that what you really think?" she said, trying to soothe me.

"Well, how else did it end up that way? You said it was all pretty much planned out and... "

"Hold on, don't drive off the cliff just yet. Do you remember what I told you about taking on another incarnation? About who decides about returning to Earth for another life?"

"You said that I decide," I said, resigned.

"Right. And, while this might be hard for you to understand, before a soul takes on that life they agree to most of the basic circumstances of the life they will take on," she said.

"So we write our own fate?"

"Hmm. Write is okay. The trouble with what you said is with the word fate."

"Why?" I asked.

"Well, the way you say that, it sounds like you're suggesting that all of the events are pre-ordained. That the entire life is a foregone conclusion and that you're just there to go through the motions that have been completely planned out in advance," she said.

"I thought that's what you were saying?"

"No."

"So what's the difference then, if there's no fate?"

"I didn't say that either," she interrupted.

"Then what **is** fate?" I was becoming exasperated.

"If I had to sketch it out, I would say that fate is an agreement – a condition of a given life – that you will show up at a certain inter-section at certain time. The thing is when you get there, when you arrive at that intersection of opportunity, it is *you*, the driver, who has your hands on the steering wheel and, the option to hit the gas or, step on the brakes."

"And who makes sure that we're at that intersection at the right time?" I asked.

"Anyone who happens to have agreed to be at that intersection at that time of course," she said.

"I'm lost."

"You're making this a lot harder than it actually is. The planning for your next lifetime doesn't take place in a vacuum. We've already talked about the fact that you incarnate, more or less, with the same groups of souls over and over again. So, when the life-planning ses-sions are going on, you make certain agreements with other souls to try to work things out by connecting at various points in that lifetime. That way you can have a stage upon which to attempt to sort out your issues – and karma – with those in your group," Kalista explained.

"Is it really all that scripted? I mean, how am I supposed to remember all of the places that I'm supposed to show up, and recog-nize who I'm supposed to meet up with? How are those people sup-posed to know its me? Maybe my life isn't all that I want it to be because I've missed a few appointments that I forgot about?" I asked.

"First of all, it's not that inflexible. Second, there aren't *that* many intersections to remember, just a few major ones. Last, you know the souls that you will meet up with pretty well. Remember that you've probably lived many lifetimes with them in different roles already. Think about it. The people in your life that are really important to you – wasn't there some real familiarity when you first met them? Didn't you get a sense like the connection with them was much deeper than if you just met a stranger on the street?"

I thought about that, and it was absolutely true for me. Of the handful of people in my life that were genuinely important to me at the time, there really had been some sort of strong and definitive connection that occurred almost immediately when I first met them. It truly felt as though I had known them much longer than the few minutes that had actually passed.

"So that's how it works. I always wondered about that. It's recognition from previous lives that allows us to know the other souls so well over such a great period of time." I felt enlightened.

"There's something else," she said.

"Oh?"

"Usually, the souls agree to certain very simple recognition codes," she said.

"Recognition codes? I know there's a punch line coming in all of this."

"No, I'm serious. In the process of planning out the next lifetime, souls will talk about special ways that they can be recognized by the other soul in the upcoming life."

"Why can't they just say, 'I'll be the tall one with black hair that...'"

"Doesn't work. There are too many tall people with black hair. No, what works are certain very identifiable and unique signs and signals, such as 'When you're in your twenties, I'll be the one with the pink umbrella with teal stripes' – things of that nature. Usually, the soul doesn't remember the exact details but, they'll see the umbrella with the teal stripes and it will trigger just enough of something deep in their minds to make them stop and take notice. From there, though, it's all up to the free will and initiative of the people involved."

"Hey, wait a minute; is that where déjà vu comes from?" I asked.

"Good guess," she smiled.

"I don't understand, Kalista, you said that sometimes people agree to horrible lifetimes with suffering in them for reasons *other* than to repay negative karma that they have accumulated. That it's not all about making up for mistakes that we have made."

"Yes. That's right."

"But, why would they do that?" I asked.

"Some people think they deserve it. Maybe they just don't think very much of themselves. Possibly they feel the need to be punished for having made mistakes in other lives. Others are still angry at themselves for having separated from Source – in essence having abandoned a perfect existence – that they feel a need to be punished in general. Many recognize that they have fallen into a cyclic existence. They are so furious with themselves for not knowing how to get out of it that they basically rant, rave and flog themselves over and over, lifetime after lifetime. Along the way, they pick up other negative relationships and have to go back and work that all out," she explained.

"I thought you counseled these people between lives though. Why don't you stop them?" I asked.

"I told you; there are very few truly inflexible guidelines. There **is** one though that says a soul cannot interfere with the travels of another soul. We can advise. We can try to influence their thinking. But in the end, if a soul wants to take on a lifetime full of aggravation, suffering, sadness and pain, we let them. Hopefully, after that lifetime, they will be able to see that doing so might not have been in their best interests. They would see that there are other ways. They recognize that they possibly learned less along that pathway than they could have otherwise. However, sometimes they *do* learn a great deal on that path, even if it's learning by experiencing what not to do rather than what to do."

"Sounds like a waste to me," I said.

"New souls are not known for their long-term thinking," Kalista said.

"New souls?" I asked, raising an eyebrow.

"Oh yes, in the grand scheme of things, the Universe is actually quite young. As such, the preponderance of souls in the Universe are relatively what you would think of as quite new. Perhaps 'inexperienced' would be a better word."

"So, is that why I took on the lifetime that I did, because I'm so *young*?" I asked.

"Actually, you're not really one of the young ones in the group. Why do you think you chose the life you did with all of its pain and challenges?"

"I always assumed that it was because I had done horrible things in my previous life. That I was a guard in a Nazi concentration camp or something like that."

"Not at all. You happen to have taken on a life this time that, while quite difficult and has had lots of suffering in it, has provided you with tremendous opportunities for positive learning. It is not a coincidence that you are so sensitized to other souls who have also taken on particularly difficult lives. They, like you, they did so for the potential to learn significant lessons."

"Is that why I did it? So being beaten to a pulp and abused as an orphan is... what word did you use... an opportunity?" I asked somewhat defensively.

"Have you learned?"

"Well, I think I'm starting to. I mean, I guess that some of it is beginning to come together for me."

"Is it in spite of or because of all the suffering and pain that you endured that you have begun to learn so much?"

Her question stopped me cold. My thinking had always been twofold. When things were not going particularly well for me, it had to be either very bad luck or, as Kalista had said earlier, my misguided belief that God was getting back at me for some of the less than ideal things I had most likely done in my life or previous lives. It would not have occurred to me to see those trying times as learning opportunities. At least not opportunities to learn anything positive. The way Kalista asked the question I knew what the answer was supposed to be. I opted to investigate that line of thought further. "I know you're going to say that I've learned as a result of all the suffering."

"Don't just say that because it's what you think I want you to say. Tell me, what have you learned?"

"Well, compassion. Compassion for anyone who is chronically ill. Compassion for anyone who is helpless at the hands of someone who is bigger, stronger or in a position of authority over someone else. You get beaten enough as an infant and you're bound to learn that one."

"What else?"

"Hmm. Recently, I've started to gain some compassion for pretty much anyone who has not gained insight or understanding about the purpose for their being. They can't see that the life they are leading is just what you and Tresden said, an illusion designed to help us learn certain things. People who are frustrated to the core, who feel that they have no purpose in life," I said, thoughtfully.

"Are you seeing a pattern in any of this?"

"I must have missed it," I said.

"Well, the word 'compassion' was in all of your answers," she smiled.

"Yeah, I guess that's true."

"So I'll ask the same question again. Is your learning now in spite of all that you have endured, or **because** of it?"

"Because of it for sure. But why does there have to be so much suffering involved in learning those lessons?"

"Remember when you were trying to get your son to stop going near the stove because you were so worried about him burning himself?"

"Yes."

"You must have told him a hundred times not to go near the stove."

"Two hundred easily," I interrupted.

"But he still didn't really get the lesson. You told him over and over again. So finally, one day, you didn't leap in as he got nearer to the stove and he touched the edges of the oven. You knew that it wasn't turned up to a hot temperature, so you let him touch it. As I recall the story, he pulled his hand back so fast and yelled at the top of his lungs so loud that they heard him down the street. So tell me, how many times did he touch the stove *after* that experience?"

"None."

"Right."

"So you're going to tell me that as life counselors, as our soul counsel, you sometimes let us take on lives that have a certain amount of pain in them so that we can learn the lesson in a very permanent way. So we'll not be tempted to touch the stove again?"

"How's your son's hand?"

"What?"

"His hand, how is it?"

"Today? Well geez Kalista, that was years ago," I said.

"How's his hand Chuck?"

"Well, it's just fine Kalista but... "

"But what?" She teased me with her smile.

"You're going to say that there was no real damage to his hand. Not really. Rather he learned and kept the lesson forever. And in the same way, souls come here, learn their lessons or not. But if not, they come back and learn them some other time. However, there's no real damage to what we actually are, which is pure soul energy. But we do, eventually, learn the lessons that we come here for. In any event, the *diamond*, as you and Tresden call it, is completely unharmed."

"I'm grateful that you didn't make me say it. Well done," she said.

For me, this was another bolt of lightening insight. I had on so many occasions pondered the meaning behind not just my own discomfort, but the broader and deeper suffering that went on in the world every day. I'd watch some horrific story on the evening news about some drunk mowing down five people on the sidewalk, including a pregnant mother, and end up nothing but frustrated that I couldn't make sense of it. Kalista's explanation allowed me to see that in reality, there are few true accidents. I also saw that virtually everything that occurs in the world has lessons within those events. At least, the opportunity for lessons, if only we will look for them.

How often had I endured some form of discomfort or unhappiness and walked away completely ignorant of the opportunity to learn from it? Worse, I walked away angry with someone or something that I couldn't understand, which had to be the root cause of whatever suffering I had just endured. My tendency had been to suffer through life's storms and difficulties without coming away from those experiences with learning the essential lessons that were right there, as gifts, in front of me; wrapped up within the problem itself. Now I needed to understand what happens when we don't see the lessons at the time they are offered up to us. What happens when we don't learn the lessons we set up for ourselves?

"Kalista, I've wasted so many opportunities to learn from all that I have faced. So many chances squandered. I feel terrible!"

"Don't be so hard on yourself, Chuck. Remember, I told you, life is set up in such a way as to make it very hard to remember that there is a much deeper purpose to it. Until you attain some level of awakening it feels like you're in a shooting gallery and that you're the target. It can be a pretty tough place to make it out of, she assured me.

"So I'm not the only one missing the lessons that are there?"

"To be honest, the vast majority of people don't even realize the lessons in life until their lives are over and they are reviewing that lifetime from the unique perspective of the life review with one or more of their soul advisors. It's only when you reach a point where you are right now, that you make real strides. Because once you understand that all hardship and difficulty holds great opportunity to learn, you stop suffering so much. And with suffering relieved, your heart – and more significantly, your soul – begins to focus on the bigger picture. You start to accept the challenges and take in the learning offered up to you in every day of living."

"How do we stop suffering?"

"A couple of ways. First, once you realize and accept that the challenges that you face in life are not being sent down on you by an angry God or the Devil or whatever target you have chosen to attribute your misfortunes to, you become less resistant to what comes your way. Your vision and your attitude becomes one of acceptance and, more importantly, you adopt the posture of a student that has been challenged to learn. This is a far different perspective than adopting the posture of a victim of unexplained misfortune. This awareness brings about a tremendous and ever-growing peace within you.

Second, when you reach a point where you truly grasp that whatever is going on in your life, that it is either of your own making or, that you agreed to it as a lesson, you will become much more accepting of those things that feel so challenging, even painful. This way you will find that there is a reason for everything that happens and, that accepting what occurs as opposed to expending great amounts of energy fighting it will accelerate you several steps down the pathway toward true inner peace. That is the point when real learning takes place," she explained.

"But I still miss many, many lessons – many opportunities to learn. Not to mention all of those that I have missed long ago."

"We've told you Chuck; the Universe has forever – longer than that really – for people to learn all that they have to know. Above and beyond that, every lifetime has a few core themes, or major lessons, as the basic construct. In that way, even though you might miss several opportunities along the way, you can be assured, that more opportunities to learn those same core lessons will continue to come along."

"But what if we miss those opportunities? What if we just bounce along believing that life is just an experience and we somehow manage not to learn anything along the way?"

"You know the answer to that, you just don't like it," she said.

"We go on to another lifetime and try to learn those lessons in some other way?"

"Exactly."

"So, would you say that, the harder a life someone is having that the more opportunities they have to learn major lessons?"

"Probably, but not necessarily. In some cases, people that are living lives of great misfortune and pain have taken on that life because they want to deal with past bad acts that they have committed – lessons they failed to learn. As opposed to taking 10 or 50 lifetimes to deal with all of their negative karma, they arrange a life where they take on a large part of it in a fairly short period of time, maybe say one or two lifetimes," Kalista explained.

"Other than that, are there any other reasons that people have lifetimes that have a lot of suffering and trouble in them?"

"Only what we've talked about before; that some people are so angry at themselves for having not made it back to Source – or having left it in the first place - that they take on lives where they are punished over and over. They believe they should be miserable so, they place themselves into a miserable life with lots of suffering and discomfort through writing truly miserable scripts for themselves. What's most unfortunate is that the punishment they take on will **not** help them get back to Source any quicker, but they will become so angry and hurt in the process of being the target of those miserable scripts that they end up lashing out at others and creating even more bad karma for themselves in the process. Thus, they create new cycles that forces them to take on incrementally difficult lifetimes to resolve it all. More inexorable cycles spiral them downward."

"So, there's no real way to, look at a really unhappy person and determine if they are that way because they are trying to move ahead in their spiritual development, or have taken on a hard life to learn those lessons?"

"Actually there is. But it is more important for that person to go through the process of understanding *why* their life is the way it is. Once you understand and accept that, whatever difficulty you have in your life, it is an opportunity – a true gift – for you to learn from, you are genuinely on your way to making major leaps forward in your spiritual development."

"How so?"

"Because all of the other potential reasons for anyone to take on or endure great suffering, pain or unhappiness in their lives are, in the truest analysis, empty reasons."

"I don't think I understand. Empty?"

"Listen, if you, as a person look at your life and say 'Hey, I'm really suffering here; I wonder why?' None of the answers that you come up with really make any difference. Not in reality. Let's say that you contemplate it deeply for a long time and determine that your suffering is due to bad karma that you have earned. So what? On the other hand, maybe you're unhappy because you hate yourself for being separate from Source. So what to that as well. No matter what the perceived reason might be that you are suffering or enduring great difficulty, the singular and only thing that makes any difference at all is your learning from that suffering. What are the lessons that you have chosen and agreed to take on? Every person, every soul, has two choices; resist and fight off the lessons that come your way or, learn from them. The first alternative will bring you only more and more lifetimes where you will suffer even more than the current one you are experiencing. The second choice, accepting that you are here to learn, is the pathway out of the cycle of lifetime after lifetime of suffering and, not coincidentally, also is the pathway that leads home. What's so frustrating is that so many souls choose the first alternative many, many times before they recognize the merits of the second."

"But what if the difficulties I happen to be enduring **are** from negative karma?"

"It doesn't matter. If you adopt a philosophy that says, 'no matter what, I'm going to learn from this and come to understand that perpetuating negative cycles is definitely not going to help me.' Then in the long run – over the course of your entire existence as a soul, literally forever – you can only come away from whatever experience you are enduring in a positive way. Learning having been absorbed. However, if you adopt an attitude that says, 'I am not going to earn any more bad karma and commit that no matter what happens; you are not going to be the person to perpetuate or initiate any more negative cycles, then all that will be left for you is positive learning."

"But, people fail so many times in that process. They get so wrapped up in the day-to-day life stuff that they lose sight that underneath all of it, exist lessons or, at least the *possibility* of lessons, if we will only open our eyes and see them. Their ego basically says, 'shut up... that bastard did me wrong and I'm going to go and slash his tires.' The opportunities for absorbing the lessons get run over and lost. We fail all the time."

"Chuck, there is no failure, other than a failure to learn. And as I have said, you have all the time you need to learn," Kalista assured me with a compassionate smile.

As with the other times I had spoken with Kalista, the insights she was sharing seemed incredibly clear to me as she was communicating. I still believed then, as I believe to this day, that when communicating with me, she has the ability to enhance the clarity of what she is saying far beyond the limitation of the words being used, the ideas being imparted. Still, within the scope of what she had said there was great hope for me. That there is a purpose to this life and, that even if we weren't necessarily aware of it from minute to minute in our lives, there was always some form of learning, even if not major learning, going on. At a minimum, there was the prospect for it. The rest was up to us.

Kalista had said that the only real failure in life was failing to learn. That afforded me a real sense of peace. I believed that even if the lesson at hand at any given time is an unpleasant one, as long as we make the effort to take in the essence of what there is to learn, we have accomplished something. Among other things, this instilled in me a true sense of purpose. Taking that concept to heart helped me feel very deeply that there was the potential for good. Although much was required to make the world a better place, in the end, there was purpose behind everything – even what seemed like the "bad" things – no matter how disorganized and riotous the world seemed.

I remained troubled that, people without these insights were probably going to remain consistently unhappy in their lives – probably for a long time. The longer a great number of people remained unhappy, the greater the likelihood was that the world would continue to be a pretty unpleasant place to be. The more I pondered this the more I got the image in my head of what New York City was like in the past, like the day after the Yankees or the Giants lost a major play-off game. The whole place was just that much more unpleasant. The people, as a whole, were just that much less enthusiastic for life and the effect hung in the air like a dense blue fog.

As I perceived the world then, the spiritual team had not had a winning season in quite some time, and a similar blue fog was hanging over everyone pretty much everywhere. Selfishness, greed, pride the need for retribution and anger were on the rise. Compassion and love for other souls who were sharing the planet on their missions to try to learn their essential lessons was down. Why did it have to be this way? I hoped Kalista would have some further insights.

"Kalista, why does the world need to be such an incredibly unpleasant place? I mean, on average, people are pretty unhappy. The world does not seem to be a place that is particularly conducive to learning."

"Good question. I have a great idea; let's ask Tresden."

With that, I heard the sound of very light footsteps behind me and then saw Tresden coming across the bridge that led to the shore. I had since figured out that the garden was, in fact, on a small island in what must have been the middle of a river as opposed to a lake or larger body of water. Tresden was dressed as she had been before, in gardening attire. I remained as up in the air as I had been about Tresden's gender and was still, very frustrated about it.

"Good day, Chuck! How are you?" Tresden greeted me enthusiastically.

"Great, Tresden. Good to see you again. Before we go any further though, I just really want to know; did Kalista call you just now or were you on your way here and she just *pretended* to call you?"

"I'm afraid I don't understand," a smug smile beginning to form around the corner of her eyes.

"Well, my back was turned and, for all I know, you were walking across the bridge and Kalista was, well I figured that... oh, never mind."

Both Kalista and Tresden broke into one of their light giggling fits for a few seconds. I felt like the only person at a party that doesn't hear the punch line to a joke that everyone else is laughing at.

"Don't get too wrapped up in all that Chuck, as it happened in this case though, I had asked Tresden to stop by, the timing just worked out."

"Pray tell, what's the problem today?" Tresden asked.

"I want to understand why the world has to be such an unhappy and unsettled place. Wouldn't it make a much better school if it was peaceful, quiet and everyone just got along?"

"That would depend, I suppose, on what sort of lessons needed to be learned in the school wouldn't you think?" Tresden shot back.

"What do you mean?"

"Well, as a primary example, if one needed to learn how to get along with other people it would be a pretty difficult lesson to learn if everyone **already** got on just merrily with each other wouldn't it?"

Tresden's British accent was theatrical now.

"I guess so. But... "

"You also have to remember that, over the course of time, there's been some pretty bad feelings built up between all sorts there. It's not just the karma of individual people but of peoples and cultures as well; countries, nations, tribes, ethnic groups and so forth. Across America, Northern Ireland, the Middle East and across the entire Earth. That can't just all go away over night. It all has to be worked out," Tresden explained.

"Hmm, I guess not. But, why do people have to be the way they are? Why can't the more advanced souls just stop everyone at the life review and say 'look, you're really screwing the place up and, it's completely unnecessary. Straighten out'?"

"Well, we... "

As Tresden started to communicate, I saw the look on her and Kalista's faces change dramatically. It wasn't that they were frightened or even startled. The impression was more of stunned surprise which, for some reason, I had thought was well outside of anything they might experience. I figured they were at a stage where they were beyond such reactions. Kalista actually stood up and Tresden moved very slowly to her left side. As I was about to ask Kalista what was going on, she interrupted my thoughts and communicated very quietly in a calm but forceful inflection.

"Chuck, listen to me. There is someone coming across the bridge. He is, I suppose you would say, a very substantial soul. He is very old and learned. He is substantial, ancient and enlightened. Very enlightened. And even though we all like to joke around here now and then as part of your teaching, I would have to advise against doing so in his case. I've no idea why he's here but you'd would be well-advised to see this as a once in a many lifetime opportunity and treat him with great respect."

"Who is... "

"Shhh, you probably want to go with the 'speak when spoken to' approach with this one," Kalista advised.

With that, I turned and saw an older man, just stepping off the near side of the bridge. I'd have guessed him to be in his late fifties or early sixties. As he approached, I could see that he was a genuinely radiant man, charismatic to the point that there was a palpable change in the area's overall atmosphere as he neared. The energy of the entire place was just greater as he approached. It could actually be felt in the air. Unusual barely covered the concept of what was occurring.

He was not a tall man, probably 5'11" and slight. On the athletic side without the usual middle-aged spread most men have at that age. Moderately balding. He had a perfect sun tan, neither over, nor under-done – similar to that you might see on either a tennis player or avid golfer. He was dressed in very dark slacks – I'd have guessed gabardine had I been in an office environment – and an unusual, very dark blue pull over shirt with a neatly tailored half sleeve. The shirt was not tucked in at the waist and hung down to about mid thigh. It was an odd look.

Similar to Kalista's, on his left wrist he had on a bracelet made of some soft metal; again, I thought it was probably platinum, with an intense deep blue or maybe even purple stone in it. He had light gray eyes that were very gentle but, also like Kalista and Tresden, they had an eerie glow to them, which made it quite difficult to look into them for any extended period of time. Still, his eyes conveyed a pervasive and definitive peaceful – even placid – look to them. The effect of his eyes and, for that matter, his overall presence, was extremely calming. The general effect, save for his unusual shirt, would give anyone not looking carefully, the impression of a man that would be found in any Board Room just about anywhere in a major business city.

I could see that Kalista and Tresden remained somewhat on the guarded side of alert, which was quite unsettling to me. There was nothing about this man that seemed in any way threatening and I just couldn't think of any circumstance that would exist in the spiritual plane where there would be any need to be on the defensive to any significant extent. Just as I began to ponder this, Kalista interrupted my thoughts.

"Chuck, this is Geradl."

It was obvious to me that Kalista and Tresden considered this person to be someone of great importance. I was very careful to listen carefully to the impression of his name as Kalista articulated it. Taking

Kalista's guidance to heart, I opted not to speak first and was grateful when Geradl proceeded.

"Kalista regards you very highly. I am given to understand that your learning is accelerating. That you have taken the insights to heart," Geradl said to me.

"Thank you Geradl. She is a very patient teacher. So is Tresden."

As I transferred this thought, something came over me that felt like a vague need for caution. I'm rarely nervous when meeting people for the first time but, in this case, I decided to stay on a conservative side of caution and see where the conversation led. I also wanted to learn what it was that I was sensing from Tresden and Kalista about Geradl. There was something else too; Geradl had a way of looking at me that made me feel close to naked. Somehow I knew that, just by looking at me, he knew all there was to know about me and probably all there ever was to know about me. It was quite unnerving at first. I was grateful when he stopped examining me and decided to move forward with the conversation. Tresden and Kalista, from my point of observation, still seemed more than a bit on edge to me.

"You are frustrated that the human form is so compromised? You note that souls who have chosen the human form of incarnation behave with some substantial disregard for each other," Geradl said.

"Well, actually, yes."

"Would you hold yourself up as someone who has met some ideal in this regard, even in the life experience that you are in right now?"

"Well, no, not really but, I always considered that I was at the back of the class. I expected that everyone was far ahead of me and as such, that they would treat other people as I would expect more advanced souls to," I told him.

At this, Geradl looked directly at Kalista for a few moments. I don't know how, but I simply just knew that they were communicating something directly that I was not supposed to "hear." Just as clearly, Geradl must have had the ability to block my perception of the communication that was not meant for my consumption.

"Your assumptions in that regard is not correct," Geradl said.

"Which one?" I asked.

"All of them, except for your inference regarding certain more advanced souls."

I started to ask for a clarification and, the way I had intended to ask might have been construed under the wrong circumstances as somewhat flippant. Before I could get the first word out Kalista gave me a look that would have frozen a freight train. I immediately rethought how I would seek further clarification from Geradl and decided that in this case, discretion probably was the better part of valor. Still, I knew that, whomever Geradl was, it was very unlikely I'd ever have access to such a soul again and decided to risk a few well thought out questions. "So, when Kalista told me that most of the souls on earth are still fairly young, I should just be more under-standing of the way that they often treat each other?"

"Why does this make such a difference to you? Why would you care about a thing unless it is *you* that is being unfairly treated?"

"I'm not certain. It just bothers me. It has always bothered me. I need to understand why we can't learn the lessons that we need to without having a world where people are amused by leaving tire marks on someone else's back. Why must we murder to settle disagreements? I'd rather study in a school that was peaceful," I tried to explain.

"I understand Chuck. Really I do. But, in order to move forward as a soul you absolutely have to master forbearance. Patience. Compassion. Things of similar construct. You simply must learn to accept that, in any school there are both more and less advanced students. You can no more blame the first grader for sounding out words phonetically, than you can a twelfth grader for reciting the Gettysburg address," Geradl almost smiled at me.

"I don't mean to be disrespectful at all Geradl, but I assume that all of that means that it's simply unrealistic to expect the world as a whole to change. To improve?"

"In the time frame that you'd like it to, yes, that's probably right. But, you should feel free to try. You never know what might come of efforts in a few hundred or a few thousand years," he said.

"So it is up to us as individuals to master patience with others?"

"And through that patience and compassion you can bring about the change that you desire."

"In the world?"

"He had an even chance at that one. You have to admire his sprit," Tresden said,who tried to lighten the discourse with a smile.

"I take it that means that the only change that will take place is the one in me."

"Believe me, you will come to understand that as individual souls change they, in reality, also change the world. More than that, souls effecting change cause a shift in all that there is. When you change in such a manner it is immediately reflected at Source level. When you change in a significant way, the Universe also changes. You might not think so, but it is so. I promise you." Geradl's tone had become compassionate.

"I don't understand that," I said.

"Give it time, Chuck. Give it time. You will come to understand all of this and it may be sooner than you think. Kalista, I think you should consider taking him to the gate," Geradl instructed.

In ten years of my interactions with Kalista and Tresden I have seen Kalista genuinely surprised only once. This was it. While her eyes didn't exactly pop out of her head it was close to that. Whatever it was that Geradl was suggesting, surprised her in a substantial and meaningful way. It was clear to me that, in whatever way the disincarnate world works in terms of hierarchy, that Geradl was someone substantial and, absolutely someone to be reckoned with. I sensed that one did not debate or discuss alternatives with Geradl. You just did what he said. I would learn – although it would be many years later – just how true all of those assumptions I'd just made actually were.

"Of course, Geradl. It would be my honor to do so," Kalista said, picking up the conversation.

"Let me know how it goes, Kalista," said Geradl.

"Of course," she replied. Kalista said, maintaining her composure just below the surface.

"Be well Chuck. You have come this far this time. Do not let up in your pursuits," Geradl said.

"Will I? I mean, thank you. I'll... "

Kalista waved me off with a very subtle shake of her head. It was clear that this part of the interaction was over and that my assignment at this point was to say no more. Geradl looked at Tresden for a few moments and then went through the same process with Kalista. With that, he raised his left hand in a sort of half wave good-bye and left as quickly as he came, over the bridge. It seemed to take some time for Kalista and Tresden to regain their balance but in reality it was only a matter of moments. It was Tresden that broke the silence first.

"What the heck was that about?"

"I'm not sure," Kalista said shaking her head.

"What are you guys so wound up about?"

"Do you want to tell him or should I?" Tresden asked.

"Go ahead Tresden, try to explain it to him."

"Let's see. To start with, in my entire existence – what you would perceive as thousands of years – I've only seen Geradl twice. That includes today. And, I never saw him when I was still incarnated."

"Well gee, Tresden, what's the big deal? I mean, he's not Jesus Chr...."

"Don't even think about saying that," Tresden cut me off with a hard stare.

"O.K., O.K., sorry. So, who – or is that what – is he?"

"There's no real way for us to explain it to you. Let's just say that he is a genuine elder of the Universe. Part of the true, essential mechanism I suppose. And most definitely at a place in his developmental pathway where parts of him are indistinguishable from The Original Center of All Things," Kalista said.

"Meaning?"

"Meaning, in your terminology, he's no more than a shading of hue away from Source, if that."

"I'm sorry Kalista, I have no frame of reference for any of that. What does that mean? In English? How many steps are there?" I asked.

"It's not like that Chuck. There's just no way for us to explain the importance of what just happened here," Kalista said.

"All right, stay calm, stay calm. What was he talking about – something about a gate?"

"Something he wants us to show you," Kalista said, looking over at Tresden.

"So what's the big deal with that? I mean, a gate's a gate and... "

"The big deal is you'll never, ever be the same again. Ever. That's if you survive the experience with your sensibility intact," Tresden smiled, sending a sideways glance of acknowledgement back toward Kalista.

"But I... what are you guys talking about?"

"Never mind all of that right now. Go back. Rest up. Come back soon. We'll take you there. We'll all go together," Kalista said.

"But what did he mean when... "

"Chuck, listen to me. You fortunes may have just turned in a way that you can't even conceive of. Those major intersections that we were talking about before when you asked about fate? Well, this kind of intersection comes once every few thousand lifetimes. Probably not that often. Do what I tell you for now. Come back when you are ready," Kalista said, with a tinge of urgency.

"I don't understand... ready? Ready for what? Kalista... "

This conversation was obviously over. From my perception, Kalista and Tresden began to fade into the background like a television picture that has been switched off. The images of them simply receded into nothingness. I regained my bearings in my study and began to furiously scribble notes to myself. Trying as desperately as I could to get it all down before my mind lost its grip on the events.

I was as much excited as exhausted. I wanted to make my return trip right away but something told me that I needed to heed Kalista's advice and rest up. I went to sleep that night wondering what the gate might be, who Geradl really was, and just where this journey might lead me next.

CHAPTER FIVE

Out of the night that covers me,
Black as the pit from pole to pole,
I thank whatever gods may be
For my unconquerable soul.

In the fell clutch of circumstance,
I have not winced or cried aloud.
Under the bludgeonings of chance,
My head is bloody but unbowed.

Beyond this place of wrath and tears,
Looms but the horror of the shade,
And yet the menace of the years
Finds and shall find, me unafraid.

It matters not how strait the gate,
How charged with punishments the scroll,
I am the master of my fate:
I am the captain of my soul.

- From Invictus, by William Ernest Henley

It took several weeks until I could arrange enough latitude in my schedule so that I could have an adequate time for another visit to the garden. Above and beyond the normal business scheduling challenges that I had to deal with, I had some trepidation about the way in which the last session had ended. Kalista, Tresden and Geradl obviously had something specific in mind. And from what Kalista had inferred, it was something substantial. It was likely to be another overwhelming

109

assault on my senses.

With this in mind, I concluded that whatever the specifics were, this was going to probably be a lot for me to deal with. Looking back, at a subconscious level, I suspect that I was stalling, as I remained somewhat uneasy over not having any inclination at all of what visiting the gate might entail. I wanted to be as certain as I could that I had enough time to recover from whatever the experience entailed.

I was also confused about the entrance into the scenario of Geradl. Who – or what – was he? Why did Tresden and Kalista show such great deference to him? If he was as advanced a soul as Kalista had gone out of her way to make clear, why had he taken an interest in me of all people? All of these thoughts and insecurities had me on edge and forced me to think carefully about whether I was really ready to proceed to whatever came along next on this pathway. I spent a couple of days leading up to the next session working on basic meditation in order to get myself into a calm and relaxed state of mind. It had marginal effect on me at best.

When the Sunday that I had selected to go to the garden finally came, I somewhat reluctantly made my way to my study in a half-excited, but still nervous state. It seemed a bit odd to have such mixed feelings about having the opportunity to learn more on the subject I had spent so much of my life's effort pursuing. I should have been itching to go. But I was unable to put my finger on what it was that had me so unsettled and uneasy.

I had some initial difficulty settling my mind enough to attain the early stages that were required in order to connect with the proper meditative state. As frustrating as it was, after applying some routine meditation techniques to calm myself down I was finally able to reach the middle state that occurs right before the image of the garden begins to take focus within my perception. From there, it was once again merely a matter of clearly recollecting the warm blanket feeling that I associated with the garden. In a matter of a few moments, I found myself standing by the hanging baskets.

My first observation was that whatever gardening Tresden had been applying in my absence was having the desired effect. My basket was again beginning to look similar to the others that grew with such vibrancy and flowed beyond any gardener's imagination with volumes of huge and perfectly formed flowers. Kalista was over by the pathway bordered by the roses, trimming some of the more colorful foliage there. She called me over almost immediately.

"Hi. How wonderful to see you."

"Thanks Kalista. Your garden looks amazing today," I said.

"Well thank you. So, tell me, do you think you're ready to take the trip that Geradl talked about?"

"Trip? I thought it was just... "

"Well, trip might be a bit of a misnomer. Still, it is a bit of a walk from here."

"Kalista, what is the gate? What was Geradl talking about? Why were you and Tresden so nervous when he showed up? What was that all about? Who is... " my questions poured out nervously. I was running on without even thinking about what I was asking.

"Slow down, Chuck. You're getting far too excited over all of this. First of all, Tresden and I were just a bit surprised when Geradl came here. Besides everything else that he said, he's never been here before. It's just not like Geradl to just show up someplace without having a very good reason. Tresden and I were really caught off guard because, even though Geradl is on your soul counsel, he very rarely appears unless it is at some major juncture when real decision-making is about to be made. Although you probably don't remember it, the last time you saw him he was there for a grand total of about ten seconds right before the beginning of this lifetime," Kalista explained.

"O.K., I can accept all that. But there's nothing that you can tell me about this 'gate' ahead of time? I mean, there's no way for me to get ready for whatever it is?"

"No, not really. It is not a test Chuck; it's not like you can study for it or even anticipate it in any way. Like all other kinds of learning, you're either ready as of now to take in the knowledge from this particular experience or you're not. If you are, wonderful, if you're not, there's absolutely no shame in it whatever," she gave me an assuring smile.

"Is Tresden coming with us?"

"Tresden is going to meet us somewhere on the other side of the bridge. Are you ready to go?"

"I guess so. But I think... " Despite Kalista's reassurance I remained nervous.

"Never mind all that. Let's get going."

We set out walking toward and then over the bridge that led from the small island that held Kalista's garden over to the shore. I hadn't been up to the bridge before and upon closer examination, I was very impressed with both the construction and intricate design of it. Clearly it was made of some type of hardwood, possibly oak. It had brilliantly ornate and creative hand-carved designs and detailed wood-working in many different places throughout the entire span. Overall, it must have been some forty or fifty feet in length, and about fifteen feet wide. Like the trellis-like structure that held the hanging baskets, the bridge was painted in a subtle off-white with brilliantly ornate gold antiquing that was thoughtfully laid in at artistically appropriate places.

Similar to all the other design elements of Kalista's garden, the bridge gave every appearance that artisans had taken untold years to create this finished effect. The overall impact was magnificent while somehow managing to stay just within the range of under-stated.

As Kalista had suggested, Tresden was standing on the far side of the bridge waiting for us. She was dressed mostly as she always was in her off-white T-shirt and green shorts, but had opted to shed her gardening smock for today's outing. As we neared to within a few feet of her she picked up the conversation.

"Good day Chuck, Kalista. How are you?"

"A bit nervous actually, Tresden."

"Hi Tresden. I'm fine. Quivering Chuck here is a bit on edge," Kalista smiled.

"Hey guys, I'm fine. Really, I can take it. So what do we do now?"

"Now? Well, now we walk."

We set out walking at first down a narrow pathway along the shoreline. After a few hundred yards the pathway turned slightly to the left and led into some dense forest. Much like Kalista's garden, the forest was filled to overflowing with more varieties of richly developed and vividly colored foliage and exotic plant life than one could possibly imagine. As we continued our walk down the poorly defined pathway I recall thinking that this must have been what it was like in the jungles when the dinosaurs walked the earth some hundred and fifty million years ago. With little human intervention to wreak havoc on the environment, plants, trees and flowers simply grew to their absolute and fullest natural potential. The effect of the variety, size and color of the plant life growing there was staggering and held me in rapt fascination as we made our way up the path.

After a while, I lost track of time. I was that distracted by the beauty of the forest. After some period of time that I had difficulty fixing, we emerged from the dense woods into an enormous field of wildflowers. At least, I believed them to be wildflowers of some sort. It must have been the effect of perceptional walking or possibly, the overwhelming optical impact of such an immense field of brilliantly-colored flowers because I started at once to lose my balance from just looking at the field. Tresden steadied me by taking a gentle hold on my elbow and after a few brief moments, I regained my normal equilibrium.

As I looked out onto the field, I saw that it was actually a moderately sized, gently-sloping hill, saturated with these other-worldly colored flowers that stood some three or four feet high. The flowers were swaying rhythmically in the gentle breeze that seemed to come out of nowhere in particular. If you looked carefully, you could just barely make out the continuation of the pathway winding its way up in the hillside through the field of flowers more or less in the shape of a gigantic "S."

I began to study the flowers more carefully from where we stood. As I did so, I became more and more overwhelmed, not only by the sheer **number** of flowers – the impression I had was that there were easily hundreds of millions or even more of them. The vast variety and intensity of coloring of the field was so vivid that it defied any meaningful attempt at description. I've tried many times since that day to detail the absolute staggering brilliance of the colors there and have since surrendered to the frustration that there simply are no words or concepts that can begin to even vaguely explain the beauty and impact that the field had on me. The range of vibrancy and sheer, seemingly endless span of colors there far exceeded a simple multiple of the rainbow. The overall effect of the combination of color, volume and intensity was overloading my senses to the point where I was close to passing out from what I assumed was intense sensory overload.

Sensing my frustration and sensory imbalance, Tresden interceded by taking me gently by the arm and leading me up the pathway. As the slope of the hill increased gently the path seemed to meander its way through the wildflower field in no particular fashion other than to generally continue in the direction of the peak of the hillside.

My sense of the events as they unfolded was that it took quite some time for us to make our way up the serpentine pathway. As we approached within what looked to be fifty feet or so of the top of the hill, Kalista broke in on what had been a silence that had held between all of us since we had first entered the forest.

"How are you doing back there, Chuck?" Kalista asked.

"Well, I'm just fine Kalista, not tired at all really."

"Golly Kalista, he's not tired, can you imagine that?" Tresden giggled.

It didn't seem to matter how focused or determined I was to maintain perspective on the experience I was going through. My efforts to keep in the front of my mind that we were negotiating a perceptional pathway and not a physical one – or so I believed – continuously fooled me. Yet the environment felt so completely realistic in every sense that I would constantly forget where we actually were. Whatever methodology or techniques Kalista and Tresden were using to maintain the impression or illusion that we were negotiating our way through a physical reality, it was nothing short of miraculous. Over the many years spanning my numerous visits to the garden and the surrounding area, they would occasionally throw in a comment like this to subtly remind me of the reality of the circumstances. Kalista would also use this kind of scenario to force me to think about just how solid my grasp was on my own day-to-day reality. Of course, none of that did anything toward clarifying just what the true reality we happened to be in at this particular moment really was. Irrespective of this confusing dynamic, after making their point, they opted to proceed with my indoctrination of the day's objective.

"All right then. Chuck, there is a reason that the pathway up to this place leads through the field of flowers that so dramatically affects your senses the way it does," Tresden said.

"What do you mean?"

"Well, if we just dropped you at the far edge of the pathway on the other side of the gate it might be a bit overwhelming. We've learned that if you take a soul up through the flowers and condition their senses a bit in advance, it makes the overall experience that occurs later on a little less jolting."

"What do you mean when you say take a 'soul' up here?"

"Oh, well, this is not someplace that we usually take souls that are still incarnated. This is not a place that is particularly conducive to interaction with souls that are still in a physical form. Most often, souls come here between lifetimes or, if they are having trouble understanding certain things about life or other complex aspects of the Universe," Tresden said.

"If you're trying to make me more relaxed you're going about it the wrong way Tresden," I replied.

"You'll just have to believe us, Chuck, that this is nothing bad. There's nothing genuinely shocking here. But many come away from this experience completely overwhelmed. Often from a kind of information overload."

"Why can't you just tell me what's there? Maybe if you told me about it before we got there that would take some of the edge off of it. Make it a little less frightening," I said.

"I would if I could, but I just wouldn't know how to do that – how to explain it," Tresden replied.

This was not particularly a surprise for me. In the weeks that I'd had to ponder and anticipate what might be forthcoming from this experience, my working conclusion had been that unless Tresden and Kalista were purposefully being overly-dramatic, anything that Geradl would treat with such sincerity would likely be a major test of my will, as well as my perception.

I'd tried to envision what the gate might look like and what the experience might entail. But it was clear that I didn't even have any real frame of reference for any of what had already happened in my experiences with Kalista and Tresden. Thus far, my journeys into this spiritual realm when I had foolishly tried to project with any degree of reliability what the upcoming experience might hold was unlikely to yield much for me except for frustration. Guessing what might be coming from this set of circumstances simply didn't work. Still, I tried once more to seek some degree of clarification from Kalista and Tresden before we arrived at wherever in this spiritual realm they were taking me next.

"Tresden, with all that you're *not* saying, I can't help but to think that there is something potentially fearful about the gate and the experience you're setting me up for," I said.

"Oh good gracious sakes; not at all. In fact, I should expect it would be quite the opposite," Tresden said.

"Chuck, you need to learn that, in the world you come from there are often perceived reasons to be afraid of the unknown. In this reality though, there are no such demons and dragons hiding behind obscured entryways. In the spiritual realm you will not only learn – but come to know with absolute certainty – that fear is not only an illusion but a totally empty illusion," Kalista said.

"Oh well, that's a relief. I still don't understand why you can't just tell me more about this though before we get there," I whined.

"Well, one reason is that we are there," Kalista announced with a broad smile.

Kalista's comment had surprised me in a way. As I looked just ahead of us I noted near the top of the hill, that there was a beautiful and perfectly appointed white picket fence. The fence was about four or five feet high and cut through the field of flowers, in what appeared to be a fairly arbitrary placement. The fence spanned the entire width of the hillside in both directions. Literally, as far as the eye could see. Somehow though, the fence seemed quite out of place there, seemingly just dropped down in the middle of nowhere.

The fence itself was perfectly maintained, giving the impression that someone had finished painting it only a few minutes before we had arrived. Directly on the pathway ahead of us was the only visible break in the entire fence line where there was a simple swinging gate with a fairly plain black painted latch along the top.

I noticed immediately that the gate was broken at one of the hinges and that two of the slats in the gate were in substantial disrepair. Quite noticeable was that the gate itself was not painted adequately and even had some areas where the paint was cracking, as well as peeling badly. The defects in the gate were so obvious that the entire impression of it seemed out of place. The broken gate was in such stark contrast to everything else there – the perfect field of flowers, the freshly painted fence seemingly dropped out of the sky into the middle of the field of pristine, magnificent flowers – that it almost ruined the ideal rustic impression the rest of the scene afforded. Beyond that of course was the stunning impact made by the beautiful field of flowers that also stood in sharp contrast to the unsightly gate. Without giving the matter any thought at all I chose to comment immediately on this to Kalista and to Tresden.

"Hey guys, I hope this isn't the gate that you were talking about because this thing is really quite a mess. If you have some tools and some paint I'd be happy to take a shot at fixing this thing for you," I offered.

Kalista and Tresden looked at each other for a few moments followed by Tresden erupting into one of her giggling fits. It was subtle at first. I could tell she was trying desperately to hold back more substantial laughing out of deference to the seriousness of the moment. I could also see that Kalista was expending a great deal of energy trying not to break into outright laughter herself. In between her bursts of giggling, Tresden managed to continue.

"Oh, Kalista, isn't he wonderful, he wants to fix the gate."

"What the **hell** is so funny about that?" I asked indignantly.

"Never mind that. Everyone just get a grip," Kalista suggested.

"Am I to take it from your outburst the gate is broken for a reason?"

"Well, let's just say that, had you thought about it, you would have realized that it would have been pretty easy for us to fix if we had wanted to do so," Kalista said.

"You will however, be known forever in these parts though for being the first person to ever offer to fix it," Tresden said.

"Don't start up with all that Tresden – we may lose it again,"

Kalista tried not to laugh. "Let's move on."

I helped Kalista get up from where she had decided to sit down on the side of the pathway. The three of us continued toward the gate. I noticed as we approached the opening in the fence that just immediately on the other side of the gate, all of the flowers there seemed to be dead or dying. They were certainly not the same vibrantly colored flowers that comprised the field we had just walked through.

As I studied the area on the side of the fence immediately opposite the gate more carefully, I noticed that it was generally run down. Completely dissimilar to the beautiful forest and field we had just walked through. As we passed through the gate I noticed that a short distance ahead – maybe another twenty-five feet or so – the path turned to the left and that in fact, this run-down area was no more than fifteen or twenty feet deep. Just beyond the dying foliage and, just a bit further past where you could see if you were standing on the wildflower side of the gate, there was an outcropping surrounded by a cluster of small boulders. Interspersed throughout this clearing were even more unusual plants, with mystical intense other-worldly coloring. This included one plant that was similar to a hydrangea, whose color appeared to shift from a brilliant pink to a deep navy blue as the wind shifted from one direction to another. I was completely mesmerized as I watched this particular plant traverse the full range of the rainbow as the wind changed direction several times.

Unlike anything I had seen in Kalista's garden, the forest or even the incredibly brilliant field of wildflowers that we had just come through, the foliage in the area immediately surrounding the outcropping was genuinely mystical beyond words. There were bright purple fern-like plants that grew to well in excess of ten to twelve feet tall. Those emitted an eerie low-pitched whining sound now and then. There were a few bushes that appeared to be roses except each bush had at least a thousand blooms on them – of every color and pattern imaginable. Kalista and Tresden both looked at me with a kind and knowing smile that conveyed a total understanding that the imagery of the flowers and the surrounding scenery was having an overwhelming and magical impression on me, much like a child seeing a rainbow for the very first time.

Kalista motioned with a subtle movement of her head for me to look back down the pathway that we had just traversed. As I did, I was shocked to note that from where we stood, it would have been impossible for a person standing on the far side of the gate to see the miraculous foliage and the outcropping. Or us for that matter. I didn't even vaguely understand the optical physics involved or the mystical effects that could affect perception in this way. But I immediately appreciated the irony. Had anyone come up as far as the gate and bothered to look at only what was immediately just on the opposite side of it they would have seen nothing but a small area of dead and dying foliage. Had they not walked the additional fifteen or twenty feet up the pathway to where we were standing, they probably would have turned away and walked back through the field of wildflowers. They would have believed that all there was to see of any real interest was on *their* side of the broken-down gate. Because from the far side of the gate, the visual impression was that there was simply nothing but dead and dying flowers and desert beyond the gate. In fact, when I thought about it, had Kalista not led me through the gate herself – literally, taking me by the hand and leading me – I would have just turned around at that point figuring the fence was the end of the wildflower field or anything worth seeing in that vicinity.

Tresden came over to me and took me by the left hand indicating that we were to walk a bit further up the pathway. Kalista took up a position just on the other side of me. We continued ahead for another 20 feet until we came to the end of the cleared out area that was a few feet or so from the very top of the hill we had been climbing since we came out of the forest. Kalista took my other hand and began to communicate in a very quiet but sincere tone.

"Chuck, we're going to move forward together. Let Tresden and I guide you. Don't be afraid. Stay focused but relaxed and just take in whatever happens here. Remember what you learned about the early stages of meditation; breath in, breath out."

"But I... "

"Shhhh, just watch," Tresden said.

With that, Tresden, Kalista and I took the remaining few steps to the very top of the hill together. As we took the last step, Kalista and

Tresden tightened their grip on my hands – I thought as a signal to stop – but then I realized that it was to hold on to me in case I fell over the precipice.

It turned out that holding on to me was a good idea too because as we took the last step, I realized that the top of the hill was, in the only words that I can think to use, virtually the end of the reality of where we were. It was as though God's architects had drawn a line right there at the apex of that hill and said, "on this side this is 'here,' and out there is something else." In this particular case, "there" was someplace, or possibly "something," that defied my ability to even remotely comprehend. To even vaguely define in any way that uses words beyond suggesting that the experiencing of it was a powerful and all-consuming emotional feeling. A sense of perception unprecedented in human terms.

Somewhere out beyond the ledge we were on – out in the nowhere – was a dimly lit space that was close in brightness to half moonlight. Overhanging that dim glow there was a surrealistic, very soft light yellow, hazy fog that seemed suspended over the entire span of the vista. I sensed, as opposed to saw, that the void held something unknown, miraculous and without any question, endless. I recall thinking at the time that what I was staring into was true boundlessness – far beyond what we experience when we peer into the night sky wondering where it all might end.

Looking into whatever it was, I experienced a knowing deep inside of me, beyond a certainty of intuitiveness, that whatever was out in that particular aspect of reality was the very source of the insights and enlightenment that I had been searching for in all of my spiritual pursuits. Desperate to know more, I somehow found a way to break through my awestruck state and prod Kalista for clarification.

"What is this place? What am I looking at? I sense something but... "

"Language is an obstacle to any explanation here. But if I had to attempt a clarification, I would say that you are standing on the shores of the River of Knowledge," Kalista said, softly.

"I don't understand. What does that mean? River?"

"Out in what you probably perceive as emptiness there is a river from which all knowledge – all insight – is available to you," she said with an air of mystery.

"River? I'm sorry Kalista, I don't see anything and certainly not a river. What am I looking for? When you say 'all knowledge,' do you mean... "

"Quiet. Again, language makes this difficult. 'River' is only a way of talking about the flow of insights that are available to you from this place. Look very carefully. Anything and everything that you want to know is out there in front of you."

I looked over at Tresden and then back to Kalista. They were both standing on the outcropping, quite rigidly staring out into the misty, yellow haze. I had the impression that they were looking intently at, or for something. But as I peered into the void I couldn't make anything out. As I began to adjust my perceptional focus with greater determination on what at first appeared to be a boundless empty space, I realized that what I had thought was a hybrid void of sorts – what I had been calling "there" – was actually filled to overflowing with some "things" that were slowly moving past us.

I was having great difficulty understanding the nature of what I was looking at. Part of the challenge was that "looking" was not a function that would yield results in this exercise. That much I had figured out on my own. One had to experience the content of the void with perception. Non-focused perception of a kind. But at the very moment when I would believe that I was about to comprehend in some manner, what it was that going past us, I would lose my perceptional grip on it entirely. It was much like being at the point of remembering something that you've been frustrated trying to recall all day long, like someone's name, and then just at the very instant you are about to get it, it slips away from you. Kalista sensed my dilemma and offered to help.

"Don't try so hard. You don't have to tackle it, just read it as it comes past."

"Kalista, I don't understand. Read it? What is this place? What is it that I am looking at? Just when I think I'm going to be able to see clearly what is floating past us, I lose my grip on it, whatever it is. Read what?"

"I told you; think of this as you standing on a shore. A bank on the River of Knowledge. What is floating past you are, ideas, information, concepts, insights and answers. There's more than that really but, learning to extract just that much will do for a start," she said.

"I still don't get it. So, what do I do, hold a question in my mind and the answer will just come to me while I stand here? Are you saying this is some magical place where the answers just come to you?"

"No, at least not in the way that you're thinking of it. The insights, ideas and answers are contained with the forms floating past us here. All you have to do is read them. Maybe it will help you to think of it as absorbing the content of the forms," she suggested.

"Read it? Absorb it? What the heck are you talking about? Read what?"

"Here, I'll help you. Most of these are just simple essential ideas going by. Some are lessons. Others are, well, here, let me show you. Look at this one."

It must have been Kalista's unique gift for being able to help me see things beyond just the scope of her words, her communications, because as she said this, I "saw" that the thing approaching us and floating by was actually a completely self-contained idea. My perception was very clear that the concept floating past was complete and absolutely comprehensive in every possible way. Perfect. There was simply no question or doubt. Everything there was to know about any given topic would be conveyed to the perceiver by careful examination of the form floating past in front of you. The idea of such a thing was so foreign to me that I had a great deal of trouble adjusting to even the concept of it, much less accepting even the vague notion of such a technology.

The prospect of watching an idea float its way up to you and then to be able to look at it – interact with it, examine it from any and every point of view – was so mind boggling that I was grateful that Kalista and Tresden were still holding on to me. The sheer impact that this form of revelation was having on me was so overwhelming that I drifted in and out of a state where I nearly lost consciousness several times. Kalista managed through some tactic that I didn't fully understand to stabilize me and at the same time, help me focus on the learning at hand.

The idea formations were magical things. They were far beyond the limitations of any unabridged encyclopedia or academic library. Our books of learning that we use in daily life are prehistoric by comparison. The forms, "threads" Kalista called them, provided one not just the basic explanations on a topic, but somehow conveyed the full experience of every possible facet and dynamic of that particular topic as well.

Kalista showed me one thread that afforded a perceiver information about a fairly banal subject, water. All of its uses, physical properties and so forth. From experiencing the thread on water, I not only was exposed to the most wide-ranging broad technical explanation imaginable about water – including chemical composition, uses in nature, pollution of and so forth, literally everything that we would learn by reading an encyclopedia on the subject – but much, much more than that. Before we released the thread containing the "water" explanations by ostensibly placing it back into the river, I had directly experienced from the thread itself what water felt like. The thread accomplished this "learning" by seemingly splashing me in the face with its form. The thread did the same with what ice felt like, what steam felt like and so on.

The threads were designed and constructed to function in such a way that a user could, if they spent enough time and examined the thread extensively enough, come away from the experience of accessing them with the full, comprehensive and essentially absolute range of knowledge on that topic. This included the basic information (Kalista called it the "text"), physical sensations, and emotional aspects/sensations relating to the subject of the thread you were experiencing. It was a learning tool that seemed so complete and absolutely comprehensive that it told a user far more than they would ever learn by experiencing what we would call the "real life" version of whatever was being taught. At that moment I recall thinking that the threads had to be the equivalent of God's dictionary on all things in the Universe. Kalista would only say that my observation was an interesting "starting point" for what the threads actually were.

Kalista also explained to me that I would forget most of what I learned by reviewing the threads that day. I had started to call them *ideaograms*, which Kalista thought was an accurate depiction. But she and Tresden assured me that they would review the content of anything that was genuinely important to me at some later date. Tresden explained further that, since I was still within incarnate form, my ability to absorb the full range of information from the threads – particularly the ones addressing certain very complex spiritual topics – would be somewhat limited. She also told me that, my absorbing the information now would be a lot like downloading a computer file in compressed format. Tresden and Kalista explained that, at later dates I could essentially "decompress" the file and, re-experience all aspects of the threads as a kind of reinforcing of the learning that I had received from experiencing the thread on that particular day.

The experience of scanning the forms passing by in the "river" and thus absorbing the learning that they offered was astounding. At the outset, my efforts in taking in the knowledge were quite awkward and my perceptional skills were not very adept. With some concerted effort, Kalista went on to help me interpret in greater detail one particular thread that we were looking at.

"See, this one is about some of the core emotions that souls experience when they take on an incarnation. On this part of the surface you see it is describing everything about the concept of fear. See how it tells you where fear comes from and why it exists? What its uses are and, how to control it? It also shows you how people respond to fear in different ways. Now it will let you sense what fear feels like in different forms of the emotion," she explained.

It was an awe-inspiring experience. At the very moment that Kalista said that I would begin to experience the emotion, in a very brief burst following, I "felt" fear in a number of different ways. I experienced the kind of absolute terror one might feel if they were being chased by a wild animal in the jungle as well as the unsettling kind of fear you might feel if you received an audit notice from the IRS. I also experienced many of the feelings ranging in the full spectrum in between those stages of fear. The difference between having someone ***explain*** what those emotions might feel like and actually *feeling* them only drove home the true brilliance of the threads as teaching devices. The threads assured that the perceiver would be fully exposed to a totality in terms of all the aspects of the explanation. Kalista continued with her explanation of this specific thread.

"... directly connected to it – different sub-facets of the concept of fear – are hate, greed, jealously the other aspects of the emotion of fear. See how it shows you that all the parts of it are directly and indirectly related to that emotion. If you study the thread very carefully you will see that the way the various parts of the fear emotion are illustrated within the interconnecting facets. It also clarifies how the different emotions directly and indirectly related to fear actually work. If you flip the thread around just a bit you will see that it shows you how fear can manifest as anger, hate, defensiveness, rage and so on."

I was completely overwhelmed by my experience with the thread that Kalista was showing me. The learning, the actual academic aspect of the information itself was one thing. It afforded comprehension beyond imagination. But experiencing the *actual* range of emotions as an incremental learning tool was exhausting. Still, it was so far beyond any other form of learning and total insight that referring to it as some kind of super encyclopedia would be wholly inadequate. As Kalista was showing me the "text," even though there was no text per se, I experienced directly, through the full range of my emotions and senses everything that the text was addressing. Beyond that, there were simply no words to describe the totality of the learning experience that the thread conveyed. I was desperate though to get some further detailed insights and clarifications about the human emotion thread we were still examining.

"Hold on a sec, Kalista; why is 'anger' here and over on that other facet as well? And why is 'anger' in one 'color' on the part directly connected to 'fear,' and another shade on the part of 'anger' that is directly connected to 'love' as an emotion?"

"Here; look just below those specific facets and it will provide clarification on that for you. If you look right here... "

Kalista went through the process of showing me new and seemingly boundless levels of insight offered within the threads. She showed me that there was even deeper information that was ostensibly "underneath" the two facets of the thread that I was examining.

125

Almost as though underneath any small part of the "explanation" that you were examining on the thread – if you really needed even further and deeply detailed information – a kind of galactic bibliography could be found in the spaces "below" the subject area. This indicated an entirely new level of depth to the information that could be gleaned from the threads. I considered asking Kalista just how much depth there was underneath any given facet but decided that it was obvious that the depth would likely been interminable.

"Now, if you rotate the concept over more you will see that another major facet related to all of these is 'love.' Note that 'love' is not, as many people think, directly on the opposite side of 'hate,' or even 'fear,' but notice how those emotions in a person are very indirectly interconnected to 'love' and all of the other emotions. If you rotate the 'love' facet sideways, you will note that 'love' has a depth to it that seems infinite and, not coincidentally, it is."

Kalista then showed me how to look deeper into the thread that contained the details, description and particulars of the concept of love. It was actually comprised of a virtually endless number of more detailed explanations and examples that were represented by what looked like little thin wafers stacked on top of each other. These wafers comprised the complete length of an endless cylinder meant to represent the concept of love. Each wafer had even more detailed examples of the totality and limitless concept of love. Some were just examples of acts of love ranging from love between family members to acts of kindness and love between near strangers. Others illustrated concepts of love on higher spiritual planes.

I marveled that what at first blush had appeared at first glance to be a basic concept represented by a kind of unusual geometric shape, seemingly just floating by within some void, had turned out to be a near endless source of absolute comprehension on the topic of basic human emotions. And this was just **one** form. There were hundreds of different ones going past as we stood there. Probably more than that. Here, standing on what would otherwise pass for a simple nondescript outcropping at the top of a hill that most anyone would have walked past without giving the place a second thought, was a vista that would afford anyone standing there – if guided by some advanced soul like Kalista or Tresden – insights into literally all of the secrets of human nature, probably all nature for that matter – and the concept of existence and untold perspectives well beyond that. For some reason, at that exact moment, I flashed back to our walk up through the field of wildflowers and focused on the stunning possibility that it would have been incredibly easy for me to have looked at the broken gate and the dead flowers just beyond them and not continued the few feet up the pathway to this amazing place.

I remember Kalista's communication trailing off in my mind as I got lost in my own thoughts. If I could just stay here for a whole day, I'd know everything, I mused. Kalista immediately jolted me from my partial daydream.

"Chuck, you could stand here for many lifetimes and still not know everything."

"You would end up knowing an awful lot though. Oh look, I like this one. Chuck you try it on your own this time."

The thread Tresden had pointed out was small and only conveyed to me the impression of any geometric shape that might have been recognizable by a student of geometry. I tried to mimic what Kalista had done when she "read" the previous thread and almost immediately saw inside what resembled a series of inter-linked three dimensional triangles.

"Cool, this one's about chemistry. It shows how different elements are directly and indirectly related to each other and how all of the basic elements are really just switched around combinations of energy and nothing else. It indicates that there's no substance at all to matter and that all matter is really just essential energy arrested and suspended temporarily at different levels of resonance. It also shows how to change those energies so that you can effect shifts in what precise form the matter takes."

That was a concept that I knew I'd never thought about in that way before. Kalista and Tresden had broad smiles on their faces, obviously proud that I had managed to pick up the basic technique so quickly. Kalista wanted to know if I could figure out how to make it through the more complicated process of examining the thread itself. If I could look inside of the concept in various ways to learn the infinitely greater detail that was available and the individual facets and detailed parts of the thread.

"Very good. What else does it say?"

"Hmm, I'm not sure, how do I find that out?"

"Well, so far, you managed to arrest the thread and read the legend. You have to learn the whole process."

"What does all that mean?" I asked.

"When you have more experience at this you'll learn that you can identify what the concept of the thread is from a distance. You can sit here and sort it out as they go past. Pick out ones that interest you. Let the others simply drift on by. From there, if you want to learn more from one of the threads you simply stop the form long enough to take in the content. Every individual form has a legend that summarizes the essence of what information is contained within the basic idea. You correctly determined that the shape in front of you now is about chemical dynamics and compositions. If you want greater details, you need to learn to manipulate it and look into the thread with your perception and your will."

"How do I do that?" I asked.

"Like anything else that you want accomplished; think it through as though it were already completed. Imagine you have succeeded in the task already and what that image of success would look like to you. See the place on the thread that you want to look at – hold it in your mind – and it will ostensibly take you there."

It felt like magic. I looked at the legend on the base triangle in front of me and saw that, among a lot of other summary information, there were some references to heavy elements, something that I managed to remember a little about from freshman chemistry. I held that raw concept in my mind and the thread gave the impression of rotating around until that particular facet was directly in front of me. From there, I found that the specific detail that I wanted, down deeper, below that particular facet.

It was like pulling a book off the shelf at the library and then flipping through the pages of it to find the exact page that had the specific information you were looking for. This process was more detailed, intricate and automatic. What would have been the pages, had there been any, turned themselves. The technology of it was mesmerizing. It was not so much that it was a toy that overwhelmed me so but the reality sinking into my head that, the ultimate and all-encompassing reference library for the entire Universe was floating past me, waiting for me to look up anything and everything I ever wanted to know.

Other types of idea forms – those pertaining to advanced spiritual concepts – came about less frequently but, as the next one came by, Tresden pointed it out to me and then stopped it for us to look at together.

"First look very carefully at the general appearance of this thread. This one deals with the concept of multiple incarnations as well as all of the information about the guidelines for reincarnation. Notice that both the tinting of the largest part of it and its overall shape in general are different than a concept that would deal with say, something that only would be experienced in your more ordinary issues in daily life, like your chemistry triangles."

Tresden went on to explain that this particular overlook (what I had called the outcropping), was a place for intensive learning, usually used by souls in the discarnate world. She explained further that, often, souls would come to a place like this shortly after finishing a lifetime in order to gain deeper insights on some particular issue that they had experienced difficulty with or, to review something that they felt they had not learned to the degree that they had hoped for. I told Tresden that my understanding was that, if soul failed to learn something in a given life that they would just return to learn it in the next one.

She countered that coming here did, in fact, afford a comprehensive level of learning on any given subject, but that it was not in any way a viable substitute for actual interactive experience such as one would get through living an incarnate life and dealing with people and complex situations on a daily basis. I got the sense that she was trying to explain to me that the threads were a form of background material, research for souls before they went on to assume the next or another incarnation.

Sensing I had learned most of the techniques, how to access the information from the threads and that I had more than saturated my brain with new information, Kalista suggested that it was time for us to move on for today. Before doing so, I shared my concerns and frustrations with Kalista and Tresden that I was very troubled about my inability to remember a lot of what I had already absorbed by reviewing the threads.

"Hold on a minute Kalista. I'm already forgetting a lot of the information that I got looking at the threads. I really, really want to be able to hold on to that insight. How can I do that?"

"You will initially lose some, maybe even a lot, of what you learned here today. It's very difficult to hold onto such learning when you are still in incarnate form. But, as time goes by, Tresden and I will go over many of the more important lessons that you absorbed here today. Because you absorbed those things directly from the threads, the comprehensiveness of the explanations that you received will be deeply implanted within you. Almost like a computer disk that has software copied onto it. As we review aspects in the future, it will be like reminding you of what you already know, like opening the files that are already on a computer disk, and in no time at all, you'll recapture a lot of what you learned here today for good. That learning will remain permanently, over all your future lifetimes. All that you were exposed to here today you already have within your essence. You just don't remember, yet."

"But what if I don't do very well at remembering – holding on to the insight, the information? What if my long-term memory isn't that good to start with?"

"Your memory is just fine Chuck." Kalista gave me a reassuring smile.

"What do you mean? How do you know how good my memory is?"

"Well, you remembered how to find the garden didn't you? I mean, I only gave you those instructions once and that was several lifetimes ago. I told you that if you got to a point in any lifetime soon when you thought you were ready to jumpstart your spiritual learning to just meet me at the garden. You just showed up. So, I'd have to say from my point of view, your memory is just fine," she said.

I was shocked. Kalista was telling the truth, I just knew she was. But I never imagined that my finding the way to Kalista's garden several months back was part of some ancient instruction that she had given me several lifetimes ago. I started to ask Kalista how all that could happen, how it all worked, but I thought better of it.

I was exhausted. Kalista took the lead for the trip down the hillside. We made our way back down the pathway, past the patch of dead wildflowers, and went through the broken-down gate. When we were about fifteen feet past the fence, Kalista stopped and slowly turned around to look back at me. I could tell intuitively that she was thinking about saying something but, I had no idea what she might have to share. After a few moments she began to communicate in a slow and deliberate fashion.

"Chuck, look back at the fence and the gate there. The issue that you raised with us and Geradl about your frustration with the human form; about how insensitive, harsh, judgmental, unforgiving and dis-compassionate people are. About how poorly they treat each other. The gross inconsiderate nature of man toward fellow man and even animals on the planet you live on and so forth. You are so intensely focused on and disturbed by man's failure to move forward spiritually, morally and ethically even as time – millennia – continues to pass by. You feel like most people don't even care about all of those things but only about themselves," Kalista said.

I nodded in agreement.

"I suggest to you that instead of focusing solely on those souls in your current world – specifically, their failures and shortcomings – that you make the effort to see humans in much the same way as you would when you look at the broken gate there. That you reach deep inside of you in order to look beyond the broken gate to the absolute, undeniable perfection and beauty that lies beyond it in much the same way as you were able to find so much incredible beauty, insight, learning and peace as you made the effort to go past this broken gate today. And as you found some of what you were looking for on your journey today by ignoring an ugly broken-down, badly in need of repair gate as well as the foundering flowers just beyond them.

I promise, if you will open your spiritual eyes and look past the superficial imperfections and deficiencies that seem to be an integral part of the human form – of what you see on the surface of every person – that you will eventually see the absolute perfection that lies just beyond the superficial actions of all people in very much same way."

I stood there staring at the decrepit gate in the fence that was in a state of complete and utter disrepair for what felt like hours allowing Kalista's words to reverberate inside my mind and permeate my soul. At that moment, I felt as though I had been blind for my entire life and that Kalista had, in some manner, found a way to impart sight to me for the very first time.

Everything that Tresden and Kalista had said before about people not only having Source within them but in fact, ***being*** Source as their true, innate, unchangeable and absolute nature came completely raining down into focus for me in that one instant. I saw with immutable clarity that, irrespective of our perception or biased beliefs at any given time, people – all people without exception – can no more be separate from the Source-God than, as Tresden had said, a wave can be separate from the ocean. Souls that take on the human form, despite all of their outward selfish conduct were no different than the broken gate that Kalista had pointed out to me. Beyond it, just beyond it, if we would only make the effort to go a short distance farther – much like I had to walk the extra twenty feet to the immaculate outcropping – there was more beauty and more perfection within people – within all people – than we could ever imagine. Or dream.

Whether we continued to walk down the pathway all the way back through the forest and back to Kalista's island, I simply do not know. I was so completely elated by the weight, depth and overwhelming impact of what Kalista had said as well as the stunning insights that I had garnered by studying the threads while standing on the vista, that I simply disconnected from everything else around me.

I was soaring. So many of the things that had mystified me in my life were all of a sudden becoming clear beyond my wildest dreams. This was mostly attributable to some learning and specific insights that had come to me through a few select threads I'd experienced, along with additional explanation on some of the fuzzy areas from Kalista and Tresden. It was tremendously calming for me to see that.

It was now poignantly illustrated for me with what Kalista had shown me about the broken gate. At their core, people are actually perfect, despite the fact that so often they choose to behave otherwise. They couldn't help but to be good – better than that actually.

I also saw that this difference could be overcome. More importantly, I saw that we can, and in fact, **have** to, start this process first within ourselves and not by pointing out the weaknesses of others.

For the first time in my life I knew, at a very deep soul level, that I would ultimately find the absolute peace, complete and all encompassing joy, total happiness, the love of the Source-God and the boundless enlightenment that I had so desperately sought for so long. I experienced a warm, all-pervasive contentment as a perfect peace came over me when I reached the realization that all that I had sought would come to me if not within this lifetime certainly the next one, or possibly the one after that. It no longer really mattered how many lifetimes it would take because, I knew that it was all there to be reaped. All of it, everything that all of us dream about, is there for us if we will only make the effort to cultivate and re-perfect our innate nature. To listen to the distant music that beckons us on our own pathway home.

My version of cracking the code and finding some significant part of life's most important answers was only a matter now of continuing the rest of the way down this pathway I had found. To do that I needed to allow Tresden and Kalista to help me recollect what I had learned in all my previous lifetimes. As I had learned so clearly just that day, from the insights that came to me from the River of Knowledge and in all my other visits there in earlier lifetimes. The same exact knowledge that all people already have within them.

My last thought that day before I drifted off into the most peaceful and all-consuming sleep I had ever experienced was my recollection of Kalista's words several months ago when she told me that we're all *going home*. Now I actually believed it, felt it, knew it at the depth of my soul, and with every part of my being.

CHAPTER SIX

*The woods are lovely
dark and deep.
But I have promises to keep,
and miles to go before I sleep,
and miles to go before I sleep*

- From "Stopping by the Woods on a Snowy Evening" by Robert Frost

Almost immediately upon reentering my normal routine over the course of the next few weeks, I began to notice several changes in my overall state of mind, which had shifted from fairly apathetic to genuinely enthusiastic about life. There were other changes. Most noticeable was that my insight and intuition skills in relation to people whom I dealt with on a day-to-day basis were substantially greater than they ever had been. Even dramatically so.

It was not as though I had developed ESP or anything even vaguely close to that level of psychic skill. I was, however, quite adept in my ability to read people's general emotional states as well as their underlying mind set and motivations, with very little effort. These abilities went far beyond merely guessing in broad generalities where someone was coming from on the basis of a strained inflection in their voice or because they had a distressed look on their face. After my visit to the River of Knowledge, I had clearly developed a very real and consistent skill for sensing someone's overall emotional and psychological state from when they entered the room and onward.

Often, I got very specific and precise impressions and, as time passed, those turned out to be more and more accurate. The ability

135

was so pronounced, that it took me several months to adjust. Irrespective of the level of my enhanced intuition, it was clear that the increase in those abilities correlated directly with my visit to the River of Knowledge. I made a mental note to ask Kalista about this.

There were other mental developments that had occurred since I had experienced my journey past the gate and the River of Knowledge. These were most often things that I would feel as though I knew, or was somehow certain of, without really having any established basis to understand whatever it was I was so certain about. In essence, it would be like knowing the first names of all of the players on a professional baseball team even though you had never studied them. All of them. It was obvious to me that I had been exposed to certain insights and information on my journey that had, in some manner that I didn't really understand, been absorbed beyond my conscious level.

By no means was this knowledge far-reaching, comprehensive or necessarily even useful at times. There were just notions that I would know, or feel more than reasonably certain of, without having any real understanding as to how I knew them. These perceptions related for the most part to the emotional and psychological wiring and intellectual reflexes of people. My insights were just that much clearer when compared to my previous abilities to read people. It wasn't even a conscious awareness. It wasn't as though I asked myself "I wonder what they're thinking?" I just knew, had a sense of it. This evoked a period of deep introspection where I pondered more and more what the true nature of the River of Knowledge actually was.

There were other consequences from the experience that frustrated me. I knew that Kalista and Tresden had reviewed a number of threads with me when we were at the River of Knowledge. While I had no specific recollection of it, my sense of it was that we probably explored at least 10 or 12 different threads in total while we were there. The trouble was, I knew that I had consciously forgotten virtually everything that we had reviewed together. In spite of my newly-discovered enhanced abilities supporting deeper insight into people and the other similar perceptional skills, I was more or less a blank on this topic. Had anyone asked me to talk specifically about what I had learned from even one of the threads, I couldn't answer.

This would not have been so aggravating except that I was able to vividly recall that, at the time that I was actually reviewing the threads, I was completely overwhelmed at the depth and reach of the knowledge I was gaining there. Staggered in fact. It was all absolutely clear to me then. The content was so comprehensive and fascinating, that the only thing that mattered to me at the time was remembering it. I had the vivid recollection that, while we were at the outcropping reviewing these insights, I was continually reminding myself of how crucial it was to remember certain specific aspects and the precise details concerning what I was absorbing. A month or so after it all happened I had literally reached a point where the only thing that I could actively remember was that I couldn't remember anything, except that it was very important for me to remember everything, which I didn't. It was very frustrating.

I had, for a long time, been overly sensitive to the fact that there were certain major subjects regarding the spiritual realm and related questions that had always troubled me. In spite of my recent journeys to Kalista's garden, many of those questions remained unanswered. Ever since my visit to the outcropping I had a vague recollection that, while we were examining some of the threads, I believed that I had made significant progress in my understanding of many of the major items on my life-long list of spiritually-related issues and questions.

The fact that I was completely stumped at this point meant that I had either misunderstood some of the insights that we had reviewed or, possibly, that I had received the explanations that I had been seeking, but had simply forgotten the details. In either event, I found myself wanting for answers to some of the more complex spiritual issues.

Because the broad range of questions that I wanted to explore with Kalista was fairly lengthy and complex, I blocked out an entire weekend for my next visit there. I had originally planned to prepare for the process by doing some regular meditation, just to relax, on the Friday evening before my planned visit. In the midst of this exercise, however, I made up my mind on the spur of the moment to shift directly into the hybrid meditative methodology that had always led me to Kalista's garden. My transition to the garden was uneventful and I found Kalista sitting quietly on her bench as though she had been waiting for me.

"Well, hi there. How are you?"

"I'm well, Kalista. Actually, a bit better than that. I feel like I owe you a debt that I will never be able to repay. The visit to the river has done me a lot of good. So did your analogy about the broken gate. It really made me think quite a bit," I said.

"You're quite welcome, but you and I stopped keeping track of such things long ago, Chuck. I'm very happy though that our little trip seems to have given you a boost," she replied, mysteriously.

"It has Kalista. Really it has. But, I'm very frustrated that I seem to have forgotten just about everything that I learned at the river."

"I know it might *seem* that way but, believe me, you've retained – and recollected – far more than you know. In fact, a lot of what you already acknowledge that you do know was learned previously in other lifetimes and, by virtue of other trips to the River of Knowledge or similar places of learning in the alternate realms," she said.

"I don't think I understand that," I replied.

"I told you, the kind of knowledge that you are seeking is acquired and retained over a great period of time. Lifetimes. Eons. Essential lessons, spiritual knowledge and all other forms of learning are, in some ways, much like what you call karma; it travels with you from lifetime to lifetime. You can change what you look like physically a hundred times by taking on new bodies in different lifetimes. But what you know, what you've learned and what you essentially 'are' stays with you. It is never lost. The issue is whether you actually remember – are conscious of – what you have learned or not. In any case it's there, within every person. An unchangeable part of every soul, whether they are consciously aware that they have already learned it or not."

"But Kalista, it's not much good to me if I can't remember it. I mean, that's a lot like telling someone that is locked out of their storage unit that you're absolutely sure that they memorized the combination to the lock. If they can't remember it, they're still locked out."

"Tresden and I told you when we were at the outcropping that you would forget much of what you learned there in the near-term. We also told you that, we would help you remember what you forgot by going over those lessons with you. You just have to understand that, as souls – even souls in human form – a big part of the work is to remember what it is that we already know, then integrate that knowledge into our daily lives. In essence, to recall our true connection with the Source-god and then manifest that knowing into outward action. In so doing we help others remember as well," she said.

"How do we do that?" I asked.

"It takes time. The more complicated the lesson, the more intricate the knowledge, the more times it has to be reenforced in your essence before you garner a real and consciously emerging command of that knowledge. Tell me what's most in your mind at this point; what general subject area do you think you have forgotten the details of that you feel is essential for you to recall?"

"I vaguely remember looking at a thread that had to do with the parameters of reincarnation and things like that. I know that, at the time, I was really awestruck at how complete the explanation that the thread offered up actually was. Even with everything that you and Tresden explained to me before, I guess I'm still stuck though on why some people end up with such difficult lives and some people seem to have it so easy."

I knew, even as I was asking, that we had spoken extensively about this topic with Tresden less than a few months ago. It wasn't that I had forgotten what they had told me as much as my frustration that I had been overwhelmed by the deeper insights that I received when we looked at this one particular thread together. I was hoping that Kalista would review for me the essential portions of those insights, so that I could move whatever knowledge there was from my passive, deeply implanted memory and integrate it into my conscious mind in a more productive way. If the understanding was there, I wanted to be able to actually use it constructively.

"What you're really asking is about the people that seem justified when they say 'why me?' People that appear to be suffering inexplicable injustices in their lives."

"Yeah, I guess that's the essence of it. It's just very hard for me to accept that some woman that's in the church choir, volunteers at the hospital aid society, adopts three children from some poor African country and so forth gets raped. Then while she's recovering from that, they find out she has cancer and has three months to live. Then you have this other guy that parks in the handicapped zone, leaves two percent as a tip at restaurants and is rude to everyone he comes across in life. He scratches off a lotto ticket and falls into a pile of money and ends up set for life. That guy goes around being inconsiderate, selfish, arrogant and otherwise generally obnoxious to everyone – as though it were the very purpose of life itself. He never gives a penny to charity and he only gets more and more wealthy. Never gets sick. Never suffers any misfortune. It just doesn't make any sense to me."

"And then?"

"And then what?" I asked.

"Exactly!" she said, appearing genuinely enthused.

"I'm lost."

"What happens to the wealthy guy you're talking about? He has all this money and he's running his life like there's no tomorrow and then what?"

"Well, I guess he dies just like everyone else. So what?"

"Do you see any ATM's around this place?"

"Oh. So you're saying that... what *are* you saying?" I asked.

"Remember back to when we were looking at the thread that illustrated the pathway of reincarnation? Do you recall now that, outside of the issues directly relating to karma, which are separate considerations – that the next life we lead is **most** affected by the compassion and love that we conveyed in our current lifetime? In essence, what we gave to others," she said.

I thought about that for a few moments. I had a vague recollection that the thread had indicated just such a basic universal concept. Guideline was a better word since it suggested that without much room for equivocation, that the compassion, empathy and love for everything and everyone that we mete out in our lives was the major factor in determining the tenor of incarnation we would take on in the next life. It was as though in order to move onward, we ostensibly raised our own essential spiritual level by learning to conduct our lives in a compassionate, loving and empathetic way. There were other factors that affected our future incarnation, such as the resolution and balancing out of certain karma issues with our major contacts, the people in our daily life, as well as how well we dealt with carry-over lessons from even earlier lifetimes and so forth. But these were the major factors that determined the nature and composition of one's next incarnation. It was pretty apparent that how we dealt with the hand we acquired in our **current** lifetime definitely was the main factor in determining the details of our next life's script.

The more thought I gave to how Kalista was explaining this to me, the clearer it became. The greedy, insensitive guy in my example, who was not very considerate to his servants, partners and other people in his life, would have a pretty good chance to come back to a life where he may be the butler, or some equivalent. He may be subjected to a not very compassionate, considerate master or someone equally as unpleasant as he was in this lifetime. What better way to learn what he had failed to absorb as key lessons in his current life and, in the same life, have an opportunity to balance out some of the karma issues that he created in his last life?

On the other hand, I also got the distinct sense that, the woman in my example, that expended so much effort applying compassion and empathy so generously and unselfishly, was more than likely already on some moderately advanced spiritual pathway. Her lessons, although challenging and painful, held tremendous learning potential in them. The only question was whether she would be able to take advantage of the learning opportunities. The suffering that she had endured would be far more likely to pave the pathway toward a future lifetime with even greater learning potential and possibly less suffering, depending on her other karma issues.

Kalista made it fairly clear to me that such a life – one where there was tremendous learning potential – even though often fraught with difficulties and challenges that "seemed" unfair to the person living it, was about as good as we can hope for. It is not that we should necessarily seek out a life full of pain, suffering and stress but the reality is that such a life offers tremendous opportunity to deeply accelerate our learning should we become aware that we are in such a situation. With

a life like that you have the *potential* to move forward in a very meaningful way.

The other choice is to complain about your lot in life, waste inordinate amounts of time trying to assign blame elsewhere for your situation and accomplish ultimately nothing. Doing so only assures that
you will have to come back and lead another life very much like the
one you are complaining about – over and over again – until you finally recognize the opportunities for learning and absorb the lessons
offered by that lifetime. As clear as all of this was a number of details
remained unresolved in my mind so I sought greater insight from
Kalista.

"Kalista, I'm getting the impression that, those people that are
experiencing very difficult lives or have endured some major trauma –
physical, emotional, psychological and spiritual are pretty much all on
some advanced learning pathway. Am I remembering what the thread
suggested about that aspect correctly?" I asked.

"You're missing some subtleties. First of all, no matter what,
whenever there is great difficulty, it is always an advanced opportunity for learning. That is the most important point to remember. A
woman gets raped, a child gets beaten; truly terrible events of that
nature are opportunities to learn multiple lessons out of the same
ghastly event. The question that you're really asking is, '*why* the event
happened?' Did that person write the script that way – or, agree to it –
purely as some form of very painful lesson? Did it happen as the other
side of some karma issue? Are they being paid back in kind for something that they did to someone else earlier in this or even in some earlier life? As I already told you, it really doesn't matter why it has happened. What matters – the *only* thing that really matters – is whether
the person learns the lesson or lessons that are available to them
through the event. Do they respond to whatever happens to them
with compassion? With empathy? Do they seek out the loving pathway or choose anger, hatred, vindictiveness, retribution and other
non-compassionate alternatives?"

"But doesn't it matter to the person who is on the receiving end
of whatever happened in terms of the karma part of it? If a guy comes
up to me and hits me over the head with a hammer, doesn't it make a

difference to me whether he's paying me back for something that I did to him some time ago or whether he's just a jerk who decided to hit someone? And then, because he did that, I have to track him down either later in this lifetime or next to hit **him** back over the head – in essence to pay him back for what he did?" I was confused.

"Ah but you see, that's the whole point; that's **exactly** what I'm trying to tell you. It doesn't matter whatever whether he hit you first or if it was the other way around. In the example where the woman was raped, she has a crucial spiritual choice. She can feed her fear, anger, hatred, sense of feeling incredibly violated and all of the other negative emotions that are natural products of enduring such an event. Or, she can choose to feel those things and then make a deeply advanced, conscious spiritual decision **not** to perpetuate the cycle. She can decide right there and then to either perpetuate the cycle or end it. It doesn't matter at all any longer why it happened – whether it was a new act or an act of karma repayment. In fact, in the grand scheme of things it never **did** matter why it happened. The only thing that really matters at that point is that she summons up the spiritual character to commit herself to not perpetuating another extremely negative cycle," she explained. "Because if she responds in kind – retaliates in some manner against her rapist – she only extends the cycle of violence and karma further. Part of her major learning is finding a way to put together the insight that, if she doesn't stop the cycle right then that it not only could, but **will** carry on for potentially many lifetimes into her future. Nothing good ever comes out of perpetuating a negative cycle. Ever. Yet, people expend such great amounts of energy perpetuating them. I wonder why?"

"Gee, Kalista, that all sounds pretty good but, I think the emotional side of that has got to be a difficult thing to ignore. I mean, a lot of what you're telling me is absolutely clear when you talk about it in that way but, when you're living it, it's easy to get caught up in the reality of the moment and respond in a very non-spiritually advanced way. It's just hard for me to imagine a woman having gone through that kind of intense trauma needing to find a way to get a firm hold on her spiritual awareness right then in order to see the bigger picture."

"I know what you mean," she said, very sadly.

Right then, the deeply increased level of intuition and insight that I had mysteriously acquired since I had returned from our journey to the far side of the gate kicked in. I "saw" with total clarity that Kalista was not speaking purely from a theoretical point of view, but that she had some unfortunate real-life experience to back it up. It occurred to me that it might be very insensitive of me to broach the subject but, for some reason, I felt as though I needed to know.

"Kalista, I get the sense that you're not talking about this woman that was raped from just a theoretical perspective," I said.

"That's right, Chuck. Your intuition is definitely on the increase," she said, then smiled, but weakly.

"I'm really sorry Kalista, it's probably insensitive of me to even ask about this."

"I don't mind. It was some time ago, and the fact is that I overcame it. I rose above the rape itself and saw the opportunity to grow by breaking the cycle through total unconditional forgiveness. This was a major change in my spiritual pathway and a turning point – in reality, **the** turning point – of the greatest significance for me. Finding the courage to forgive my assailant and to empathize with him – even though I definitely could not sympathize with him – turned out to be the last hurdle that I needed to overcome in order to move ahead spiritually to the next level. As I advanced spiritually, I became consciously aware that I had set up that rape to give myself the opportunity to either learn the remaining major lessons about empathy and forgiveness that I still needed to recollect at that point or, to fail in that learning and kick off a whole new downward spiral of negative events and emotions. As it turned out, I summoned up the energy I needed to make it past all that. But just barely. It was a big risk for me to take but, I knew the odds when I agreed to the script in the first place."

"Were you, I mean was it... "

"It was in the late 1800s, the last incarnation that I had on earth. I was a nurse at the time in a very rural part of Ireland," she explained.

"I wish... I wish I could have been there for you; helped you somehow."

"You were Chuck. You did."

"What? I... what?"

"Let's move on to something else."

Kalista didn't appear upset or emotionally affected, at least out-wardly. It was clear to me though, that there was simply nothing else to be gained by taking this part of the discussion any further and she obviously felt it best to move on to something else. I was completely fascinated though by what Kalista was inferring; that she and I had crossed paths before when she had lived the life of a nurse in Ireland in the late 1800s. As she requested, I moved on to another issue, but still related to the general subject we had been exploring.

"Kalista, what you're saying is that, in order to move forward spir-itually that we have to change how we behave in the current lifetime. That we more or less set up the next lifetime for better or worse dependant upon our level of spiritual learning in this one?"

"This is important; there's nothing that says that you *have* to change. That you have to prospectively set up more productive spiri-tual behavior. However, if you don't, you will just perpetuate cycles that you're already locked inside of. You'll add more and more fuel to karma "fire" that is already bringing you the very things that already are making you unhappy about your current life – the exact things that people find themselves complaining about day in and day out. If you don't break those cycles, you'll have more future lives where you'll still be unhappy. But they'll likely be more complicated and challenging because each life that you fail to move forward, sets up a next life where you have to deal with those lessons again as well as any new karma that you acquired in the last lifetime."

The fact is that, it is people themselves who perpetuate their own cycles. It's neither the Devil nor an angry God doing it to them. Until they learn and accept that truth they are likely to continue to suffer very challenging cyclical existences. People want to think it's God or the Devil creating the circumstances that are making their life appear difficult because they don't want to accept the universal fact that they – and *only* they – are responsible for their own dilemmas in life. The reality is, if someone is complaining about how unfair life is, about how badly things are going for them, it's pretty much a sure thing that it's their actions in their previous – or even current – life that have brought them to that very place. The only way for that to change for them in the future is for they themselves to make changes in the way they are conducting their lives in the present."

"So what you're saying is that in order to be happy or at peace or whatever it is in the next life that you desire you need to break all of the negative cycles that you're involved in?" I was still a bit unclear.

"And not start any new ones. That's where most people get into trouble. They get it in their minds that life is a one-time thing and figure, for example, that if they have an affair and their spouse doesn't find out about it, that they're home free and that there are no repercussions if they don't get caught. But remember, there's really only one test, one real judge and one standard; was what you did loving, compassionate and did it reflect the highest practices of empathy? The ultimate judge is you, yourself and only you. What you observe directly are the effects and outcomes of your actions on the other people involved in your interactions.

The venue for your decision-making about what you really caused is the life review where there is absolute and indisputable clarity of the actual resultant feelings and impacts that your actions caused. Not what you *hoped* the outcome might have been and not what you ***thought*** the results of your actions or in-actions should have been. If the results after reviewing the outcomes of your behaviors are, "No, I wasn't very compassionate or loving when I did X" then, you've either started or perpetuated some cycle or triggered some component of negative karma that you're going to have to deal with one way or another."

"What do you mean when you say one way or another?" I asked.

"For the most part, the only way to reconcile karma is to pay it back – work it off. That doesn't mean necessarily that, if you were a murderer that you must come back and experience life as a murder victim. You might decide that there are other scenarios, other ways to absorb the impact of your non-loving, non-compassionate actions. Most souls, because of the absolute clarity afforded in the life-review process, usually decide to experience the victim side of the negative acts that they committed in order to reconcile their actions.

There is always the possibility though that you can resolve your non-compassionate, non-loving actions by genuinely acknowledging what you did wrong and why it was wrong. From that point you need to take yourself to a place where you deal with what you did, or did not do. If you really see that what you did was wrong; if you feel it at the core of your essence and truly reconcile yourself with it – at the very deepest level of your soul – then you can attain a genuine state of self-forgiveness. You can thus possibly avoid resolving the karma through actions, in essence dealing with the karma as a victim of one sort or another in another lifetime."

"I'm not sure that I understand all that." I was secretly hoping to learn more about this method of reconciliation in hopes that I might be able to side-step some of what I had created in my current lifetime.

"It might be most effective if I gave you a real-life example. One that you could relate to directly."

"What do you mean?"

"What if I could show you what your next life might turn out like by taking you through this current life in the life review mode?" Kalista asked.

"I don't think I understand. You mean do a life review for my current life right now? Here? Today? This minute?" I asked, almost dumbfounded.

"Well, yes. What I'm suggesting is that I'll run your life review for you as though your life ended right now, today. It will be completely realistic. In that way, by seeing what you have and haven't learned in this lifetime you'll be able to get a pretty good idea what your next lifetime *might* be like in order to absorb and reconcile the lessons that you haven't taken in yet in this life. How you might deal with the karma that you've created, the lessons that you haven't embraced," she said.

What at first blush had sounded intriguing and like a great tool to amplify Kalista's teaching, was all of a sudden not a good idea to me. Not at all. In a mostly panicked state of mind, I was trying to create a quick mental inventory of all that I had done – and not done – in the most sensitive areas that might count toward spiritual advancement or demerits. I was also thinking about how I might stack up when measured against the universal standard that Kalista had described where compassion, empathy and loving behavior were the ideal.

As I raced through the highlights of my life in my mind's eye, I was becoming more and more desperate – trying to find areas that I considered to be even vaguely redeeming, when compared against all of the things that Kalista and Tresden had told me was optimal conduct. Desperate to defer this exercise until I could think up some of the more beneficial things that I might have done in this life, I attempted to gently move Kalista toward an alternate plan.

"Gee, Kalista, I don't know. Your explanations are really pretty good, I just wanted some clarification on... "

"I understand, Chuck. Really I do," she smiled very compassionately. "But the reality is that you will have to face up to this life review, just as you've had to face up to all of your other life reviews for all your other lives in exactly the same way as every other person who experiences any life does. There is no escaping it. I just think that, if we go through the exercise now, for your current life, it might have an educational impact on you and potentially give you an opportunity to think about the approaches that you have been taking in dealing with people, with the challenges you've faced and other learning scenarios in your life. Besides, it will illuminate whether or not the way you've been doing things will lead you to the kind of lifetime that you really want the next time around."

The idea was sounding worse and worse with every word that Kalista communicated. I remembered all too vividly the last time Kalista had run me through just one simple event in life review format, when I had shot out our neighbor's picture window with a BB gun. The sense of stunning reality that I felt from that experience was still with me. Haunted me in fact. I could still feel the anger, fear and resentment of our neighbors as each shard of glass went flying through their house.

The idea of experiencing all of the feelings that I might have caused in my still relatively young life, as well as feeling the repercussions of all of my actions was making me ill at ease and getting worse with each passing moment. I could sense that Kalista was determined. She saw this as an opportunity to clarify for me the concepts that we were discussing about what kind of future life people will get under the Universe's guidelines of reincarnation. She also must have seen a chance to help me experience – with crystalline clarity – the true consequences of all my own actions and the potential benefit that doing so would have on helping me plan my future.

"Kalista, I really think that..."

"Chuck, you should do this thing. I believe because of where you are in your spiritual pathway at this time that it has a tremendous potential for positive impact on you."

"O.K., but, go easy on me will you. I know I've made some mistakes and... "

Before I could complete what I was saying, Kalista backed up a few steps and half closed her eyes. In a few moments, I began to experience my very early childhood in exactly the same surrealistic manner as I had when Kalista had taken me through the scene when I was ten and had foolishly shot out our neighbor's window. As with my earlier experience with the life review, the sense of realism was so intensively vivid and detailed as to be beyond description. The sounds, emotions and feelings of every person in a scene were so complete and pervasive as to be dumbfounding. It was, simply stated, an experience far in excess of the full range of senses that we experience in real life. I could see and feel everything that everyone, in all of the scenes that were playing out before me actually thought and felt. I sensed everything about the overall perceptions of everyone in my life at the time as well. There was no room for equivocation. The accuracy of the technology was almost frightening. I braced myself for the inevitable that I knew was coming next.

The review process moved in short bursts through my early childhood years. I observed with great interest the first foster home that I was placed in, where the beatings and other merciless physical abuse began. In this venue, I was now an observer and not a direct participant. The physical and emotional sensations perceivable within the scene, the torture being inflicted on the infant that was me, although quite realistic, were not as frightening to me as when I experienced them as that child. Since the pain was not being felt directly, I was able to experience an odd form of fascination in my observation of the intense, overwhelming sadness and self-hatred that the male figure who was the primary guilty party in doling out the physical beatings was feeling.

I was only seven or eight months old at the time, but the vividness of the life review process gave me insight into the inner feelings and anger dynamics of this man. He was in such a dark place as a soul that taking out his self-hatred on me was, to his distorted and obviously twisted thought process, his only viable course of acting out. How could anyone so deeply invested in anger take on that level of self-hatred? These were my thoughts, as I watched scene after scene of senseless physical abuse and non-ending psychological warfare that was imparted on this child. Seemingly out of nowhere I found that, similar to what Kalista had just said about her rape assailant, I could actually empathize but not sympathize with this terrible person.

I sensed by virtue of the technology that the female figure, my foster mother at that time, was obviously paralyzed from fear and basic incompetence as an adult. She was simply over her head in terms of having any abilities to deal with this man and his actions. She was equally as incompetent at defending herself against his assaults. Up until that moment in my life I had nothing but resentment and hatred toward these two people, even though I had no specific recollection of them. The specifics of who they were was blocked from my conscious ability to recollect. The abuse they doled out however – the intense physical and emotional pain they inflicted – wasn't blocked. The police reports I'd seen much later in life validated more than I ever really wanted to know about what they'd done. Still, from this unique perspective of the life review I saw that this woman was not in fact, the evil person that I had always imagined, but simply a terrified person frozen from taking action. Much like a deer frozen in the headlights of an oncoming car. As the scenes unfolded, I somehow found it within me to muster up a generalized empathy for her.

Kalista ran through a few other scenes in my early childhood that were more or less the same deeply abusive scenarios, but with different foster parents. The one happy foster parent relationship that I experienced was short-lived, as the foster mother died from breast cancer less than a year after my arrival. From that juncture, it was back to the orphanage and more abuse from some of the same foster parents that had treated me so poorly in my first year or two when the police removed me from their custody.

As I watched these scenes play out, I remember thinking about how imperfect the system is and how much empathy I truly had for anyone stuck in the orphanage or foster system today. I watched yet another scene of terror brought on by still another of the abusive male figures in my early life. As I did so, Kalista unexpectedly froze this scene and turned to me. She had a very intense, but at the same time deeply compassionate, look.

"Why did you choose this? When you wrote this script for yourself, you must have had some learning – or potential learning – in mind. What was it?" Kalista asked.

"I guess I... I don't remember." I was still deeply shaken from viewing the events as they had played out in the scene.

"Yes you do, try harder. Where did this incredibly terrible pathway take you? What did you learn from it? Why did you choose an early life that had only pain, suffering, abuse, sheer terror and bottomless sadness in it?"

I was a bit surprised by Kalista's aggressive tone. She obviously had a genuine need for me to deal with this now and not to side step it as I had been inclined to do up until this point in my life. "Kalista, honestly, I'm not sure. I really don't know."

"Let me try another way. Anyone else who endured this kind of abuse would have either completely collapsed on at least an emotional level or, would have become an incredibly abusive and angry person themselves. They would have probably been violent and antisocial. Most likely, worse. You did neither of those things and in fact, chose precisely the opposite pathway, one of compassion. Why?"

"Because it's not in my essential nature to be abusive. I guess I had enough experience with that as an infant and as a child so that I learned that I never, ever, would want to be a part of anything like that," I said.

"That's right, Chuck. Inhuman as that abuse was, no matter how many beatings and how much torture you endured, you ultimately responded to it by *not* lashing out against others. That alone was amazing to me. What else?"

"Strange as it may seem, while I was watching that scene I actually began to empathize in a way with the man. He was in such an incredibly horrible place. He was so unbelievably unhappy and completely invested in self-hatred. I never would have believed it was possible but, I actually felt sorry for him; the guy that beat me bloody more times than I can bear to think of, the man I thought I hated with all that I was or could possibly be, I actually felt sorry for him."

Kalista looked directly at me for a moment – something that she did only on very rare occasions and for barely a flash of a second even when she did so. She had a blank expression on her face and I wasn't sure what she meant to convey. There were no thought impressions of any kind coming through to me at that moment. She turned to look up the pathway where the roses were and I couldn't see her face for a few seconds. If I didn't know any better I would have thought that she was crying, something that I was sure was completely beyond her. In a few moments she turned back to me and picked up where we had left off. "That, Chuck, is a major leap forward."

"Why Kalista?" I asked.

"Because, the ability to afford genuine, from the soul, empathy to others – particularly others that have directly wronged us, maliciously and mercilessly tortured us – is a major spiritual accomplishment. Some people are able to pay lip service to the concept, 'Oh, yeah, I forgive him completely,' but, they don't mean it. Gerdal once told one of the souls that I watch over that, 'When they can go to a movie and genuinely empathize with every person in every scene completely that they will be ready to move forward.' I think that your empathy for that man who was so abusive to you is a brilliant step in that direction."

"Geradl knows about movies?" I asked, teasing her.

"Don't start," she said, restraining a smile.

Kalista continued on with the life review process, moving me through several interesting but relatively unimportant events in my early years. Just as I was about to comment about how relatively painless this process was, Kalista slowed us down to a scene from when I was sixteen years old. There is nothing to be learned by going into the specifics of the scene. However, after I absorbed the full impact that my actions and attitude had on others that were involved in the life scenario that had been played out before us, I was genuinely shocked at how insensitive and selfish I had been.

For some reason, I felt as though I really needed to understand the details of what had occurred and asked her to replay the scene over several times. Each time I experienced it, it actually made me feel worse and worse, adding vivid punctuation to what was my insensitivity toward others at the time. The technological attribute that allowed me to feel what everyone else in the scenario was feeling – in essence, what I had made them feel through my insensitivity – was incredibly sobering for me. I was genuinely disheartened. Even more so because I couldn't do anything about it now.

As Kalista moved me forward through my life review, I began to notice a pattern that was quite unsettling to me. I found myself cursing my own actions and inactions over and over again. What was most striking to me was that, at the time the events that we were viewing actually occurred, I had no sense of what the other people might have been feeling or thinking. More to the point was that going through this life review process emphasized to me that stylistically, my general manner of conduct was to operate without giving much thought to how other people might feel or be affected by my attitude and my actions. For most of my life I had been concerned almost exclusively with how *I* felt about what others were doing *to* me.

Scene after scene I watched with growing disgust as I trampled through scenarios of interaction with others without allowing reasonable regard for the effect that I was having on their feelings. On their ability to proceed through their daily course. The more I watched the worse I felt. Kalista would comment – although with great sensitivity and empathy, and always constructively – now and then about how I might have done something differently. How I could have approached something with compassion and love as opposed to lashing out and using fear, resentment or anger. How I could have taken a less than ideal outcome as a lesson as opposed to reacting and responding like a victim. After a while, I asked her to stop the process so that I could ask a few questions.

"Kalista, I just can't believe what an incredible jerk I am. How insensitive to the feelings of others I have been. I always thought of myself as being a compassionate person and it looks as though I am anything but that."

"Actually, Chuck, you are very compassionate. Obviously by your own standards you believe that you can do better. Awareness that you can and want to do better, is the seed of actually accomplishing more. This is one of the reasons that I agreed to take you through this advanced version of your life review and to give you the opportunity to see for yourself specifically where you think your weaknesses are. This gives you a chance to do something about it before the end of this particular lifetime."

"Does everyone go through this? I mean, are most people incredibly shocked at the negative effect that their behavior and attitudes have had on other people?"

"Pretty much but, people tend to be their own worse critics. You have to remember something very important in this regard though. The traditional religious institutions have worked very hard to establish the image that the life review process is administered somewhat sternly by some deeply advanced and relatively non-compassionate soul. They have created the expectation that the standard for the life review itself is some preset agenda of strict, harsh and inflexible rules and regulations as each religion itself has proscribed; this is a sin, that is a sin and so forth. The expectation is that "hell" is coming is, omnipresent.

Most people are surprised to learn that, while the life review process is aided by a spirit guide in terms of process, the ultimate "judge" as it were, is the person themselves. The "evidence" is what that person learns by virtue of seeing the direct effects that *their* actions had on others with the only real measurement mechanism being how their actions withstood the only meaningful standard; the degree to which they were compassionate, loving and empathetic. Guides are very gentle and sensitive to he fact that virtually everyone is pretty disappointed that they didn't do better in this regard as they participate in their life review."

"So my experience isn't that different from where most people come out?"

"In reality, you are moving ahead fairly quickly at this juncture. It takes most people quite a while before they get to a place where they attain a level of sensitivity to their own insensitivity and where they can muster genuine empathy for true villains in their lives. Most people finish their lives still holding onto a lot of carry-over anger and cycles that they've perpetuated in one way or another.

"During the review process, they realize how completely unproductive and self-defeating such behavior is because, since they brought it with them to this point, they'll probably decide to take on another life in an attempt to deal with those things then. They go on to the next lifetime – with the best of intentions – to try to resolve those issues. Sadly, most of the time, they get so wrapped up in the details and interpersonal interactions and complexities of the next life, in repayment of old cycles and starting many new cycles that they end up creating all sorts of new issues to deal with. As a result, they just keep on coming back over and over again. Perpetuating cycles, holding onto grudges, carrying forward one side or another of a vendetta and creating longer and longer lists of unresolved karma.

"They are mystified that their lives are so miserable because they don't make the connection that it was **their** own actions that set all of their unhappiness and poor circumstances up in the first place. They keep looking around for the person, or supreme entity, that is responsible for their sorry lot in life and never find them because their ego won't even allow them to consider the possibility that it is *they* themselves that are responsible."

I began to think about the effect that going through this life review was having on me. I knew, beyond a shadow of a doubt, that experiencing this life review in this manner would cause me to change my life going forward in many dramatic ways and that the changes would start immediately. My goal, I decided at that very moment, was to become completely aware of the potential impact that all of my actions – and inactions – might have on others. I also made a commitment right then to shift my conduct in such a manner that I would take full measure of any possible negative outcomes that I could be responsible for going forward. I needed to find a way to make compassion, love and empathy my style and not just an idealized concept that I read and heard about others adopting.

As I was considering this, I began to wonder about the possibilities of other people jumpstarting their lives in some similar way. I wanted to know if there was some technique that could be applied that would ostensibly display a life review for others before they got to the end of their current lives? Doing so while they still had a chance to make meaningful change in their current life without having to wait for the life review when it was too late to change this current life.

"Kalista, why don't the advanced spirit guides take the people that have really fallen off track or the ones that are potentially really close to moving forward in some major way and run a mid-stream life review process for them? I mean, this has had such an incredible impact on me that I simply have to believe that if you gave other people a similar opportunity, they too would change dramatically for the better."

"Such things happen when people are ready for them to happen. In reality, most people are ready when they reach a certain point where they have enough experiences to review to be meaningful and, they agree to pass on back into the pure spirit realm for a while. Then they have a chance, through the life review, to take the time required to contemplate their last life. If they choose, they can visit the River of Knowledge and other places in the spirit dimensions that provide other kinds of insight and learning to prepare for their next life and hopefully, set a course that will move them in a more productive way through all of their cycles and karma issues.

Running a life review before the end of the actual life is not something we're really supposed to do because most souls aren't ready to accept many of the realities of existence while they are still incarnated. In this case, I just saw it as a potentially great opportunity to help you take some major steps forward on some important things, so I took the chance."

"But there must be some way for other people to get that same advantage, that edge. There has to be a method that can help them see the consequences they are creating for themselves without having to wait all the way until the end of their current life," I said.

"Sometimes we whisper a hint directly to people that they can accomplish most of the effects of a life review if they do a life inventory. By doing so they quite often reach many of the same conclusions – garner a preponderance of the insights – about their conduct and certain changes that they need to make to begin the process of moving forward in a constructive, as opposed to destructive, way."

"Inventory?"

"It's not that complicated really. Time consuming but, not complicated. I actually did it in my last incarnated life in Ireland about 10 years before I passed on. What people do is go to a very quiet place where they can be completely alone for several days. From there, they begin to review their life meticulously within their minds; people they've met, a very detailed examination of the interactions that they've had with the significant people in their life and so forth.

Most people make extensive notes about things as they think them through. What they did. What they said. What they didn't do. The effects that they had on other people, and in particular, attempting to perceive the effects they had on others from those people's perspective, not their own. They carefully try to chronicle the things that didn't turn out the way they had hoped and search for an explanations as to why those events turned out the way they did.

If they can do so honestly, they write down things that they have done to others that were not very positive or beneficial no matter what they were. This simulates in its own way what the life review accomplishes when you experience directly what others felt when you did some particular thing. Writing it down sort of drives it home. Spiritually advanced souls always have a vague recollection that the life review – or the logistical equivalent of it – is coming at some point in their continuum of life anyhow and going through this inventory process is a way to begin to deal with all of that. It also gives the person performing the inventory something to look at, a guide as to specifically how, they can change their behavior.

Most important is that the inventory constantly assesses every event, every interaction from the perspective of how loving, compassionate and empathetic each item in the inventory was and how the person conducting the inventory feels that other people they interacted with felt from that perspective. The last part of the process involves the person thinking through how they could have handled each major event and interaction item in their life that wasn't very loving or compassionate in a way that would far better reflect those standards."

"Does it work?" I asked, completely fascinated.

"If the person doing the inventory is honest with themselves and takes the time to execute the process thoroughly, then yes, it does. Quite well in fact. The challenge is that, many people that attempt the life inventory try to gloss over things or rush through their most negative or irresponsible actions which ultimately, detracts or even negates the entire process. Much like the life review, the results are often so sobering as to result in a kind of shock or short-term spiritual depression. It is far better than the alternative though which is to continue on with patterns that will only perpetuate a cycle of lifetime after lifetime of *not* moving forward and, of having lifetimes where sadness and suffering are perpetuated indefinitely."

Kalista returned me to the life review process and continued to take me through my twenties, and then my early to mid-thirties. There were several scenes and periods that brought me to the edge of physical illness. While I had never broken the law, part of me thought that doing so might have been less painful and in some cases, less offensive. I simply hadn't learned how to be as sensitive to the feelings and interests of others as I knew, particularly based upon this insight, that I should have been.

I made a serious commitment to myself right then and there that I was going to change. And change substantially. I had forgotten completely what Kalista had said when we had begun using this process to project what my next life would be like on the basis of how I had done so far in this one. About that same time she decided that I had enough of the review process and the imagery faded away as she began to talk about the next phase of this procedure.

"So, let's think about what kind of life script you'd need to write for yourself in the next life in order to help you learn what you had as weaknesses this time and, deal with the karma that you created for yourself."

Kalista's words made me feel as though someone had shocked me with a cattle prod. Thinking back over the things I'd just witnessed myself doing, or not doing, the people that I had not treated very well and the issues that I had sidestepped throughout my life gave me a sharp sinking feeling in the pit of my stomach. I began at once to understand how people end up with lives that have some very difficult and challenging scripts in them. They end up that way, I thought, because they run around being inconsiderate and not very compassionate to people in their current lives.

I began to think through what kind of life would, in fact, be best suited to correcting the shortcomings that I'd seen in the "me" that was reflected in the images that had just been played out by Kalista. I didn't like the script that seemed fully appropriate for reconciling those particular shortcomings and sought to appeal to the only higher authority that was present. Kalista had, as always, been reading my thoughts.

"Don't come running to me. You made your bed, now lie in it."

"But Kalista, this is so unfair. If I had only known I would have... "

"You'd have what?" she said as she flashed me a genuinely warm smile.

"Oh, you're going to say that, now I do know and, armed with that insight, let's see what I can actually do with that going forward with this life."

"Pretty much that is what I was going for. Just one thing; you're pretty hard on yourself. Even the people that you didn't exactly make very happy in your life wouldn't be nearly as hard on you as you tend to be on yourself. You might want to take that into account in the future."

"Kalista, I want to be able to not lose my grip on this. What I learned at the River and have since forgotten, I need to be able to recall that and, the details of this life review so that I can use it as motivation to make myself better."

"O.K., consider it done."

"What? What does that mean?"

"It means, in this case, you'll remember all of this. Everything."

"Gee, thanks Kalista. There's one other thing: how do I possibly deal with what I have just seen?" I asked.

"Deal with?"

"Well, before, you were talking about there being a way to resolve our mistakes, without necessarily having to come back and lead lives where our acts are paid off directly to the person that we wronged."

"Oh. Well, sure, you can do that. Don't confuse me saying that with any ideas that you might get that it would be easy for you."

"How would I do it?"

"First, you need to think very, very carefully about why what you did was not as loving and compassionate as it should have been for each situation that you're recalling. You have to genuinely understand it. Absorb the details of it deeply. You have to truly see where your actions could have been perfected by manifesting compassion and love and empathy. To comprehend and see the "correct" resolution to it – is essence, identify the proper compassionate response that *should* have taken place – at a soul level. You must be able to see that with great clarity in your minds' eye and, at the same time, intend it at the depths of your being. Last, you have to seek forgiveness."

"How do I do all of that?"

"That's up to you to figure out."

"But Kalista... "

"Oh, and there's one other thing – a really important thing actually."

"O.K., I'm ready. I can take it. Give it to me straight on."

"You have to forgive yourself for making the mistake. For not acting compassionately, or lovingly or in an empathetic manner. None of it means anything if you can't acknowledge that you're in a school and that you are not perfect as long as you are *in* that school. Just by virtue of living a life – which takes great courage, in most cases – you have to learn to accept that you will make mistakes.

The idea is to make progressively less of them as you move closer to adopting compassion and love as a pathway. You have to abandon the errant belief that compassion and love are some idealized destination that maybe you'll arrive at someday; they are, in fact, pathways to walk not end points that you reach. In any event though, in order for the process to be complete and meaningful, you must find it within you to forgive yourself and, to forgive yourself completely."

Kalista went on to explain to me that it would take much longer for me to ultimately reconcile my lives if I remained the way I was and didn't change anything. She told me that, reaching a point where we first understand – far beyond the intellectual level – that our actions have real consequences and impact on others is a major achievement in spiritual learning. Making a commitment to change in such a way that our effect on people is more positive from a spiritual perspective is the next major stage. This step also included learning to be more compassionate and loving to ourselves. Actually doing something about it, taking action, was the third major step in this process.

At that time it felt as though my task was insurmountable. It was as though there couldn't possibly be enough time left in my life to make up for all the mistakes that I had made and, to make meaningful enough changes that would make a real difference in the momentum of my life. I told Kalista that the life review had drained me completely and that I would return again soon. She nodded, then smiled at me and waved as she got up to walk across her bridge. I left the garden that day a deeply changed and determined man. The return to my study was uneventful, as I had pretty much mastered the process of going to and from the garden at this point.

My mind was inordinately heavy with the experience of the life review that I had just experienced. More than anything else I wanted to crawl into bed and rest. But the life review process and Kalista's words had a sobering effect on me. I found new energy in my purpose and determination in my desire to manifest true change in my life's path. Instead of sleeping, I sat down at my desk and immediately began writing.

Dear _____

I hope this letter finds you well and, in whatever ways are meaningful to you, at peace with the world. It has been some time since we last spoke, and I thought this might be an opportune time to make an attempt to touch base and to possibly make peace with the past.

I recently had an experience that gave me cause to think back on what happened 12 years ago and how poorly I ended up treating you at the time. As I think about it, I simply can not imagine what...

I ended up writing 14 letters that night, all different and all personalized to the best of my ability. Unfortunately, not everyone's address I needed was available and this frustrated me. I ended my day by staying up until well past four in the morning to complete all of the letters. As I sealed each letter, I meticulously replayed in my mind, in painstaking detail, what I had done that I felt was not particularly loving, compassionate or empathetic to this person and carefully thought through how I could have handled the situation with much greater empathy and love if I had it to do over at this point, fully armed with all that Kalista and Tresden had taught me. As I placed a stamp on each letter I said a silent prayer hoping that each person would find it in their heart to forgive me for the insensitive mistakes I had made.

Finally, as I tossed each letter into my out box, I felt as though some small weight had been lifted from me – as though I was actually lighter with each letter that left my hands. That feeling has stayed with me to this day.

The next day, I reviewed as many of the life scenarios that were bothering me the most in as much detail as I could remember. I also tried to perform the last step that Kalista had mentioned – forgiving myself for what I had done, for my failure as a human being. This was clearly the most challenging step in the process.

Nevertheless, with the passage of time and great effort over the course of several months, I managed to forgive myself for each of my failures. It was one of the more challenging exercises that I have ever gone through. There was, however, a distinct benefit that I felt when I mailed each of the letters that I had written. I felt lighter – and spiritually exhilarated – as I found it within me to afford *myself* forgiveness for each issue.

My overall peace of mind and feeling of well-being were increasing dramatically with the passing of each day after having gone through this effort. I found myself wondering at times just how much we might be able to ratchet down the overall anger in the world if everyone performed such a introspective task. A dream. But a beautiful one nonetheless.

Whatever subconscious, spiritually intuitive insights that had been implanted within me by virtue of my experience at the outcropping were, as Kalista had promised, beginning to unfold and take root within me. It was like a seed at the early stages of germination. I became more aware that there were certain insights that were accessible to me that simply had to have come from my experience at the River of Knowledge since I had no conscious recollection of ever actually learning many of those things.

There were still several threads that I had barely a vague recollection of. A kind of faint echo of a thought reverberating somewhere in my subconsciousness. I still could not recall any of the specific details about many of them though. One in particular was causing a consistent, nagging feeling in the back of my mind that I couldn't seem to get rid of. Of the little I was able to bring into conscious focus, I knew that it had something to do with understanding in some depth and detail the concept and the particulars of what Kalista had constantly referred to as the Source-god. All I could recall was that, when I was experiencing that particular thread, I was completely awestruck – paralyzed by the feeling of total elation and all-consuming peacefulness that the experience had conveyed to me.

I recollected that the feeling that I got from the thread must have been to some fraction of a degree, the sensation of the absolute and boundless nature of the love and compassion that the Source-god emits. But there was more to it, much more. I just couldn't remember it, which frustrated me.

Determined to pursue this knowledge and reconstitute this enlightenment and pervasive feeling of bliss that had become a nagging awareness within me since our visit to the River of Knowledge, I promised myself that I would return to the garden the next day. But first, sleep. I just desperately needed sleep.

CHAPTER SEVEN

The most beautiful of all emblems
is that of god,
Whom Timaeus of Locris describes under the image of
"A circle whose center is everywhere
and whose circumference is nowhere"

- Voltaire

The weight of having gone through the extensive life review process and facing up to the fallout and outcomes that derived from my past decisions in life was stressful and, in some ways, troubling. The entire event caused me to sleep very poorly over the next several weeks. I continued to have flashes of specific scenes from the life review that Kalista had conducted for me. It made me wonder what other people might have to wrestle with if they had to experience the life review. How would they respond to the reality of coming face-to-face with what they had done to others and how they had made those around them feel?

I had originally set aside an entire weekend for sessions with Kalista, to make an attempt to garner some progress on the one specific thread that had been nagging at me since my trip beyond the gate. I had learned from my previous experiences that it was usually very difficult for me to make the connection to the garden if my energy level was low. Nevertheless, I felt a burning need to find out what I could about the thread that dealt with the details relating to what Kalista had referred to as "Source-God" For obvious reasons I was very anxious to re-experience the thread that was apparently designed to convey the feeling that many people might equate to the love of God. I remember thinking that, if I could learn anything about the true nature of Source that it would be worth any temporary physical and psychological toll that the effort would take on me.

With a determination and focus to get to the bottom of this topic, I mustered the energy needed to make it past the exhausted state I was experiencing. I managed, in spite of a significant lack of sleep, to make the transition to Kalista's garden without encountering any meaningful problems at all.

Kalista was sitting on her bench, reading a book of some sort, which I found odd. Over the course of all my visits to the garden I had never seen anything that looked like a book nor any printed or written material of any kind. I noticed at once that this was no ordinary book. It was constructed of some type of pure crystal material. From what I could tell, based upon the unusual angle where I was standing, it seemed as though multidimensional pictures arose from the pages, which were made of leaves of crystalline material that appeared to be about a quarter inch thick. As the details of the garden came into final focus, Kalista closed the book without saying anything about it. She then looked up and smiled at me.

"Hello Chuck, how are you?"

"I'm okay Kalista. Still a bit uneasy over my life review. I guess that's why they only do it once in a lifetime, huh?"

"Well, imagine what the life review feels like for some who lived a genuinely far less compassionate and non-loving life in the world. I suspect that someone you've complained about before, Adolph Hitler, is probably down the hall *still* going through his life review." She was smiling, trying to keep things from starting off too heavily. But, she was also reinforcing it for me.

"I meant to ask you about that; wouldn't it be better if people could remember that they're going to have to face up to the life review process at some point? What if people actually knew that there was no escaping the day when you have to feel everything that you caused others to feel – bad and good? Then deal with the true impacts of the less than stellar actions and in-actions that we have caused. I think the world might become quite a bit more peaceful a place to live in if it worked that way."

"But they do know, Chuck. Most people either don't want to remember, or they think that they'll be able to rationalize their way out of it in exactly the same way that they try to rationalize their behavior when they're living their current lives. But it's not until they actually get to the life review that they remember that there is no dodging the process, and that they will feel precisely what they caused others to feel. That they will experience the consequences of what they did or didn't do and that compassion, love and empathy are not simply words, but the fuel that powers the engine that drives souls forward, or backward, depending upon how they acted along their developmental pathway. In this case, their lives on earth."

"Kalista, what do most people do after their life review? I could barely sleep at all just thinking about all of the things I could have done better."

"Well, a fair amount of souls take some time to think about it. They go off to some beautiful place – you know, we have a few of those here in the spirit dimension – and just think about what they saw and felt during their life reviews. They try to sort out why they did what they did – good as well as what they could have done better – and, how they might structure their next life and lessons in such a way that they can resolve some of those things more productively. They take time to ponder the lessons that they have learned and, the ones they haven't learned. They examine what they will need to work on the next time around. They also have the ability to go to places where there are records so that they can look up other lives that they have had and how they have handled things in previous lives.

If they want to, they can go to the River of Knowledge, or similar sources of insight, in order to learn more about certain understandings where they feel they have weaknesses. Many souls prefer to digest and review their life experiences in the equivalent of spiritual classrooms with others that they shared their life with. Those settings are facilitated by more advanced souls that help move the discussions along. Others still prefer solitude to contemplate their past lives. But, no matter what venue the soul chooses to ponder the past, it is through processes like this they can gain deeper insights into what they didn't understand or, what didn't work out. When they've made it through all of that and they've begun to formulate some ideas about what they might need to do next, they usually track down their soul counsel and begin to explore what their life options are going forward."

"That's pretty cool. How long does all that take?"

"What do you think?" she flashed a broad smile.

This had become a kind of running joke between Kalista and me. Kalista had explained many times, in a variety of different ways, that the universe allows us to take as much time as we want or need to make it down our own, individualized pathway in the process of re-perfecting our soul. She reached a point where every time I slipped, or suggested that the answer to such question might be anything *other* than "as long as it takes," she would try to embarrass me in a very friendly way, by drawing attention to my mistake in an overly-exaggerated manner. She was obviously doing it again, and I silently cursed myself for falling into the same trap.

"I know, I know, as long as it takes. What I really meant was what's normal? How long do most people take after they die before they're actually going back to start the next lifetime?"

"I don't know that I'd really want to try to fix a number as being 'normal' because every soul's pathway is as different as the soul themselves. Since I know you won't give up until I give you an answer, I'd say that it equates to something like twenty-five to one hundred years. Even as I say that, I have to tell you that there are some souls that decide to go right back in what is the equivalent of a few years and some that have taken a thousand years or more to sort things out before going back. Some, don't go back at all. They choose to learn in other ways. The real answer is more complicated than that but, for what you're asking, it will do for now," she said.

"Now we're getting somewhere! What if a soul really, really doesn't want to go back? What if yesterday was the real thing for me and after I thought about it I came to my soul counsel and said 'look, I've had it with paying taxes, traffic jams, a corrupt society and so forth. Yeah, I know that I've left some unresolved karma behind and there are some essential lessons that I haven't exactly earned top marks on yet but, I'm really tired of it all. I just want to stay here and work things out.'"

"That's definitely a choice that you can make. But the reality is this; when souls return to the discarnate world they are no longer confounded by the ego and the other distractions that incarnate life throws in their pathway, most notably fear. Once a soul takes the time to think about their life review and talk things over with their soul counsel, it's usually their choice to seek us out and begin the dialogue about returning. Often the desire is to return to an incarnation where they can get back to sorting out their karma issues and, learn the lessons that they want to master. Sometimes we have to slow them down a bit in order to make all of the arrangements."

"And the ones that don't want to do that; I mean, there have to be one or two every now and then that... "

She smiled. "You're not going to be satisfied until you make me say it at least once today are you? All right, they can go off and think about it for as long as they need. Someone from their soul counsel will check in on them every now and then to see how they're doing; see if they have any questions; ask them if they are ready to talk about ways to sort through their issues. Soul counsels are infinitely patient with all souls, but particularly the ones who are going through a period like this. We let them know anyone can take as long as they want to, but that eventually, they're going to have to deal with what they need to. Learn what they have to. In the end, everyone comes around. Now, are you ready to talk about what you really came here for today?"

"Absolutely. But, this time, I want to be able to actually remember what you tell me about Source, not just enjoy the experience of it and then have this annoying feeling that I have forgotten it all by the next day," I said.

"You will remember what you are meant to. I think this time you're likely to recall much more than the first time you experienced the thread. However, I won't be explaining any of this to you directly," she said.

"We're going back to the outcropping? Cool."

"No, we're going to be staying right here, Chuck," Geradl said.

I had neither seen nor heard Geradl come up the pathway

169

through the rose garden and take up a position directly behind me. At least that's what I assumed he had done. In the process, he scared the hell out of me – possibly exactly what he intended. I'd seen no direct evidence that he had a sense of humor but, then again, Geradl was not an ordinary sort; there was no telling what he might have intended. After a few moments I regained my composure and tried to pick up the conversation while trying to appear to be unshaken.

"Hi Geradl. You know, we need to put a little bell or something on that pathway. You could give someone a heart attack doing that."

"Sorry, Kalista called me and I didn't want to interrupt your conversation."

"I knew you wanted to discuss Source and there's just no doubt that Geradl is far better equipped to help you with that than I am."

Much like before, Geradl peered directly at Kalista for what seemed like a minute or so. During this time, I didn't sense any thought impressions of any kind. My assumption was that they had the ability to block me from reading any communication that they wanted me not to overhear. I noted that Kalista gently nodded her head a couple of times and looked in my direction as she did so. Before I had a chance to even think about saying anything, Kalista smiled, sort of patted me on the back gently and then walked in the direction of and then over her bridge.

I wasn't particularly uncomfortable at the prospect of being alone with Geradl. His presence gave the irrefutable sensation that he was the most compassionate soul with whom I had ever come into contact. The feeling that I got from being around him defied words. It wasn't anything that he said, as much as a feeling of complete and calming absolute peace that clearly emanated directly from and throughout the entire area around him.

Still, the events surrounding our first meeting remained fresh in my mind, particularly the considerable deference that both Kalista and Tresden had shown to Geradl. And even though I have never had the honor of meeting His Holiness the Dalai Lama, or His Holiness the Pope, I felt at that moment as though I was in the presence of someone of equal spiritual stature. I was imbued with a sense of absolute awe and wonder. I was anticipating Geradl sharing insights with me that were far beyond what I ever expected to learn when I had set out on what I considered, was a simple mission, almost a year earlier to find a new method of meditation. I pondered the odd outcome that my experiment in meditation had grown into, then Geradl interrupted my thoughts.

"Kalista told me that you did very well at the River of Knowledge. Your desire, your capacity to learn and move forward spiritually is very high. You remain quite impatient though. Driven I would say. Reminds me of someone I once knew."

"Impatient?"

"Most souls are satisfied if they master a major essential lesson over the course of several lifetimes. I understand from Kalista that you are unhappy because you cannot recall all that you were exposed to at your first trip in this lifetime to the River of Knowledge where you experienced 26 threads."

I was stunned. In my mind, I retained a vague recollection that, with Kalista's and Tresden's help, I had experienced possibly six to maybe ten threads on our recent trip beyond the Gate. Geradl was suggesting that the number was almost three times what I thought I had experienced. I was unclear on what Geradl was trying to tell me about mastering one essential lesson over several lifetimes and how that might compare to experiencing several threads at the River of Knowledge.

"Geradl, are you telling me that experiencing a thread is the equivalent of mastering a major essential lesson?" I asked.

"If you could completely absorb all that any thread contained on a given subject – something that you saw for yourself is a very difficult thing to do – you would have been exposed to all of the raw information relating to that essential lesson. But, it would not be the same as having the actual experience related to that subject," Geradl explained.

"I don't understand."

"You could experience the thread on one topic of, for example, human emotions. Part of that particular experience, as you saw it for yourself, was the thread communicating to you, the perceiver, what love feels like. But no matter how deeply you went into – immersed yourself inside the substance of that thread – no matter how much time you spent experiencing the full range of it, it would not be the same as taking on an incarnation. The reality of falling in love with someone and learning through incarnate life experience what it feels like to love, to be loved and experience the near endless range of extremely complex issues and feelings that are part of any love relationship. That same condition would hold true for all threads. The basic information to the nth degree is there for consumption within every thread. But the depth of it – the full knowledge experience – is in learning the nuances of reality through life. That is what adds the crucial dimension to the lessons."

"Is that one of the main reasons that we take on actual lives; so that we round out certain knowledge? In your example, the River- or similar places of learning in the spiritual dimension – gives us the raw information. However, to fully understand all of the finer details and practical parts of the lesson, we have to take on the actual life experience in order to gain that enhanced knowledge here, in that way?"

"Exactly. Think of threads as a multidimensional, layered galactic encyclopedia; they have extensive information but, without the practical life experience to back them up, no matter how brilliant the threads are in their inter-workings, they are an augmentation to, and not a substitute for, life and genuine life experience."

"So what Kalista and Tresden told me about life being a school is accurate. More than anything else, it is a school for practical – as opposed to book-type knowledge. And that's why we come here; that's why we take on various lives. We need to supplement our learning, our knowledge."

"Some of your words could be more precise but, you have it fairly well pegged now. You must remember, at this point, all people alive on Earth are there, living those lives in order to perfect, essentially re-perfect, their knowledge. To resolve issues that they have created with others in earlier lifetimes and to remind themselves within the unique opportunities that only an incarnate life can offer up that they arose from, they are forever inexorably interlinked with – and are on a journey to return to – Source."

Over the course of many years after this day I would replay those words that Geradl spoke, over and over in my mind. In one brief paragraph, he had answered in absolute comprehensive terms the question of why we live; why we're here; why we need to bother with doing any more than just going through the motions in our lives. Between what he and Kalista had explained, it was clear that, while the Universe was infinitely patient in allowing us whatever amount of time we needed to learn our lessons and resolve our karma, that those were two things that *were* going to get done. Period. The irrefutable spiritual fact was that, it was completely up to us to determine whether we took a more or less direct pathway in pursuit of these objectives. God neither pulls us along behind Her nor holds us back. Neither does the Devil because, the only real Devil turns out to be the darker side of ourselves. What Kalista had called "the convenient excuse we create for explaining inconvenient behaviors."

I also began to replay in my mind what Kalista had said to me about making a conscious decision to break our negative cycles. It was clear that, the more time and energy we invested in perpetuating those negative cycles and life threads, the more off-course we become in terms of learning what we need to. It is essential that we do not create further negative karma issues that will require more and more energy and lifetimes to resolve.

All of these insights taken in combination, it was becoming more than obvious to me what Geradl, Kalista and Tresden were telling me. That, in order to follow the most ideal pathway – the one that leads home to Source-god, eternal peace, the end of all suffering and the realization of immeasurable happiness – we need only recognize and accept our mistakes. Then we must resolve them and fully accept that we are on a pathway of learning – relearning, the construct of our true nature.

From there, we must focus on our lessons – learning or relearning our basic connection to compassion – and make a genuine effort commensurate with the goal of returning home to Source. To God. To limit the negative karma that we take on. At the very moment we make that commitment, truly obligate ourselves at the level of our essence, the pathway back home begins to illuminate on its own in front of our very eyes. In my case, as I became deeply committed to this goal, as I became determined to discern my true nature and mission in this life, the pathway to Kalista's garden became apparent to me – even without my being consciously aware of it at first. There was still more learning, and a lot of it, that could not be accomplished without a deeper understanding of what "home" was all about; what Source or Source God really was... and is.

"And the thread that deals with Source?" I asked.

"As you experienced yourself, this is by the very nature of the subject, an ornate, intricate and complex thread. Most threads are very comprehensive by nature. But the thread that deals with the topic of Source is limited because, among many other things, Source can only be talked about indirectly. This particular thread can – and does – give many examples of what Source is and is not, but in the final determination, The Original Center of All Things can only be experienced. And the fact is that it can only be experienced to different degrees dependant upon the level of Resonance the individual soul has attained," Geradl explained.

"Geradl, ever since Kalista used the expression "Source" I've been confused; is Source the same thing as God? And, when you say 'The Original Center of All Things' do you mean that to be the same as Source?"

"Let's approach it this way; take a few moments first to think through, circumspectly, what God is or means to you."

That was not what I expected from Geradl. My hope had been that he would dive right in and provide the insights and clarifications that I was so desperate for on this essential topic. His question, although seemingly very direct on the surface of it, was, of course, the one that had been challenging mankind for as long as there has been recorded history – probably even longer. The manner in which Geradl asked this question jolted me into a state of acute sensitivity. Despite all of the reading and thinking that I had done on the subject of spirituality, I was probably no closer to having any meaningful insight or even a defensible answer for this than when I had first begun to contemplate such matters, somewhere around my twelfth birthday.

"That is one of the most difficult questions for me to answer. But

I think of God as the entity; the originator and guardian of the known and unknown universe. All-seeing. All-knowing. All-loving. All-compassionate. It is the plain vanilla explanation that most people have, I think."

"And you think of God as an individual entity?" Geradl asked.

"You mean an old man in a long white robe?" I countered.

"Is that what you think?" a hint of bemusement was arising around Geradl's eyes.

"No, I guess not. I suppose that the only answer that I'm remotely comfortable with, is the one I already gave," I said.

"Have you ever thought about *why* you think that?"

"I'm not certain. I suppose because it's what I had always been told. Parents, teachers, religious leaders and people who we're supposed to trust to give us answers. They just tell us as children and we believe them," I said.

"Of course that is where most people's concept of God comes from. Few people ever question it much beyond what they are told early on in their life. Or, if they do, they quite often end up returning to whatever they were told originally because they were unable to come up with a better explanation on their own. Before we go any further, are you certain that you are genuinely open to an idea or concept that goes beyond that?"

"Why wouldn't I be open to another view?"

"For most people, their concept of God as being the eternal, unchangeable, all-powerful and omnipotent being provides their greatest security. If that is challenged, they feel as though there is little left for them to grasp onto. Just the possibility of a different concept or practice of God has brought people to fight great wars on Earth. Those wars have been fought – millions of people killed – because someone said they wouldn't believe someone else's concept of God, or how they choose to worship that God. In some cases wars have been fought because people chose to pronounce "God" in a different way. That sad state of affairs continues up until today."

"Yes, that's all true. However, the explanations and rationalizations that have been commonly used to support the concept of a God, those that I've heard so far in my life, don't make complete sense to

me. If someone wants to burn me at the stake for thinking differently, so be it," I said.

"Meaning?"

"Well, for example, whenever there is some disaster in our world
such as the Holocaust, religious leaders and their most fervent follow-
ers don't want to have to deal with the prospect that an all-loving, all-
compassionate God would allow something like that to happen; so
those people feel compelled to jump in with rationalizations – even if
they fly in the face of sensibility or dogma. They are so determined
to defend their religion and their inflexible concept of what God "is"
and "is not" that they manufactured explanations out of thin air."

"Explanations?" Geradl seemed closer to the edge of amusement.

"Well, sure; if we go back to the Holocaust example, the more
fundamental religious types will claim in that case, that 'God allowed
it to happen because He loves us so much that He didn't want to com-
promise anyone's free will. So, God has to let things like that happen.'
In that case, I assume they're referring to the Nazi's exercising their
'free will' to murder six million Jews. The other favorite of the fundamental religious thought is the 'devil made someone do it.' None of
that makes sense to me. Never has."

Geradl was not one for showing emotion of any kind, but, now I
could definitely see the very faint hint of a smile creeping up around
the corners of his lips. Knowing that he was by far the most compassionate and sensitive soul that I had ever met, I knew instinctively that
he was not amused at anything that I had said about the Nazis. My
newly emerging intuition told me that Geradl must have had some
experience in at least one of his lifetimes with the religious fanatics
who were so inclined to convenient rationalizations. I surmised that
what I was seeing in him was not amusement, but recognition of the
very same type of people that he had encountered. Before I had an
opportunity to call him on it, he preempted me and answered my
question.

"Yes, I seem to recall coming across that unique form of thinking
a few times while I was still incarnating. So, is it your belief then that
there is no God or, that there is a God but he/she doesn't care? Are you
suggesting that God simply allows freewill to dictate the course of all

events? You must have spent some time thinking about all of this."

"Is it possible to say that I definitely believe in God even though I am uncertain what God is? I know I believe that, in the case of the Holocaust, there are more than enough lessons to go around for everyone. In that case, there must be great volumes of karma being sorted out one way or another when something that spiritually vast occurs. But it's very confusing to try to understand all of the nuances and implications of it."

If what Kalista and Tresden explained to me is accurate, karma and the other guidelines that determine how the universe functions will eventually reconcile all of the spiritual aspects of events like that. The Nazis will have to endure some pretty terrible lives as deeply persecuted souls. Those that helped the Nazis, but didn't actually kill anyone, will have other future lives and scripts that assure that they learn from direct experience that there are repercussions of assisting by silence. Compassion and love is the only path that is truly viable. If that is how it all works, my guess is that God just allows the essential rules and guidelines of the Universe to prevail. Events play themselves out. Karma balances. God need not intervene because God has created a system that works perfectly already."

As I was explaining my thoughts to Geradl, it occurred to me that I had not thought through what I was saying to any significant degree. In fact, not at all. Much of what I had learned, and continued to learn, from Geradl, Kalista and Tresden was still being digested in my mind. In its own unique way, reabsorbed by my soul as something that I knew, but had forgotten. I thought about what I had just said to Geradl, and it made sense to me. Our primary mission is to re-perfect our learning and to resolve issues relating to karma. Therefore, it only stood to reason that God, whatever that might really be, would neither be inclined to nor *need* to intervene – even selectively – when even the greatest disasters arose. There would be no reason to because the way in which the universe functioned, in which God set things up in the first place, was perfect. The existing mechanisms would reconcile all that occurred even if it wasn't always efficient, expedient or fair from our perspective. As Kalista had said over and over again; "the Universe has an eternity for these things to work out."

I could sense that Geradl was contemplating the most effective way to respond to what I had just said. After a few minutes passed, he stood up and signaled me with a subtle movement of his head. I followed him toward the rose garden. As we began to stroll in that direction, he began to answer me.

"What you just said is actually very insightful. In essence, it's accurate to say that Source, irrespective of definitions, is a hands-off manager of the All. The immutable guidelines that influence the ebb and flow of freewill and reconciliation work. Perfectly. Eventually, all things attain balance. To gain deeper insight into why this works, it might be most helpful to remind you about some of what you had experienced directly from the Source-thread. Specifically, that part that relates to the beginning of all incarnation. What is called Origination of the All."

As we walked into Kalista's rose garden Geradl continued his explanation. He clarified that, at some time in the past, the Source of All Things was an all-encompassing absolutely perfect love, which took the form of inconceivable light, The Original Center Of All Things. This essence of light began to create through the process of unfolding universes, dimensions and a novel variety of various realties. Source continued this process of Origination until there were limitless realties, boundless numbers of universes and immeasurable quantities of dimensions. At Origination Source allowed the All to develop far beyond human beings' abilities to comprehend its limits. Geradl called attention to the fact that all that is made by and originated by Source, itself, is essentially the "construction material" that comprises all things. The composition of all known as well as unknown constructs, including individual souls, that had been developed since Origination were, themselves, made of the same all-encompassing and perfect-light-energy and love that is Source. And only that. At some juncture, Source recognized that Origination, was now beyond infinite. This became known as the ALL.

Source then "decided" that it would cease any further direct control or influence on further creation and would allow the sheer momentum of what had already been put into motion to simply continue to occur. Since Source knew that even greater numbers of limitless manifestations would arise out of what had been created and set into motion, Source created the law of freewill so that the ALL could develop without any limitations but remaining within the boundaries of chaos.

Source also saw that freewill left fully unrestrained and unchecked held within its beauty the potential to result in development beyond chaos. Seeing that possibility, Source created a system of perfect ballast to freewill which was recognized as the law of reconciliation and balance. The two dynamics together, freewill and reconciliation were eventually recognized as one guideline. What some call karma. This was, a perfectly balanced equation designed to maintain a certain degree of constructive order in the ALL – within the limitations of chaos and without the need for direct intervention from Source. Geradl described this as "the potential for excess within control but not without balance."

As the ALL continued to unfold, an endless number of manifestations continued to develop in all of the Universes, dimensions and varying versions of reality that had been created. Source then set out to establish a way to observe the creation of the ALL. To accomplish this, Source reached within itself and spun out five perfect crystalline wisps from the center of itself; the heart of Source – and flung them into the five major universes, dimensions and realities that had been created. These five wisps, came from the essence of Source, and were collectively called the "Essential Source."

When Geradl got to this point in his explanation I was almost breathless from both excitement and sheer fascination. My mind was racing through a seemingly endless spectrum of possibilities and questions. One essential question burned at the forefront of my mind, and was so crucial that I decided to take the risk of interrupting Geradl to seek clarification.

"I apologize for interrupting Geradl. But are you inferring that there is some system of hierarchy gods in the Universe? That when Source spun out the five major wisps it was creating a system of lesser gods that 'reported' back to Source?"

"No. However, that is a common misconception. The 'Essential Source' and Source are inexorably, completely and instantaneously interconnected – they are one thing. When we say that Source 'flung these out into the other universes, dimensions and realties' it is only a manner of speaking. Those five spun-off wisps are the senses and the simultaneous presence of Source at all places, at all times, even though you might be tempted to think of them as only being pieces of the whole. There is a proclivity to think of this in earthly physical and numerical terms; that it is impossible to take five pieces from something and still leave the original source completely in tact. In reality, Source uses its own form of mathematics to disperse Essential Source out while not diminishing itself in any way. This was a simple matter for Source."

"So when Kalista, Tresden and you talk about 'Source' and 'Source-god,' are you talking about the same thing?"

"When we refer to Source, we are talking about the original Source that triggered the initial Origination of all the universes and before the 'Essential Source' was spun off. When we talk about Source-god, we are referring to that part of the Essential Source that resides and most closely watches over the Universe and related iterations of reality that you and I come from. We use Source-god only as a form of reference. All things are Source and all Source is God. The Original Center of All Things is primordial God; the origin of all things; known, unknown and unknowable."

"Then why even bother to spin-out the five wisps? Why not just acknowledge that what we all think of as God is, in fact, omnipresent, all-seeing, all-powerful?"

"Some highly-advanced primordial souls believe the initial scope of Origination exceeded even the expectations of Source – as though Source stood back and said, *'I've outdone even my own expectations.'* Those souls also believe that, the five crystalline wisps were deployed so that Source could observe the marvel of all, which develops directly. To have a form of presence in proximity to all that is unfolding.

Others believe that we simply do not know all of the reasons Source might have had to have reached inside of itself and tossed portions of its heart into the midst of creation. But we believe that it was an action motivated by pure love and compassion. That Source so loved all things that might derive from creation that it wanted to watch over all things created more closely. We believe that the details that relate to the ALL falls into the category of unknowable," Geradl explained.

"Why the distinction between Source and Source-god?" I asked.

"Source is the primordial originator of creation itself. We refer to Source-god in that way because that is the point of origination for all of us as individual souls within the knowable realities. We all trace our origination back to Source, the Original Center of All Things through Source-god; our father and mother."

I must have looked shaken because Geradl made a point of suggesting that I sit down and continue our discussion from there. As I did, the space between us unexpectedly opened once again into the unworldly form of projections and indescribable experiences that were similar to – but far more vivid and intricate – than the ones I had experienced in the life review that Kalista had manifested for me.

What unfolded next in the scenes in front of me was the most stunning display of three-dimensional images – actually far more than three dimensional – with incredible multimedia and representational graphics that I have ever witnessed, including some of the images that Kalista had shown me. It was so far superior to the imagery and sensations that I'd experienced in the life review process, in terms of clarity and richness, that the life review seemed like radio compared to high-definition color television. I wondered whether this was because Geradl was far more advanced than Kalista and possibly had greater skills in this arena.

The possibility also occurred to me that, since the life review was simply not nearly as dramatic an event as the Origination of the Universe that, the graphic impressions were commensurate with the nature of the events being shown. No matter what the explanation, I found myself speechless as the display unfolded in front of me.

As the scenes of the Origination and developments of creation played themselves out in colors, sounds, feelings, emotions, explosions of imagery and other ways that defy description, Geradl narrated the developments as they were occurring. The imagery began as an inconceivably immense swirl of enormous, blinding, brilliant, pulsating light suspended in the center of a boundless void. The light, which I took to be a representation of Source, was saturated with exponentially greater volumes of every color in every rainbow charged with a form of bounding energy that far exceeded my ability to comprehend. The volume and sheer power of the energy pulsations were palpable, yet still incomprehensible. As I was experiencing the vastness of the light swirl, I began to get a true sense of the totality of what we are as individual souls: spun-off parts of Source. The imagery in front of me wasn't a calculation of dimension as much as it was an experience of immensity. Vastness beyond comprehension.

No matter how immense I perceived it to be, at the moment I attempted to ponder an order of magnitude I immediately recognized that it was even exponentially larger than I had just perceived a second before. That perception occurred over and over again until I was no longer able to tolerate the concept of the size of what I was observing. As I was reeling from this contemplation, I noticed Geradl was trying to get my attention.

"This represents the Original Center of All Things. It is the ALL before it began the process of being unfolded by Source."

"What is it that I am sensing or seeing Geradl? It feels as though I am experiencing something that is so far beyond boundless that I can only think to call it immensity."

"That feeling is your attempt to connect with what is called the totality of yourself or, the Totality of the Soul."

"The Totality? I don't think I... "

"Take your time. Think it through slowly; its not as complicated as you are making it. Source spun-off Source-god which in turn spun-off you, me, Kalista and, all other individual souls. Therefore, you are forever part of Source, which in turn is really the same as the ALL because the ALL was created from pure Source. Therefore, the very essence of what you are made of is the same essence of the ALL. The true essence of what you are spans all eternity and all things. As I said before, this reality – this 'truth' – is called the 'Totality of the Soul.' It is there for any of us to connect with, if we only recollect the resonance that equates with that Totality which is within each of us. It is an inexorable aspect of our permanent soul-memory. It's there, more than inside of you, because it *is* you; you just have to know that you remember it and, recall the way to get back in touch with it. Once you are able to recall the 'frequency,' and you reach down a bit further, you will be able to connect to the place within you where the absolute love that derives from Source is stored. Combined, those two elements are the resonation of the Totality of the Soul."

I began to feel a sensation of being completely overwhelmed in a way I had never ever felt. Almost consumed by the explanation Geradl was sharing with me. Somewhere inside of me I connected to a recognition that, what Geradl was saying was not only true but in fact, was something that I had connected with at some earlier point in my existence, although not in this lifetime. I just couldn't quite make the connection to a specific recollection of it. I was close, very close. I could almost reach out and touch the exact recollections that Geradl was telling me about. Sensing my frustration, that I couldn't quite connect with the resonance that he was describing to me, Gerdal offered his further assistance.

"Move downward a bit from where you are. Let go. Release the ill-conceived notion that you are separate from this. The first step is to gain the confidence within yourself that the memory is there; that you have connected with it before and that you can do so again. Most of all, you need to recollect that you *are* this essence; that you are not separate from the All."

"It's frustrating, Geradl. I know that I've 'seen' this before. I just can't seem to remember what it felt like, how to get there."

"Let me help you."

Exactly what Geradl did next remains unclear to me. A mystery. From my perspective, he reached into his back pocket and pulled out a small strange looking device that looked something like a small Chinese gong combined with a miniature harp and a small drum. With that, he looked, perhaps peered would be a better word, directly into my eyes and said, "It's simple, just remember the Totality of your Soul – your origin. That you are no different, that you are in no way separate from the All."

He then struck the gong-looking device. Once. Only once. The sound emitted from the instrument was completely inconsistent with the appearance of it and is, indescribable. It was as though someone had run their hand over the entire length of a harp, run the full length of a xylophone and struck several multi-toned gongs at the same time. At the same time, the gong-like device triggered a multi-colored, multidimensional light show of mammoth proportions that completely saturated my full scope of visual perception. In one combined tone the device had emitted sounds and a multitude of other sensorial effects that far exceeded a symphony of experiences and overwhelming beauty. The effect was beyond perfect harmony throughout every sensation that I could experience and was completely captivating. Mesmerizing. Just short of being hypnotic.

As the one-note symphony began to slightly ebb and reverberate in my mind, it was as though someone had just whispered to me what I had been trying so hard to remember for my entire life. Probably all my lives. All at once the entire space in front of me opened up in a way that I could never conceive of much less describe. It was a seven or ten or twenty dimensional image, but those are only words to infer what I experienced just then. What was even more stunning was that the vision in front of me – which I took to be a representation of the ALL as it was being unfolded near its point of Origin – continued to open and unfold over and over and over again. It was as though a crumpled piece of paper was dropped and began to open up on its own.

The difference was that, the images Geradl was showing me kept opening and opening and opening. And then they unfolded again and again. Endlessly. Not figuratively endlessly but literally, endlessly. It was as though I was watching the grand finale of the universe's millennium fireworks display, enormous in its construct, except every second or two there would be another, larger explosion from within the last one. It got larger and brighter and louder. And it never stopped. Ever.

Every time I thought the scene was about to conclude, the imagery would expand once again. Simultaneously, far beyond all of the horizons ranging the full span of my perception in every direction. The absolute immensity, perfection and sheer beauty of what I was seeing brought tears to my eyes. I found myself actually weeping uncontrollably; not only at the overwhelming magnificence of the images but at the irrefutable recognition that occurred to me at that moment that I was actually recalling my own origin – the origin of all souls, all people and of all things – and I knew then that I would never forget this moment. I would resonate with this experience forever.

I was so overcome at that moment that my ability to accurately recall exactly what happened next is not what I'd like it to be. Looking back, I believe that what I experienced at that moment was an absolute sensory overload. There was more information of an over-whelming and magnificently sublime nature, pouring into my senses, brain and soul than I was meant to absorb. I remember watching the Totality unfold yet one more time and, the volume of the items in the ALL and the numbers of colors that comprised the imagery seeming-ly multiplied all at once by a factor of thousands – probably millions – I couldn't tell. It was the ultimate kaleidoscope of our own origin. Concurrently, I was perceiving a vision that reflected a representation of the Source of all things that was so immense and saturated with absolute purified perfection and joy that it was more than I could take. I was about to ask Geradl to slow the images down in order to give my senses a chance to adjust when I passed out.

I regained my bearings with Geradl standing over me. As much as I knew how far out of character it was for him, he was half-smiling. At the same time, he had a look of genuine caring and compassion on his face that clearly showed that he was concerned.

"Sorry. I guess we got a little carried away." He reached down very gently in order to help me up.

"Not at all. I... I just can't believe what I saw, what I experienced."

"Has it occurred to you that, what you saw is what you in essence, are? That the point of the illustration was for you to experience the Totality of Your Soul."

"Are? Totality?" I was still shaking off the cob webs.

"Chuck, listen to me; this is crucial knowledge. What you saw; what you experienced; the Totality of ALL that there is. You ARE that. Always have been that. Always will be that. Everyone you've ever known or will know is that."

"I'm not sure *how*... the Totality?" I had so many questions.

"I know that this is a lot to absorb. Let me try again. Source reached within and created the ALL, everything there is – no exceptions. Source reached within and spun-off Source-god. Source-god over time spun off all individual souls, you, me and everyone else. That means you are inexorably connected to it, made of it. See if that helps you remember: Source, Source-god and the ALL. More than being connected to Source, Source-god and ALL is that you ARE in fact, in every way possible, Source. Source-god and ALL, forever. Completely. Do you see that?"

I admit that sometimes I can be a little dense. There have been times in my life that it has taken twice or on rare cases, even three times for me to get something that has been explained to me. It's embarrassing when it happens. Especially when it happens in front of someone that I really respect. As Geradl explained it to me, I felt as though the light bulb actually did begin to illuminate above my head.

It wasn't a matter of understanding the words or even the concept. Those I got. It was a matter of actually absorbing at the deepest levels of all that I am, the reality of what Geradl was saying. It was really just the same thing that Kalista had said several months before. It basically came down to a very simple concept. We ARE. And we are ALL that there is because we arose from exactly the same place; Source. Source-god. God. The ALL. It was difficult to understand only because we chose to make it difficult. If we'd get out of our own way, we'd see things as they actually are: we'd relate to love because we ARE love. Source not only gave us that as an eternal gift but, made us of that. How could I have missed something that obvious for the last 40 years?

When I looked up at Geradl who, like Kalista obviously had the ability to easily read my thoughts, I thought that for a split-second he had a look on his face and in is eyes that appeared more like pride than anything else. I mused that he must have been thinking; "my student isn't completely hopeless after all." I knew he'd never actually think that. But before I had a chance to say anything, Geradl changed the subject.

"So, that's part of the challenge. Now you need to make the same connection to the absolute love that Source has imbued in all of us."

186

"Before we go on to that Geradl, I need to know about the music that I heard before I connected with the concept of ALL."

"Music?"

"Well, that's what I heard. That's how I experienced it first. That triggered the recollection for me."

"Interesting. I've never particularly thought of it like that. But, if remembering the connection to Source to or through music, or a tone, or relating to it as a specific sound or even feeling works for you, that's fine. What's most important, in fact, the only thing that is important at all, is that you do remember it. Because as long as you remember that, you will have a constant touchstone that you are forever – always have been and always will be – connected at the level of your Soul, your very origin, to all things. Every person, cat, dog, the sun the moon the stars, everything. That is the very definition of the Totality of yours – and everyone else's – Soul."

Geradl's words took a few moments to sink in because my senses had been under near constant assault almost from the moment I had arrived at the garden that day. I was most concerned as to whether I'd be able to recollect the "music" that made the recollection of the All so clear for me. I was already disoriented and confused as to whether it actually was music that I had heard or simply an impression that I received that left me no other word other than music to explain the effect. All that I really cared about at that moment was remembering some touchstone so that I could reconnect with the Totality of Soul that Geradl had shown me.

As I concentrated on recalling the sound specifically, the incredible warmth and magnificence that I had felt the first time I had the experience began to come back to me with great clarity. The imagery was not there, at least not near the vividness that was present when Geradl had shown me, but the incredibly heartening feeling of my absolute connection to all things came back to me in a matter of moments. At that very second, I remember wondering two things; would I be able to recreate this experience when I was back in my own world and, would it be possible for me to help other people share this experience?

My mind began to drift to the memory of when Kalista had simulated the life review process for me. I remember pondering just then how the world might change for the better if everyone had the realization that the day was coming – and coming soon – when they would face the consequences of their actions in this unique way. This made me wonder how the world might change for the better if everyone could experience the feeling of absolute oneness that I'd just had when Geradl showed me our undeniable and inexorable connection to all things. How would it be possible for there to be such violence and hatred in the world if people could see with their own eyes, experience with their own souls, that they were in reality attacking themselves? It seemed so obvious to me that I was dumbfounded. Knowing that in my enthusiasm for things I sometimes overlook the obvious, I thought to ask Geradl why this insight was not more broadly available to others in our world.

"Geradl, why don't more people connect with this reality - with this information? It is such a basic and immutable truth. I mean, wouldn't the world be a more peaceful place if everyone knew this? Knew that being connected to everything and everyone wasn't just a cliché but in fact, reality? If they could only see this they'd… "

Geradl replied compassionately, "but they **do** know it Chuck. They do. As you saw for yourself, it is not only inside of but an integral and crucial ***part of*** every soul's very construction. Not a, but ***the*** essential material used to create every person, every soul – no matter what race, creed, color or religious beliefs they might have. If they are not remembering that it is because they have made a decision, conscious or not, to ***not*** remember it."

"But why would they do that?" I was very frustrated.

"There are many reasons. Foremost among them is that when souls leave the discarnate world they accept the incarnate world as their reality for the time they are there. This means they have to accept certain conditions."

"Yeah, Kalista said something about 'making them drink the brew.'"

Geradl sort of smiled for a moment, "well, that's only a way of talking about it but, the reality is that unless souls that are in the incarnate world are convinced that the world they are in for that particular time is real they simply wouldn't take it very seriously. And if that happened, they wouldn't learn many of the lessons that they assume an incarnation for in the first place. So it's a trade-off of sorts. But the reality is that it isn't necessary to forget our connection to all things as a condition of incarnation. When all is said and done it is the ego that forces that reality to the side. Totally fixated on denying the reality of anything but itself. And the ego, as you have learned, is pure transient illusion. Quite a mess all told."

"But what about me? I am aware of that reality now... I'll never let go of it."

"In this case you're an exception but, if you don't find a way to put that knowledge to good use into practical application, it will begin to dissipate and eventually, you'll forget it."

"What do you mean?" I asked, fearful of such a prospect.

"There are certain intersections that all souls come to when they are at a point of potential advancement to another level of true spiritual insight. What happens immediately before these intersections are reached is that the soul experiences a burst of new information such as the insight that I just helped you to see. From there, it's up to the individual soul to either find a way to use the information to make the move onward or not. This is accomplished by actualizing the insight. In other words, moving the insight from the intellect to the spiritual core. It is the difference between understanding the insight and accepting it at a soul level. If you're ready, it happens – you move onward. If you're not, there's absolutely no shame in it whatever but, you have to re-learn some of what you couldn't put to use at sometime in the future. In some ways, it is much like having to master basic math before trying to take on algebra. And algebra before geometry. Geometry before calculus and so on."

I didn't know what to say or think. Kalista had joked with me when I first started coming to the garden that I was "close to getting a promotion," but, I never really took her seriously. Geradl made it all sound quite fascinating, but at the same time, it had the all too familiar ring to it of a pass/fail test, which was a format that never instilled a lot of confidence in me. I'd learned from my interactions with Kalista and Tresden that it was sometimes a risk to misinterpret concepts using the kind of conceptual communication used in the garden. So I decided that before I got too much momentum in a direction that might not be valid, I'd seek further clarification directly from Geradl.

"Geradl, this sounds like a kind of soul test where you find out if you've accumulated enough spiritual knowledge to move on to the next grade," I said.

"There's no test Chuck and, there would be no teacher to grade it even if there was," he assured me.

"I'm lost then. How is it possible to determine whether you move on to the next level?"

"It is all a matter of increasing your level of Essential Resonance. Based upon knowledge acquired and actualized in combination with a soul's actions in both the incarnate and discarnate worlds a soul has the potential to move on through various developmental stages. As they progress along their pathway their basic level of energy increases in terms of vibration. Spiritual Resonance actually. But in reality, it is far more than that. Knowledge in this case is a bit too broad a term to really describe what needs to be accumulated but, it will do for now. As souls acquire and are able to retain different portions of crucial spiritual knowledge and essential lessons, what we call their 'Essential Resonance' begins to increase. In more of a literal than figurative sense, their resonance increases as the development of their soul moves more and more in the direction of Source. The more consistent the soul gets at integrating Love, Compassion and Empathy into their functional pathway, the greater their essential vibration level. And the reality of that is, the greater their spiritual resonance level, the closer they come to resonating at a level approaching Source, approaching God."

I was shocked. Overwhelmed actually. Not that this was how things really worked in the Universe, but that Geradl could relate the essential manner in which souls progressed onward as though he were telling me how to fix a flat tire. In a few short sentences Geradl had just shared with me knowledge that I had been searching desperately to find for probably of all my lifetimes. A few critical details still remained unanswered.

"You said that it is not enough to know these things just as facts

– that they had to be assimilated to really mean anything. 'Actualized' you called it."

"Probably the single most challenging intersection for souls to make it past – many have taken twenty, thirty or even hundreds of lifetimes to negotiate this particular obstacle – is finding the way to move the knowledge – the intellectual understanding that Love, Compassion and Empathy are the essential components of incarnate spiritual development into a plan of action that puts those ideals into a functioning lifestyle – in short, a pathway. That is, going from knowing it to living it. Make no mistake, getting to a place where as a soul, you recognize the fact that Love, Compassion and Empathy are the keys is a tremendous move forward. It's huge. The increase in spiritual vibration level that occurs when a soul truly recognizes just that much is tremendous. But the most substantial leap forward that an incarnating soul can possibly make at one critical juncture is when they are able to actualize that knowledge by adopting a life where those become the sole touchstones – the ostensible fuel for daily living – to the exclusion of all else. In short, when they walk that path way as opposed to think about that being the pathway."

"Can we go back to the different levels for a moment? Are you saying that we pretty much progress as we assimilate critical lessons?" I felt that I was approaching an understanding of the key points Geradl was trying to convey.

"Yes, and, probably one of the more significant things that you need to know about that is that no one else determines what you have or haven't learned or put into action."

"Then how do we progress? How do we know that we have learned whatever it is that we needed to in order to move onward?" I asked.

"There are a few ways. First of all, your soul counsel, by guiding you to take on certain lifetimes and, to some extent by coaching you in between lives, makes every effort to see that you are exposed to the best opportunities that can, if you master the lessons, move you along the pathway to the exact knowledge that, as a soul in transition, you need most. Also critically important is that, when you are between lives, the insights that you had such difficulty identifying when you were, what you call 'living,' are no longer blocked from you. With the ego temporarily subdued, the soul is able to 'see' much of what it should have been understanding – actualizing in the way of essential knowledge – during the last lifetime with greatly enhanced clarity.

As this process gets repeated over and over again over the course of many lifetimes, eventually, the soul begins to recollect that it needs to remember something – some crucial message – even though it probably can't identify the details. As the soul approaches this particular juncture of development, their resonance level increases a bit. As their level of Spiritual Resonance increases, the pathways to spiritual enlightenment begin to open up for them. It's a kind of cycle from there; the more you learn, the higher your level of Spiritual Resonance. The higher your resonance, the more doorways open up and pathways illuminate for you."

I understood everything that Geradl had said to me. But this was the first time that Kalista, Tresden or Geradl had mentioned anything about Spiritual Resonance or how that was related to making progress along the spiritual pathway. Like many of the insights that I received at the garden, this one was obviously going to require further thought. I was also hopeful that clarification on some of the finer points would be forthcoming.

"I'm not sure that I really get all of that Geradl, can you give me an example?"

"Of course. This garden is one of the best examples that I can think of for you. On your own, at your current state of spiritual development, you have not yet attained the Resonance level that you would need to get – or stay – here, on this advanced spiritual plane. It's obvious that you had progressed far enough with all of your learning for you to make it part of the way here. And actually, most of the way here. Kalista had to gather and make available the extra spiritual energy required to finish off the garden and, to raise your vibration level the rest of the way. When you entered your highly creative state of meditation it allowed you to raise your Resonance level just enough so that when it was combined with your current base level of spiritual vibration, that Kalista was able to meet you somewhere in between the two realities. Kalista did the rest. The reality is that you're able to stay here on her borrowed vibrational energy plus what you have on your own. On a much grander scale, the Universe works the same way. You can get to and stay at different planes based upon the level of Resonance, or spiritual essential energy, that you have attained. You move up that scale along the course of your development over lifetime after lifetime. Stage after developmental stage as a soul. By virtue of what you know, what you learn and most importantly, what you are able to put into action from the lessons that you have assimilated, your Individual True Resonance level increases. There are a few other things that contribute to overall spiritual development – and thus, increased vibration level – that you'll learn as you move further on."

Geradl went on to explain to me that, as we progressed through various planes we are able to assimilate deeper and much more complex learning. As our spiritual energy increased, which happened by virtue of what we learned and were able to put into action from that learning, we gained the ability to move through even higher planes based upon that increased state of Resonance. To all intents and purposes, as we learn more, what Geradl referred to as our "Essential Resonance" increases. That increased vibration state acts as a kind of "pass key" to other, higher spiritual planes and "places."

There is no need at all for us to be judged by anyone or to have a test to see if we're ready for the next highest level. We determine that on our own on the basis of how much closer to Source – essentially, returning to purified compassion – we are getting. And that is determined on the basis of how well we're doing in terms of walking a pathway where we have fully integrated Love, Compassion and Empathy into our lives. In essence, integrating those elements into a course of daily living. The thing is, sometimes it can take a hundred lifetimes, or longer, to move to the next level. The good news is that, it's completely up to us as to how long it takes. We can learn or not learn. Geradl said such was part of the original bargain, a guarantee of freewill.

I was about to tell Geradl that my head was swimming with all that he had shown and told me that day. Then he started to remind me that there was still one more insight related to Source that I had experienced and needed to remember from my first visit beyond the

Gate.

"The last thing for now is for you to experience the counterpart to the creation that Source engineered."

"Counterpart?"

"That is actually only a way of referring to it. As it happens though, on that particular thread, the information regarding the immeasurable love of Source is on the opposite side of the thread that chronicles Origination. If you're ready, we can go through that now."

I felt like saying that I was not, in fact, ready. The effects of Geradl's last little light and multimedia show had made me pass out from a kind of sensory overload and the residual from that was still causing me to suffer a vague, foggy feeling in my head. Nevertheless, I managed a sort of half-nod to let Geradl know that I was as ready as I could be for whatever came next.

"The main point for you to remember is that Source does not simply manifest love; Source is love; a concept that simply defies any words that we might try to employ to provide clarity. Before we go further, do you understand that?"

"I understand the words. I'm not certain that I understand the full scope of what it means in the overall scheme of things."

"Simply put, we cannot use words to talk about the true love of Source. We can come up with expressions, analogies and metaphors that tell us what it is not, such as; 'it is far greater than immeasurable,' but unlike reviewing the period of Origination that could be experienced with your senses, the primordial love that is Source exceeds all of that. By factors beyond our imagination. Do you understand?"

"You're saying that it can only be felt," I said a bit shakily.

"No. I'm saying that only **part** of it can be felt. The Totality of that Love is so vast that you can only experience part of it; now, in your present state." Geradl had an urgency to his inflection.

I understood the gist of what Geradl was trying to say to me. The love of Source – and its truly limitless, unconditional and compassionate composition – was more than I would be able to stand as a still-incarnating soul. I was about to ask what would happen if I did receive a full dose, then I thought better of it. It was clear that this was a subject Geradl took with the utmost seriousness and there was no need to alienate him with a foolish question.

"I think I understand what you're telling me, Geradl."

"There's only one other thing; once experienced, at the very point that you are showered with this love directly from Source, certain things will be lost to you forever."

"Lost? Lost? What do you mean lost? Like what?" I felt nervous.

"Some portion of the person that you are now – I can't tell you specifically what."

"C'mon Geradl. What are we talking here; an arm, a leg, my liver?"

This was the one and only time over the ten years that I had been visiting the garden that I would ever see Geradl actually smile. It didn't last long but it was so genuine that it not only melted me where I stood, but conveyed to me without any room for doubt that I had nothing to fear from whatever was coming next.

"No, Chuck. All your essential appendages will stay in place. No organs will be lost either although some may be affected."

"What? I don't understand."

"That's all I can say. You decide whether you want to go through this experience."

I was about to launch a protest of sorts. To tell Geradl how unfair it was to ask me to make a bargain, without knowing all the terms and conditions. And then it occurred to me; part of this entire process was about trust, something that I hadn't been particularly keen on since the first several sets of parents that I'd had as an child in this lifetime had decided to use me as a punching bag – often worse. I knew that there was no mystical ritual going on here. Any preset religious practices, strictures, or any complex formal rite did not bind Geradl with specific rules governing how to do things. It was equally clear to me that he knew, in order for any of this to really mean anything to me that I had to reconnect with some essential element that had been buried deep inside of me long ago. Trust. I don't know how I knew all of this; it just came to me with total clarity.

Having convinced myself of this, I steadied my mind, took a deep breath and made a weak attempt at assuring myself that whatever came next, it was okay with me. Geradl looked at me for a few moments and then backed up a few steps. He pulled out his strange-looking gong from his back pocket and struck it once, just as he had done the first time. I heard the music and again saw the panoramic imagery that was more or less a continuation of the scenes from the Origination that we had been viewing before. At some point though, the process of universes unfolding endlessly with explosions of light far beyond all the colors in the rainbow slowed down and then, stopped.

What remained was the absolute boundless infinity that quite apparently, Source had always intended. There was a low-pitched pulsation, encompassing the sheer totality of the imagery. Close to the vague beating of a heartbeat but, in some unidentifiable way, it was just beyond that. Subtle while at the same time, seemingly louder and more substantial. Much, much slower and deeper. The faint low-pitched humming sound seemed to rise and fall with the unusual pulsations of the imagery.

For ten years, I have tried to piece together both the sequence and the actual events of what happened next. I was staring directly into the immensity, feeling the pulse of the universes in front of me when the center of the image opened up like a stage curtain. It was as though all of the imagery of the immensity was painted on a backdrop and from behind, someone was simply pulling apart the curtain where it naturally split into two pieces. The effect of seeing the pulsing universes open up was another overwhelming assault on my senses and I felt myself start to fade away. I heard Geradl urgently communicate something to the effect of "stay here" or, "hold on." I somehow managed to reach inside myself in a desperate effort to find the willpower to remain conscious. But barely.

I then saw that what I had initially perceived as a curtain opening up was actually a kind of tear in the reality; some completely non-indefinable aberration of the Universe right where I happened to be focusing right then. Or so I thought. While definitely not something that I was accustomed to seeing in our everyday world, I had almost gotten used to such peculiarities in Kalista's reality. As this tear in the scenery opened a bit further I could see that the vague, unusual pulsation that I had sensed was actually coming from this area – behind the perceived curtain.

And then, the light.

Light is not really the right word. But all at once – in the matter of a fraction of a split-second – I understood the full scope of everything that Geradl had just been saying to me. Words were ineffective. Useless. Calling what I experienced "light" would be like calling a thousand nuclear explosions a safety match. In one instant every question that I had ever had about the existence of God or Source or whatever word, or concept, anyone might ever want to use was simply gone. Every idea of love that I had up until that moment went out with the wind as well. I almost laughed at myself for an instant at how ridiculous our concepts of these things are when compared to the reality of them.

What we think of in our daily lives as love, compassion, empathy – while incredibly beautiful and comforting – is not even a faint echo of what I experienced in those few moments. I understood then what Geradl meant when he used words like Totality and Absolute. Those words were wholly inadequate to describe where and what we all originate from but, they began to afford some vague sense of concept. They almost began to approach the sheer immeasurable magnitude of it all. But, just barely.

The reality of it all was that there were no words that could ever describe the depth, breadth and immensity of this feeling. The actual, as opposed to what I had conceived of, Love of Source/god was so absolute, so consuming and at the same time overwhelming that all I have ever wanted since that moment is to return to that place and bask in that feeling. Forever. Much, much longer if possible. And anyone else that experienced that absolute, unconditional and complete love would do anything to return to it. Absolutely anything. All else would be completely inconsequential.

Questions began to race through my mind. There were a hundred, maybe a thousand things that I simply *had* to know about what I was experiencing and how I could get back here – to this feeling of total security and absolute love. Nothing, I thought, could ever exceed this feeling. At that exact moment, I realized the opening in the reality – the split in the curtain – was barely cracked. Not even the equivalent of what we would think of as a micron. Concurrent with me having this thought, the curtain began to open only a fraction of an inch more to reveal exponentially even more light.

If I had been looking at a hundred candle-power of God's love before I was now exposed to ten billion candles. It was so much more in terms of sheer volume and intensity that it completely dwarfed all concept of what Geradl called "Totality." It was Totality times Forever to the trillionth power. And still the curtain was barely cracked.

My next awareness came as I regained a degree of consciousness on the floor of my study. I reached for my notepad thinking I could steady my senses by jotting down the highlights of what had just happened to me. Nothing. My hand, although shaking violently, was ready. But my mind would not create words or images, to write. Tears were saturating the page of my notepad as I wept with recognition of what we all really are, and what we ultimately return to someday.

It occurred to me that if I got up and moved around it might help me. I decided to walk into town and get something to eat. The local diner was less than a half mile away. As I began to walk down the street that mid-May late afternoon, a feeling of immeasurable warmth and an all-pervading peace began to well up inside of me. What I felt went far beyond joy and exceeded total elation. It was far beyond any love in our world I had ever experienced. Or ever could imagine experiencing.

As I turned the last corner before coming to the diner, I laughed out loud with genuine unabated glee. Geradl had said, "No organs will be lost, although some may be affected." Now I understood exactly what he had meant. As I passed strangers on the street, I saw not just men, women and children making their way about. I saw souls on their mission to learn the pathway of Love, Compassion and Empathy.

At that moment I experienced a deep recognition that, in truth, all of us come from the same father and the same mother. Not just as a clichéd concept, but in reality. It is ***our*** reality. Finally, as I walked up the front stairs of the local diner, I recognized that in spite of my personal history that was scared in my earliest years as a badly abused orphan, I saw that in reality, my original family remained in tact. And

I loved each and every one of them. All four billion.

CHAPTER EIGHT

What we are is god's gift to us.
What we become is our gift to god.

- *Anon.*

There are certain junctures in our lives when we recognize that something within us has changed. Upon my return from most recent experience with Geradl, I developed a creeping awareness that I knew at the level of my soul, I had been changed forever. I recall thinking at the time that, we can change our hair color without much effort, but such a change wears off in very little time. However, the effects of having been immersed in the knowledge and all-encompassing enlightenment that Geradl had afforded me would never go away. And *never*, when Kalista, Tresden and Gerdal spoke in terms of an eternity, is a very long time.

Looking back, I recognized that over the course of my life, up until this point, I had become aware of life-altering intersections only long after I had passed them. I was able to see and acknowledge them only in retrospect. The experience that I'd just come from with Geradl was not like that. I recognized immediately what I had experienced, everything that I had seen, wasn't just to change the course of my daily life. The cumulative effects of what Geradl had shown me, in addition to what I had learned from Tresden and Kalista, kindled a recognition of the nature of our essence and what makes us all bonded at a place scientists can't point to. The pathway of my soul had changed. Substantially.

This was my first exposure to an understanding that it is possible to make changes that are permanent to the soul, even if changes we make in any given life can only last as long as that particular lifetime. Learning and accepting that essential truth, I learned from Kalista, is a major spiritual turning point. This was my first long-term spiritual investment and it was deeply inspiring for me. I had attained a genuine knowing that I would benefit in all of my future incarnations – no matter what form they took – based upon what I had just learned from my experience with Geradl. This realization brought into focus just how substantial Geradl and his mysterious ability to impart enlightenment directly to me really was.

As I considered the events that had unfolded over the previous year I realized, beginning with the very first conversation that I'd had with Kalista, that I had managed to jump-start my journey along the spiritual pathway. This was something that I'd always hoped for but never really knew how to accomplish. Usually, when you find yourself on a journey, you have some idea of where you're going. Each time I sat down and began to enter the state of deep calm which took me to the garden, I was painfully aware, as I approached the one year anniversary of my first visit to Kalista's garden, that I had no idea where all of this was taking me.

One thing I *did* know was that whatever my future held, if I could find the pathway and put the knowledge that Gerdal shared with me into action in my day-to-day life, if I could take it beyond the conceptual, then I knew that the destiny of my soul would be on a path for wherever it was that I was truly meant to be. When I first met Kalista I felt I was spiritually lost and had no concept of where to go or what to do in order to move forward toward enlightenment and, achieving an inner peace.

Believing everything I had been exposed to by Kalista, Tresden and Geradl and then embracing it as something that I knew without question was a genuine leap of faith. However, based upon what Geradl had just shown me, and what I was able to recollect from the powerful imagery that explained so many of the questions I had about my purpose, the leap was not a tremendous one. Only a fool would have turned away after having come this far and experiencing what I had – or a coward. I never considered myself a fool.

I was also aware that in some ways, my life had already changed dramatically. Once I began to walk this revealed pathway, I was confident that I would continue. I also came to the stark realization that there is no way to enter a pathway such as this and expect daily life to continue along the status quo. It became progressively difficult for me to conduct business with that same "take no prisoners" attitude that is a basic requirement for most Fortune 100 executives. I was beginning to fail in that regard and, I knew it.

In my personal life, my tolerance for people who were mostly driven by materialism or greed was deeply diminished. I was no longer comfortable around them. Friends and acquaintances would talk at social occasions about this car or that boat ad nauseum. I couldn't have been less interested. People who were blatantly non-compassionate and uncaring about the other souls on this planet rapidly faded into the background of my life. Many people that had been friends drifted off. Now more alone than I had ever been, I found myself much more at peace despite the dwindling number of friends around me.

By early spring 1994, I became acutely sensitized to my realization that each time I got near the end of a session with Kalista or Tresden, I actually dreaded coming back to what I thought of as "our world." Here, where we spend our days and nights. More than once I found myself hoping I would somehow figure out a way to simply remain in the garden and bask in progressively deeper levels of enlightenment. To be showered without end and with the incredible peace and that blissful feeling that I felt constantly while I was there. The idea of remaining in Kalista's garden, forever, became close to an obsession, although not one that I dared to articulate to Kalista.

Kalista knew my thoughts and dreams and, one day in a gentle way made it abundantly clear that this was not going to be my path for at least the near-term future. While I accepted this fact with a frustrated resignation, I was also quite curious to learn if this was not my near-term pathway, what was?

There were offsets, which compensated for Kalista's news that staying in the garden wasn't my near-term future. After the last session with Geradl I noticed that my day-to-day life began to reflect outwardly many of the changes that were taking place within my core spiritual being. With Tresden's instructions on how to adjust my actions and behaviors in my day-to-day life – many of which seemed absolutely ridiculous when she told me about them – I found that I was more able to make a distinction between the intent of my core spiritual essence and my ego. What Tresden called "the everyday self you see in the mirror" or simply, "the absolute delusion of an illusion."

The spiritual exercises Tresden instructed me in resulted in a sharp increase in my basic spiritual awareness and a dramatic shift for the better in my treatment of people in the world, including myself. It was clearly a change for the better. Tresden called this "shifting the essential intent of the soul." She explained that there were two simple stages of this process. First, to garner a basic awareness that, through intent and actions we directly affect others, who in turn affect the state of the world. Then we must take that awareness and manifest it into a change in our own overt actions. As we shift our behaviors for the better we trigger a chain reaction by affecting those around us more positively. They, in turn, because of our improved interactions, reflect those behavior to others.

Eventually, each soul that takes such action is responsible for moving some number of the souls in the Universe in the direction of Source. Kalista, Tresden and Geradl – much later, when I met with him again – told me that, this is one among the major checkpoints that we have to pass in order to move forward substantially along the spiritual pathway toward enlightenment.

Tresden made an effort to explain to me precisely what arriving at this particular intersection meant. I was rapidly approaching the place where you come to realize what it takes to change. At this juncture if I could gather the spiritual willpower to learn how to treat other people in the world with true compassion I would also change my own spiritual essence for the better. This comes about only when we consciously make a decision to change what we intend toward the other souls in the world around us in general and toward all creatures in specific. I began to realize through my daily activities – in a far different manner than Geradl had illustrated this concept to me – that we truly are all one, originated from one Source as our essence. As I digested that realization, beyond simply identifying the ideal of that concept being echoed through some beautiful lyrics in a song, it became impossible for me not to undergo a jolting shift in intent, in the direction of embracing and loving all people and all things. The result was a palpable and dramatic increase in my own Resonance.

I also went through a difficult period where I debated – within the confines of my own mind – whether Geradl was actually able to effect change and enhance my awareness purely by virtue of my being in his presence. I was toying with the novel idea that enlightenment might come about just by being around him. I remember thinking at the time that the only thing one can grasp in our day-to-day reality by being in someone's presence is a cold. In time though, due to the brutal, but good-natured teasing that Kalista and Tresden put me through on my insistence that Geradl had some special abilities in this regard, I came to accept that the only issue of importance was, that I was learning. The details of how that was happening didn't really matter at all. When I shared that conclusion with Tresden, she smiled like a Cheshire cat as though I'd just discovered the front door to Wonderland.

By late spring 1994, I became aware that Kalista and Tresden were focused during our time together on expanding their explanations of what they called "the true nature of Reality." This process was designed to broaden my spiritual education beyond the pure concept phase. They began to focus and instruct me with greater detail about how to take the insights and spiritual knowledge that I was absorbing and put it into action in my everyday life. Kalista called this, "walking the pathway of knowledge." Tresden explained it was the difference between doing something and intending that same thing. This difference was the key to me taking the next steps in my development. My "awakening" Tresden called it. It was what I needed to accomplish in order to increase my spiritual resonance level to the next significant stage.

No matter what it was called, it was largely about going to our true home and being able to set aside the day-to-day madness of the world. I argued with Tresden that, doing something – anything – whether it was done purposefully or by happenstance, made no difference if the outcome was the same. As such, I maintained, the intent behind the action didn't really matter. I knew she must have been exasperated, but she never stopped the lesson. Some of the examples and analogies that she used to illustrate my ill-founded arguments were so hilarious that, I still think of them to this day and burst out laughing.

Walking this pathway though wasn't always easy. Many times I had to seek out Kalista and Tresden for what Tresden playfully called "spiritual remedial instruction." I often found the people in the world around me frustrated me to such a degree that I sometimes required material infusions of encouragement to continue along the pathway Tresden and Kalista had defined for me. When you've been doing things a certain way for forty years or, as Tresden would say, for lifetimes, it takes real effort to change your basic style. I learned that there's a big difference between being told the significance of integrating compassion, empathy and love into your daily life and actually doing it. This is exemplified when the driver in the next car makes an obscene gesture at you after he cut *you* off.

Kalista reminded me with a gentle smile and compassionate voice, that our world can be a very difficult classroom. She also reminded me that the lessons that we come across each day of our lifetimes are there because that is precisely what we need to learn at the specific time. Tresden chimed in when I forgot, which was often, that no matter what was taking place in my personal vista, it was there as an opportunity to learn and master one or more lessons no matter how silly and frustrating the events of any particular day might appear. There was a larger view, she would remind me, and not all lessons are completed in one day. With infinite patience she would instruct me over again how to capture a concept and emphasize for me how urgent it was to focus on changing my intent in the direction of total compassion, love and empathy and not just my actions.

When I saw the troubling events of my day-to-day life and the world around all of us in that light, I began to recognize the gifts those problems present to us. When we accept the basic premise that the people and problems in our path are there because we need them specifically, and the teaching they can afford us if only we will adjust our perspective accordingly, our soul begins to rise to the challenge and learn. When I had some difficulty accepting this concept, Kalista took me to her favorite part of the garden, just behind the roses, and then turned to look directly into my eyes. I've never forgotten her words or the tremendous change in attitude they brought about in me.

If you will stop seeing yourself as a victim, as though the world or people in the world are doing things to you, and start seeing yourself as a student, you will rapidly learn that the lessons that life offers you are your very purpose for living. Once you realize that fact you will move forward faster and be much happier than you ever dreamed.

Kalista was right. In searching for insight in one of my own greatest challenges, tolerance toward many of the less than well-behaved people in the world – using what Kalista had just told me, I found answers. Helpful answers. Kalista would remind me that many of the souls we come across in our day-to-day travels are either frightened or, very angry with themselves. In either case, they are confused. Disoriented. Seen in this light, most of the people that we encounter in daily living who appear to be reckless and incredibly insensitive toward others, begin to fall into a zone of comprehension where what they are doing becomes as somewhat understandable.

As the weeks and then months passed after my stunning session with Geradl, I found that I had acquired a newfound, sincere interest in people as souls as opposed to my previous view that they were just distractions on my path. I became sensitized to their suffering and, their need for my, and everyone's compassion – not just the starving children in Africa and India, but the executive down the hall who was fighting alcoholism, at war with a spouse or just angry with the world. I began to observe, and attempt to treat, everyone I encountered with empathy instead of my previous inclination to criticize.

Based on conversations with Kalista and Tresden that dealt with why people in my daily life acted as they did, they demonstrated an inordinate amount of compassion with me. They explained that beings in our world – "souls in early learning transition" they called them – act as they do largely out of their inability and frustration to recollect their origin. They often feel like the orphans of the universe, as though they had been abandoned by God, since they had lost touch with the warmth and security that connection affords us. They feel an emptiness that they don't know the cause of. Tresden would explain, that people are intrinsically angry that they ever separated from Source in the first place. They act in this manner much like a small child who is angry with their mother because the child let go of their mother's hand at the mall. The rationalization doesn't matter to the child; all they know is they have been separated from their true source of security and, they're very unhappy about it. Tantrums of one sort or another follow. Seen in that light, the behavior of many people becomes understandable.

Kalista would also remind me that inside, most people are far more than what they see themselves as being when they look in the mirror but they can't remember the specifics. They have a vague and gnawing recollection that they are missing something, – but they simply can't recollect the details. It's maddening to them. Most incarnated beings try to focus on other things – problems that we hope can be solved. We immerse ourselves in work, relationships both good and bad, and other activities. Anything to keep ourselves distracted. Many of those activities unfortunately, result in less than stellar outcomes. We fall deeper and deeper into negative karma patterns and cycles.

To varying degrees, all of us feel this lack of connection. Our behaviors, are a kind of desperate attempt to "feel whole" as Kalista called it. She explained to me that, the desperation to feel whole is so pervasive and inspires such frustration and deep, spiritual pain in us that, in our often misguided attempts to fill in this emptiness, some people resort to very unproductive "solutions." Drugs. Alcohol. Food. Addictions of any and every kind, anything to relieve the feeling – to distract us from the reality – of being disconnected and lost. Even if that involves self-destructive behaviors such as suicide or other unthinkable, damaging manifestations. None of these behaviors lead anywhere, except to spiritual dead ends. Eventually, Tresden told me, everyone makes it to their pathway. It's just a matter of how much abuse one chooses to go through – to tolerate – in the process.

Some of the changes that were emerging from deep within me

were very inspiring and led to moments of extreme clarity. Even small epiphanies. One in particular changed my life and dramatically accelerated the pathway of my soul forever. While on my way to a meeting at the World Trade Center in New York one morning, I was walking through Penn Station drinking a up of coffee. At the same time, I was trying to scan an article in the *Wall Street Journal* that covered the company I was on my way to meet. Seemingly out of nowhere, my perception of the thousands of people making their way through the terminal suddenly and unexpectedly shifted. Dramatically. Spontaneously. It wasn't a vision, delusion or an illusion. I wasn't "seeing things." My perception had somehow just shifted to a place where, instead of seeing all the bodies in suits and dresses on their way to and from meetings, I perceived thousands of souls on their respective pathways of learning.

Those pathways were not to business meetings but, from the unique perspective I had shifted into, I saw these souls were on a pathway of absorbing soul lessons through daily trials and challenges. They were all on a definitive course that moved in the direction of learning at various speeds. The individual souls appeared to me as brilliant golden-colored wisps of light with various hues ranging from pale blue to yellow to very rarely, one that seemed to be of a light blue-purple hue. All of them appeared to be flowing effortlessly along their respective paths. It shocked me. The sudden shift in my perception surprised me so much so that I actually dropped my cup of coffee – the one I'd just waited ten minutes in line to get.

In a few seconds my perception had shifted from what was my "normal" view of a bustling 8:00 a.m. New York business crowd to a state of perception where I "saw" that the mass comprised of thousands of people were all not just human forms pushing and shoving their way to wherever they were headed to pursue their daily business agenda. What I saw with my spiritual eyes was that these souls were fellow travelers; wisps of spiritual energy on their own, individualized and completely self-directed, self-controlled pathways of spiritual learning and karmic self-healing/reconciliation. Pathways that they had chosen for themselves, no matter what disasters lay along those roads. It was a realization so jolting and clear in my mind, and vast in its implications that I had to sit down for quite some time. I missed my meeting. I didn't even call to explain. Something else to add to my list that was completely out of character for me.

What struck me at that moment was that most of these souls weren't even vaguely aware of this reality. They were unaware that the missions they were pursuing were far beyond the meeting they were traveling to at that hour. For a fleeting moment I was tempted to stand up and shout "hey, it's not what you think, really, it's not!" I caught myself just in time as in the back of my mind I remembered that Bellevue, and its famous padded room psychiatric ward, was just across town and down a few blocks. Nonetheless, this realization – this absolutely clear recognition of the true state of reality – sent my spirit soaring.

In spite of these advancing insights, I still had to work very hard to understand the Sadam Husseins of the world. The public prosecutor that buried evidence in order to convict an innocent man. The rapist. The murderer. And because of my experience as an orphan, my least favorite of all, the child abuser or anyone of greater strength victimizing someone of lesser ability to defend themselves.

The sad reality was that there were plenty of people right in my backyard who served as shining examples of people that took tremendous effort to love and even greater effort to see as comrades traveling the same spiritual, learning pathway. Kalista would provide comfort now and then by reminding me that, in any school there are different grades and, that students learn different lessons based upon what they have already absorbed, what they still need to learn and, their individual ability to learn certain things. In my moments of frustration, I would take a deep breath and recall Kalista's words. It always brought me comfort.

An unexpected byproduct of these insights was that I noticed that fear began to disappear from my life. Six months after the realization in Penn Station, it was pretty much gone. Around this same time another realization came to me. Upon returning from one particular session with Kalista I had a vague, yet palpable awareness that all of my trips to Kalista's garden were affording me the opportunity to accumulate a vast array of insights and knowledge. When viewed in a certain way, they were actually several different pieces of one comprehensive explanation of reality. A universal tapestry. A detailed and comprehensive explanation of the things many of us, as questioning human beings, have wondered about for as long as we can remember.

When I confronted Kalista with my theory, she gave me one of those genuine, but sincere smiles, patted me on the back and reaffirmed that I was "definitely on the right track." The only other clue that I got from her was when she was leaving that day. She walked across her bridge, turned and said, "You know, as I recall, there are some places in Europe and the Middle East where a person can work on a single tapestry for decades, even their whole life." With that, she flashed me one of those smiles that lasted a second or two. She then turned and deliberately walked across the bridge.

She said nothing beyond that, but I took her answer in combination with her demeanor to be a pretty solid "Yes, you're on target." I made a mental note to make certain that I continued to pursue this until I understood everything that I needed to know. I silently pledged to myself that if it was going to take the rest of my life to weave together the specifics of this particular tapestry that I would succeed. Looking back, I can only say that the arrogance of the lesser informed soul that I was at the time knows no boundaries. It was like swimming across a small lagoon thinking that it was a real accomplishment only to look up and see the actual size and depth of the ocean in front of you.

In my efforts to sort out the balance of the image – to begin the process of assembling the remaining pieces of the tapestry, as I began to call it – I realized that many basic questions still remained unanswered. In fact, I had learned that, in some ways, the more trips that I made to the garden, no matter how informative and inspiring any given session might be, that shortly after returning, it sometimes felt as though I had more questions than I'd had before I'd left. That the tapestry's edges became larger with every new bit of information I acquired. That should have been the first clue that I had miscalculated a thing or two.

After my visit with Geradl, I spent a week or so trying to fully absorb all of the insights that he had shared with me on my last visit to the garden. In the midst of driving to work one morning it struck me that I had left Geradl just standing in the garden the last time I was there. For some reason I had failed to make the connection that I had departed – in an unattractive fashion – without saying anything to Geradl. Not even a thank you for all the patience and compassion that he had shown me that day. I felt terrible. Horrified. So much so that I rushed through the meetings that I had scheduled in the morning and returned home in the early afternoon so I could try to make a quick visit to Kalista's garden and make an effort to apologize. My visits were becoming so commonplace at this point that I thought nothing of dashing off to the garden like most people would go down to the corner convenience store.

My mind was so cluttered with concern over having stranded Geradl and rushing everyone through the morning marketing meeting that I actually failed in a few attempts to connect with the garden before I could actually settle my mind enough to make the transition. When I finally perceived the foliage beginning to take form around me, I was so relieved that I lost my concentration completely and had to start the entire process all over again. After one more botched attempt, I was able to fully establish a firm connection and was quite happy when I saw Kalista standing by her bench with her arms folded, smiling and waiting for me.

"Are you... are you O.K. Chuck?" She was grinning from ear to ear, feigning concern. With her highly developed perceptional skills, she obviously knew that I was rattled about something and she was taking the opportunity to try to lighten the atmosphere. It worked a little but, I was embarrassed that, after all this time, I was still unable to make my way into the garden without experiencing some difficulty now and then.

"I'm fine. Why do you ask?" I said defensively.

"Well, it's just that you kept coming in and going back out again. You looked like a light bulb right before it blows out and has to be replaced." She was laughing with such sincerity and in a non-offensive way that it was impossible to really be mad at her, no matter how frustrated I was at the moment.

"That's pretty funny, Kalista. I just had trouble concentrating today for some reason."

"It wouldn't have anything to do with leaving Geradl in the lurch the last time you were here would it? Because you abandoned the highest form of soul in this dimension?" She was doing her best to restrain her amusement.

I was grateful at that moment for my evolving heightened intuition because, I could tell at once that Kalista was only trying to get a rise out of me. My intuition told me that Geradl wasn't upset with me at all. In fact, it was pretty apparent even without my advancing perceptional skills that nothing in this world or our world could ever upset Geradl. Thinking about the stresses and strains of my average workday at the time I was extremely envious on that account alone.

"Not at all. Although, I'm pretty unhappy that I couldn't even remember that I did that to him until today."

"I wouldn't worry about it. Geradl said that you'd had a pretty rough go of it and that you did extremely well. Better than I did the first time I went through all that. And a lot better than Tresden did," a mischievous smile rising at the corners of her lips.

"I feel just terrible Kalista; I can't believe that I couldn't even hang in long enough to thank him for everything that he helped me with... "

"It's okay. As you know, he is very understanding. Besides, he's attained such advanced states of development – his Resonance is so great – things like that don't even register with him anymore. You must have come for more than that, though. I assume you have your usual list of a hundred questions or so." Kalista was still trying desperately to suppress a smile. It was obvious that she was still having fun with me.

"To be honest, after I took in what Geradl showed me and thought about everything that he explained to me about Source and Source-god, and how, at some point Source-god began spinning-out individual souls, I got a little lost. No matter how hard I tried to remember, I couldn't understand one basic question: why would those souls – all of the people in our world – ever have left the spiritual plane? The absolute beauty; the perfection that I saw, the incredible and absolutely overwhelming, all-encompassing sense of peace, of living in the presence of the All; the perfect serenity conveyed directly into my soul by that Light he showed me. There was no pain, no sadness and no suffering. What possessed all the individual souls to leave such a place? Why would we ever come into the physical world in the first place?"

"I see that you're on to your usual list of all the simplest questions in the universe. First of all, it wasn't 'all of the individual souls' that came into the physical plane. Not anywhere close to that, at least not at first. Second, there's a lot more to the story: background about what was going on then, and certain dynamics about the Origination. What Source pondered. Contemplated. Had as aspirations for Creation. Why and what happened. The fact is, a lot of what and how your world is today – with all of the problems that you are so sensitive about – trace their roots back to what transpired around events not terribly long after what we perceive as the time of Origination. Before there even was time, much less the concept of time. To what Geradl has called 'the original episodes of the All,' which afforded the opportunity for souls to take on incarnations at the outset."

"I'm completely lost Kalista. Will Geradl explain all of that for me some time?"

"Actually, he said that if you asked, that I could tell you. If you'd like."

"Seriously?" It was around then that a flash went through my mind that, this was the very information that would help fill in some of the major pieces of the tapestry that I had been pondering. If I'd understood Kalista correctly, at some point, Source must have pondered the creation of individual man and woman and, created a physical world for us to work and play in. I wondered why Source would do such a thing. My ruminations in this regard, as I would learn later on, contained a number of misassumptions.

"I'll try to explain it to you in exactly the same way that Geradl first told it to me. Geradl is much better at simulating the imagery than I am, but I'll try to duplicate some of that, to help provide the incremental clarity for you. Why don't we sit on the bench. This may take a while."

Kalista sat quietly for a few moments. She seemed to be concentrating on trying to remember the story exactly as Geradl had told it to her. Maybe she was thinking about how to simulate the appropriate imagery for me. I noticed that she kept on closing her eyes and gently touching the right side of her head, around the temple. This appeared to be some kind of novel memory recollection technique. I didn't want to interrupt her concentration, because I had never seen her do anything like this before, but I was very tempted to ask her about the details.

When I got around to asking her about it several months later she smiled for a moment and then side-stepped the question. I wouldn't have thought anything of it at all except a few weeks later, I noticed that Tresden used exactly the same methodology when I asked her about how Geradl first explained something to her a very long time ago. She too evaded the question. Another mystery. I would eventually learn that it wasn't even close to being what I thought. As I became immersed in thinking I almost missed the fact that Kalista had begun relating the explanation that Geradl had passed down to her.

"Around the period when Source had unfolded all of the initial and primary universes, dimensions and realities – and well before the concept of time even began – the momentum of the initial creation was accelerating so fast that Source decided to place a portion of itself into five of the major realties. At that point, Source reached within itself and spun out portions of its heart and flung them into those universes. This part, that was derived from the perfect center of Source was called the 'Essential Source.' Essential Source was, and will always be, simultaneously, perfectly and absolutely connected in ways unimaginable to all of us, directly to Source."

"This is where I got confused with Geradl's explanation. Are you saying that God or Source or whatever someone wants to call it split itself into five parts and those parts went into five different portions of what had been created up until then?"

"No. But for this part of the explanation it is important for you to remember that Source refers to what Geradl's first explanation of Source to you was. As you'll recall, when he refers to Source he defines it as 'The Original Center of All Things.' That is why the distinction is so important. What Geradl is saying is that, before Creation – literally before there was anything that we could conceive of *as a begin-*

ning – there was only one single point. I like to think of it as the immense wisp of light that contains all things, all creation and all possibilities of all things. That same, exact Original Center of All Things still exists today."

"So you're saying that, there is some central point, let's call that the place where God originates, and still lives. But that, because of the unlimited possibilities of God, she was able to reach inside of herself and create five... would you call them duplicates, and sent them into what had been created up until them to watch over things?"

"Actually, that's pretty good. Not exactly correct but, you've got the basic parts of it. It's important for you to understand that, even as the Original Center of All Things flung out the Essential Source, it was not diminished in any way. It was not as though Source divided herself into five separate pieces. After Essential Source had been flung out, all five pieces of Essential Source and, The Original Center of All Things were all, each, as complete and capable of all things as the original Source was on its own."

"Sounds like magic to me."

"That's not the half of it. But then again, what would you expect from what you call God?"

As Kalista was relating this part of the explanation, the background of the garden faded away as the images she was describing began to take form and went into motion in front of me. The imagery itself was of a similar nature and quality as the life-review imagery with the obvious exception being there were no emotions of individuals to be felt. The imagery showed an immense wisp of light that was so brilliant and vast that it was impossible to even try to look at it directly, much less describe anything specific about it.

The immense, pulsating wisp emitted electrifying colors and hues of a deep, rich blue, almost black. Part of the spectrum had a distinctive vibrant, lustrous other-worldly golden halo-like glow mixed in. The enormous wisp was either spinning or pulsating gently, I couldn't really tell which. The images that Kalista had afforded me as illustration added so much to the explanation that all of the remaining questions that I'd had in mind immediately evaporated as I viewed the imagery before me.

In absolute awe, I had to remind myself several times that what I was looking at was only a representation and not the real thing. Geradl would tell me many years later that it would be impossible to experience all of the actual Source directly without being fully consumed by it. He added, "In your current form of existence, of course." He offered no further explanation at the time, and I was beyond mystified and intrigued by what he had said.

I stood there allowing the intense images to be absorbed by my senses with stunned fascination. From my perception, at one split second in time, the enormous pulsating wisp of light seemed to open right down the middle for a fraction of an instant. Then, five distinct wisps of a blinding, brilliant golden light all of equal size and light intensity as the original wisp – came out of the very center of the central wisp of light. These five wisps seemed to bolt out in different directions. In a matter of moments, all five wisps disappeared. The effect of all the brilliantly colored wisps of light dispersing so suddenly was so shocking that, for a moment, I was stunned and seemingly blinded.

When I was able to see and get my bearings again I noticed that the wisp that represented the original Source – Geradl's Original Center of All Things – was, hanging, suspended in the middle of everywhere, pulsating with a soft, but still completely blinding, yet irresistibly tempting, glow. I was now able to perceive that, it was both spinning and pulsating very gently. In my mid-section I felt an indistinct, low-pitched subtle humming. I sat there, in awe of what I had just seen and barely aware that Kalista was communicating again, continuing on with the explanation.

"This is the point approximating what you might perceive to be a beginning."

"Wait a minute. Hold on Kalista, You're going too fast. This is a lot to take in."

"Be patient Chuck. This is one of those explanations that, when you're hearing the parts of it, it can be difficult to understand, much less easily accept. At some point, we'll get to a place in the explanation where it should all start to come together for you."

Despite Kalista's assurances I was feeling uncomfortable. No matter what she said, the impression that I had was that God's little experiment in Creation got away from her and almost in a panic, she had to reach inside of herself to send out little "managers" to watch out over different parts of Creation. If that was true, I remember thinking, I felt just a little less confident in the true power of the God that we are all indoctrinated to believe in as the absolute power when we were youngsters.

Still, Kalista had never misled me and I knew that if I wanted the knowledge from Kalista I had no real choice other than to take it as it came. I desperately wanted to put this piece of the tapestry regarding creation and our origin as beings into place – this part of the explanation of reality. As I was about to become mired down in this contradiction, Kalista continued with her explanation.

"The important part for you to understand in all of this is that Source did not lose control, or allow Creation to run away from her.

The way Geradl explained it to me is that Source made what we would think of as a conscious decision to allow the momentum of Creation to go wherever it would. Like a scientist mixing together a few chemicals in the lab and allowing the ensuing reactions to take place in whatever way it would on its own. But Source, seeing that the momentum of Creation, if left completely unchecked, could potentially develop some outcomes that were not within the desired objectives of Source, created a few simple, essential rules to govern events and, control Creation while still allowing some significant degree of freedom to go wherever it went of its own momentum."

"And the spinning-out of the five pieces of the Essential Source; that was done to monitor the various forms of creation? Like putting video surveillance cameras at different parts of your property so that you can watch what's going on from a central location?"

Kalista was close to one of her giggling sprees. I could just sense it. It was one of my weaker analogies run amok and she could barely contain herself at my less than on-point effort to explain what was going on at the outset of the creation. She managed to contain herself but, just barely. "Video cameras. What a great analogy!"

She was teasing me and, I knew it. But my fascination with the subject matter was so great that I was somehow able to skip over the light insult. I urged her with a rise of my eyebrows to continue.

"Really Kalista. Why bother. I mean if Source, or whatever one chooses to call the originator of all things, is really all-seeing, all-knowing and all-powerful why would it have to create a system like that to watch over things?"

"It never ceases to amaze me how you can just blurt out the most complicated questions regarding reality and the origin of the universe like you are asking about the time of day. What you are asking can only be known by Source itself or, those that are much higher in energy – and closer to Source – than we can even conceive of in our current state of awareness."

I was very surprised to hear Kalista say this. I had been fairly certain up until then that she was of such an advanced state, that knowledge of the nature she was talking about, was easily within her direct reach. It was only after a few years more experience with Geradl that I was to learn more detail of the various stages that we go through in our spiritual development and, what the various capabilities are that we take on as we move through those stages. Irrespective of this, Kalista was still a very highly advanced soul compared to anyone still incarnating on Earth. "Kalista, do we know **why** Source effected Creation?"

"The sense I got from Geradl when he explained this to me was that, Source decided – or what we would think of as a decision – to see what would and could happen if she effected Creation beyond herself. There were other reasons of course but, we'll get to that."

"Please don't tell me that we're all part of some experiment gone awry. Or that we're just an amusement for Source-god? Little mice in a maze and that, in the end, none of it really matters? That we're all insignificant and unimportant."

"Not at all. Source, and in specific, Source-god – the part of Essential Source that watches over and effects the process of Creation in the Universe, in all parts of the known had something very specific in mind when creation was set in motion. And, the fact is, Creation is still occurring even to this day."

"I'm not sure I understand that Kalista."

"I'm sure that one of us has already told you that new souls are being created all the time. Are being spun-out of the Source-god even as we speak right now."

"Why? I mean, why would Source-god do that?" I asked.

"You won't like the answer," she said.

This had also become a kind of secret code between Kalista and me. It was her way of telling me to brace myself because whatever was going to come next – be it explanation or some kind of visual display like the River of Knowledge – was going to be a sharp assault on my senses. "O.K., I'm as ready as I can ever be for one of these things. Just tell me."

Kalista was grinning from ear to ear. Without even needing to ask her what was so funny, I realized on my own that I had asked her the very purpose of God's creation as though I had asked her what day her birthday was. Sensing that I had diagnosed my error on my own, she opted to proceed with the answer. Before doing so she looked directly into my eyes – something that I had never been able to really withstand for more than a half-second or so before this day – and gave her response in a deliberate manner.

"To improve Creation. To increase perfection. To create something better and broader than herself by allowing the process of Creation to run with little virtual control. To expand the All beyond the original limits of the Source."

I wasn't shocked and, I wasn't particularly surprised. Probably because I didn't really understand what the answer really meant more than anything else. It made me think for a very long time. As I mulled the possible implications of what Kalista had said, she sat patiently, her eyes still locked directly in on my gaze. I don't know how I knew it but, somehow I just knew that this was a technique that was designed to convey the absolute truth of what she had just told me and, at the same time, not allow me to lose concentration on my own train of thought.

"If Creation was effected by Source and, we all assume that God is perfect, how can everything within Creation be anything less than perfect?"

As I finished speaking, my own words carried me away to a place that I thought unreachable by me in my current state of enlightenment. I never imagined that such insight would be within my grasp. Ever. Kalista was so overwhelmed that she was close to tears. I could see it. And the tears, had they actually flowed with any volume, would have been tears of pride. She had somehow led her student – she would say a few months later that I had led myself – to a place of one of the deepest understandings of our reality that there is. I had managed to find, without being told directly, the immutable truth that, no matter how imperfect, flawed, chaotic and misguided our world might seem at any given moment in time, as part of God's Creation, it is, by definition, perfect. Always has been perfect. Always will be perfect. I still had some difficulty understanding the details, like how murder could be perfect but, in its own way, the picture was becoming clear to me. It took some time until both of us could settle down from my realization.

"Does that raise any other questions in your mind?," Kalista was still beaming.

"Well, come to think of it, yeah. I'm still stuck on how Source's objective could possibly be to improve Creation? How can you improve something that derived from perfection?"

"You know, you're really brilliant at answering your own questions. I only wish I had been that insightful back when I was where you are right now."

"What the heck are you talking about?"

"Go back to what you just said. You answered your own question."

I tried to think back in our conversation and was just about to protest to Kalista that I couldn't understand what she meant when she interceded and provided me some relief.

"You asked, 'how can you improve something that derived from perfection?' What if Source pondered that very thing? Or, what if Source pondered the question, what would happen if Creation were allowed to run its own course, if the various pieces spun-off from The Original Center of All Things could some day return to perfection without Source's help and guidance? What would happen?"

"I find it hard to believe that Source doesn't have something better to do or, wouldn't know the answer to that on her own before allowing it all to play out." I'd blurted it out before I'd taken any time at all to even think about what I had just said and, how absolutely ridiculous it was. I noted after I spoke that Kalista had framed what she had said in one of her "what if" formats. When she did that, I had learned through experience, the answer lay somewhere within what she had said, but not necessarily exactly the way she had said it. It was a device that she sometimes used to make me think and, more often than not, it worked. Still, the way I had just blurted out my response amused her and she let out a small chuckle at my hastiness.

"I think that's probably someplace that you don't really want to go. I mean, taking on me or Tresden that's one thing. But Source itself, well, that might be a bit out of your depth at this point don't you think?" She was smiling broadly but at the same time, it was a gentle admonishment for me not to get too far ahead of myself by trying to rearrange the universe as I saw fit or, to assume that I knew more than I did. Her point was well taken and appropriate considering what was running though my mind just then.

"Yeah well, I guess you're right on that. But, I still need to understand this. What you're saying is that Source wanted to see what would happen if Creation was initiated – subject to a few basic rules like karma, what you called 'reconciliation and balance.' The main objective was to see what improvements could be made or, to see if the various spun-off pieces of Source could even make their way back intact? Is that pretty much it?"

"I'd say much more the first part of what you said than the second but, it's more or less a combination of those two with a twist or three added in."

"Kind of like me watching my son grow up – seeing what he'll grow into and what he'll become?" I was getting an inkling now of where this might be going.

"Do you want your son to become more than you are... better than you are? To achieve more than you did? To go farther, be happier and so forth?" she asked.

"Absolutely!"

"Will he always still be a part of you no matter what he learns or what he does?"

"Well, of course, he... well, he came from me – is made from me so to speak. At least partially."

"Do you deny your son anything, anything at all, in supporting him in his struggle to attain the goals that you have for him: learning, improvement, being happy? Loving? Experiencing?"

"Nope."

"Any ground rules for the kid or, can he run pretty much amok if he likes to?"

"Well, we try to give him a pretty open pathway – a fairly long leash we call it – but, you know, there have always been some basic rules or things might get out of control," I said.

"Do you stand over him every minute and personally direct every detail of his life? Tell him he has to turn the wheel left to go left? Tell him what cereal to buy at the grocery? Do you give him all the answers to the test he's going to have to take tomorrow?" she asked.

"No. No way. He wouldn't learn anything then. And it's impossible to watch over him every minute – and who would want to? At some point you just have to let go and hope that the basic instructions and attributes you passed onto him are enough. I drop in now and then of course and provide encouragement. See if there's anything I can do to help. But in the end, he has to make it – grow into whatever he decides he wants to be – mostly on his own," I responded.

Kalista was smiling broadly again. She'd made her point and, as usual, done so brilliantly and in a manner that led me exactly to the place that she'd meant to while making it appear to be my own idea. It was the sign of a genuinely brilliant teacher, and I was deeply grateful at that moment for my good fortune in finding my way to her and, most of all, for her patience.

"Creation, huh?"

"Yup. Absolutely. Origination. Basic guidelines. Absolute freedom tempered by the law of reconciliation. Eternity as a running clock. And return. Or not. Then stand back and watch to see what develops."

"So, it's up to us to make thing better – to improve on the whole thing?" I asked.

"If we can," she said.

"And if we can't?"

"I think you've had more than enough for one day don't you? I think you should go think about all of this for a while," She was glowing with some pride that I had achieved this degree of understanding.

"But Kalista I... "

"Chuck. Listen. This would be enough to absorb if you took several lifetimes to take it all in. Be patient with yourself. Take some time to think it all through. See if you can get to a place where, it not only makes sense to you but, you resonate at the level deep inside of you that it is the truth that you have known going back to your own point of origin. Because, the reality is, since we are all spun-off parts of Source, the memory of the time when Creation was contemplated and effected is inexorably innate deep within our primordial memories. In a way, we were all there, as parts of the original whole. If you'll allow yourself – if you can genuinely let go completely – you will get to a place where you will know that this is true. Feel it through experience as though you are re-experiencing the events themselves. It is such an exquisite realization that it defies description. More to the point, getting in touch with that recollection will be an enormous leap forward for you spiritually. From there other memories of who and what you really are will begin to flow into your consciousness. Once attained, you will never look back again and, your connection to all things will take on a new meaning far beyond what you can even contemplate right now."

As always, Kalista found a way – without the use of words or even gestures – to let me know that I was always more than welcome to come back. I needed to be gentle with myself when I failed to understand the nature of reality in the period of a week or even a year of this one lifetime. She explained to me that, this particular portion of knowledge was like watering a seed that was already in the ground. With time and some nurturing she assured me, the seed would grow into all that it was meant to be and, that as it did, my recollection of different aspects of reality – of the history of Origination – would grow proportionately.

I spent the next several days lost in a kind of mystical haze trying to absorb the nature and depth of this reality. To grasp the concept that the Creation of all things derived from a large wisp of unimaginable light as she had explained it to me. I found it overwhelming to ponder that, even in some small way, when we return to Source – either between lives or permanently – everything we have done, thought, intended, acted upon and not acted upon – all that we have become – is reflected in the very fabric of God herself. It took me a month or so to be able to articulate that back to myself but, when I did, it rang completely true. Not in my mind but, as Kalista had suggested, somewhere within my primordial recollection. I felt some level of enhanced Resonance in my soul.

What we become in this life is our repayment to God for granting us this lifetime in fact, all of our lifetimes as an existence continuum. And since we are all spun-off parts of the Original Source – no matter how small a part of that we are – what we become, in turn, is what God becomes when we return home to her. Tresden said it this way, "God is whatever she was at the outset plus whatever all of her children ultimately become."

It was this latter realization that concerned me the most. I began to wonder; could God actually be dirtied? Be made less perfect by, a murderer returning back into spirit form? When a rapist dies, does the overall God end up just a bit more stained and thus, less perfect? For some reason, thinking this, I thought back to my time at the seashore several months earlier. The ping-pong balls, the food dye and my little experiment in trying to understand how souls reincarnate in groups.

Without wasting much time, I ran upstairs and filled up my bathtub with water and imagined that water represented the totality of God. I dropped one drop of blue dye in thinking of it as a rapist returning back to spirit form. And then another, thinking it was a person who spent a lifetime acting without compassion. And then, another. A vague panic began to come over me as, when half the bottle had been emptied into the tub, the overall water color did begin to take on a pale blue tinge. I had, for a moment, begun to worry that, with all of the marginal types in our world maybe God was, in some way, at risk. That she could be dirtied if enough of us didn't work hard enough to resonate with the original ideals of love, compassion and empathy.

In a moment, the panic began to fade as I thought about how large all of the oceans are when put together when compared to my tub. And then I thought about how large our solar system is. And our Universe. And galaxy. And the billions of galaxies that lie beyond that. And the trillions we can't even see or imagine. Then I remembered what Kalista had told me once, "All of the galaxies in your imagination are not even a single grain of sand in the totality of the All." I slept better that night than ever before.

Little did I know then just how short-lived my sense of peace, well being and security was to be.

CHAPTER NINE

Faith is not a storm cellar to which men and women can flee for refuge from the storms of life. It is, instead, an inner force that gives them the strength to face those storms and their consequences, with serenity of spirit.

– Sam J. Ervin, Jr.

Oneness. The reality that we all, in actuality not limited by a vague theoretical concept examined academically in some philosophy class, but in fact, came from a single Source at our Origin. After the last session with Kalista where she not only told, but showed me the entire truth of reality and the impact of it, I walked around for weeks in a kind of elated, but also a disoriented and confused fog.

"How could it be other than this?" I would ask myself on my morning drive to meetings. As much as anything, I wondered why this reality had never occurred to me before. But the realization that this truth was something that I now actually owned, as opposed to simply contemplating it intellectually, was overpowering. It was rapidly becoming the predominant feature in my life. It was impossible for me to see our everyday existence in the same, mundane way once this door had been flung open.

This insight also had its downsides. Because even though I was deeply immersed in and directly responsible for managing a multi-million dollar merger at the time, it felt to me as though I was a completely uncaring, disinterested observer in the transaction. The deal may as well have involved Martians and Asteroids. Because the realizations that had been afforded to me through Kalista, Tresden and Geradl were gradually shifting my awareness to a state of mind where what we all think of as our everyday world was becoming not much more than a distraction to me. I saw my everyday life as the sideshow in my true existence.

The energy that flowed to me by directly experiencing the realization that we all derived from One went far beyond anything I could have vaguely imagined just a year earlier. Back then, I had remembered driving off to work trying to figure out if there was any meaning to life at all. Based upon what Kalista had just shown me, I was faced with the obvious, but still genuinely shocking, truth about reality. The true state of affairs from A to Z. In truth, I wondered if it were more like A to D at this point. I really had no idea how much of the picture I had. Immensity is a difficult thing to quantify.

The course I set out on was a substantial pathway of learning and personal development for me to have traversed over the previous year. I often found myself mentally and emotionally drained from the experiences. It also gave me great perspective on something that Geradl had said to me. "It's not unusual for a soul to take one, or more, entire lifetimes to absorb a single major lesson. And most often, several lifetimes."

I was finally able to settle my mind and achieve a reasonable level of comfort with the realization that we are, not just in concept, but in fact, all the children of the same parents. Source definitively **is** the parent of all things. At that point of recognition a deeper and pervasively calming peace, the nature of which I never believed I could attain, gradually took over and comforted my soul. It's never left. The unshakable calm that people who know me comment on now and then is a byproduct of the realization that, I know at this point that it will never leave either.

It was around this time that I began to ponder if it were possible for others to also share this feeling of complete calm. An inner peace that cannot be shaken by outside events. I also wondered what our world might become if others could see what I had seen. To feel attached to all things at some essential level of the soul, the way that Kalista had helped me to experience. To have the incredible freedom to abandon such notions as fear, hatred and anger as viable feelings or thoughts in life; to be in a position to set them aside never to be needed again, ever. To laugh off the concept of retribution or retaliation. This needed to be shared.

It was a beautiful dream and, at the time, I didn't have the first notion about how to share what I had begun to learn from these three advanced souls. Besides, I still had tremendous volumes of learning that I needed to do. The defense system within all of us imparts some degree of self-censorship, which reminded me that, no matter how beautiful the dream might be, sharing such insights has to be performed very selectively. And since I retained my aversion to being locked up in an asylum, I kept quiet.

Something that Kalista had said before the last session ended was still bothering me. She had drawn a brilliant analogy for me concerning my son. The absolute love that I hold for him and the aspirations that I have for him. After thinking about this analogy I concluded that Source must feel the same way about all of us. As humans – Souls in Transition Kalista and Tresden called it. Source or God or whatever we want to think of as the creator of all things simply *must*, if Kalista's analogy held true, care for us like we do about our own children. Hopefully, even more.

I understood and accepted what Kalista had shared with me long ago, that one of the basic laws in the Universe is that Source had effected the law of "reconciliation and balance," karma, instead of Source having to watch over every single development relating to every one of its creations. I remained deeply troubled that there appeared to be no real protection for us as children of Source. Some kind of divine coverage against the senseless violence, pain and suffering that is so prevalent in our world.

At the same time I had come to understand that hidden within all of that pain and suffering here on Earth, by the very definitions and objectives of life – what we call life – it was clear that there will always be opportunity for learning what we need to learn. This was one of the central themes of what Geradl had taught me. What I couldn't comprehend though was why there was no intervention; no help, no guidance and precious little more than snippets of hope in the form of the promise of a better life after this one. Where was God in all of this? Why effect Creation if there was no caring and nurturing for the participants? Seeming disinterest in the outcome.

As I drove home from a meeting one day in early summer 1994, I remember thinking that I would do anything, almost without limitation, to help my son if he was in desperate straights. That didn't mean that I didn't want him to learn to stand on his own two feet, I did. In fact, I insisted upon it. But at some point, if he was in trouble – real trouble – there was no question in my mind that I'd step in. He could learn lessons later on. When I looked back at the analogy Kalista had used that day and factored in my perspective on our reality – what I saw every night on the evening news – it wasn't hard to conclude that we, as children of Source, needed help. Lots of it. Immediately.

If Source was constructed of absolute love, then our aspirations as people, as souls, was to become more compassionate as our pathway home. Why then would Source and the higher souls in the Universe allow children to starve in Africa? Murders to occur unchecked? Suffering on an enormous, virtually wholesale, scale? And all of the other events we all endure day-in and day-out that made our world seem like a genuine cataclysm run wild?

It wasn't all one-sided. I had to account for the central lessons that Kalista and Tresden had told me were the essential purpose for our lives. Beyond that, there was karma to be reconciled. Karma was its own lesson. And there were other truths of our existence that Kalista and Tresden had yet to share with me. I was still faced with the harsh reality that, it isn't compassionate to watch other beings suffer, particularly when you're in a unique position to help them. The way I saw it, Source – and all the other souls that had already made the transition into higher spirit form – were watching, doing nothing. I became more troubled as I tried to understand why. I wondered; if I was in trouble – real trouble – would Kalista help me?

I had learned from experience that when I had an issue or problem like this, Kalista wanted me to try to work it out on my own rather than running to her with every question that came into my mind. Sometimes it worked. On occasion I actually sorted it out on my own. Following this practice, I spent a month or so with no visits to the garden, trying to rationalize why Source would abandon her children, her Creation. Was she busy doing other things? Dead? Indifferent? Was it that, once the basic laws of the Universe were put into place by God – guidelines, such as reconciliation and balance – that Source wouldn't intervene in our world no matter what happened? I had no illusions about changing God's intentions about how to run her Universe, but I was fascinated to learn the explanation for all of this seeming indifference.

After exhausting myself in an attempt to sort out and understand the range of explanations for what seemed to be a blatant contradiction on compassion, I blocked out the better part of a weekend morning for a visit to the garden. I disconnected the phones, fax machine and every other potential source of interruption to my meditative state. I carefully duplicated the process that now worked so efficiently for me to enter the deep state of quiet necessary to traverse the distance required in order for me to visit Kalista's garden. This time, I was determined to come back with answers no matter how complicated the explanation was.

As the imagery of the garden began to fill in around me, I noticed that Kalista and Tresden were already there – almost like they were waiting for me – involved with some kind of maintenance chores in the rose garden. This made me immediately suspicious. Seeing the two of them together as I arrived made me feel as though some other kind of surprise was in store for me.

Another issue that put me on guard was something that Geradl had said to me when I had met with him last time. He had gone to great lengths to make certain that I understood that, souls may pass to higher realities by raising their own spiritual energy levels. I recalled that he had told me, that in my current state of development, I didn't have the energy necessary to make the trip to the garden on my own. When I thought about this, I came to the conclusion that Kalista somehow must have helped me complete the journey to the garden. I surmised then that this journey could only occur by virtue of her lending me some of her energy in ways that I didn't, and couldn't, understand yet. It was the equivalent of me ringing her doorbell and her opening the door as I began to permeate to deeper levels of my meditative state. She knew that I was coming because, I couldn't arrive without her help. This made sense to me.

When I told Kalista about my deductions and the doorbell analogy she laughed so hard that tears ran down her face. Tresden showed up moments later and, before I could even try to stop Kalista from embarrassing me with Tresden, Kalista just blurted it out. Tresden, being compassionate, did not participate in the good-natured laughter. Possibly, she sensed my sensitivity on the subject. It was quite apparent that it took some effort for her not to do so. When they settled down they reassured me that, "all things, in reality, do not make sense from the perspective of the life you now lead." It was a mysterious statement that they refused to explain.

All of this was on my mind as I tried to settle in on this particular day. As I walked over to where they were standing I cautiously eyed both of them suspiciously. I was trying to figure out where the snake-in-the-grass would come from this time. My supposition was that they were going to use one of their unique forms of dynamic imagery or other shock methods that they often employed to make their point. When they were together was the very time that they were most likely to spring one of these techniques on me. This I had learned the hard way from experience. Kalista, with a wry smile, called them "mere spiritual teaching tools."

If history was any guide, most often these little surprises had the effect of assaulting my senses to such a degree that I was left in a daze and usually required substantial rest for several days afterward. This time, I was going to be ready for it. Kalista noted my defensive state and told me that there was no reason to be concerned. As we all walked over to the hanging baskets together it was Tresden who began the conversation.

"A bit sensitive today, huh?" She gave me a gentle smile.

"No, not really. I've just learned from experience that you guys like to surprise me just to make a point. In the process of your little illustrations, my sensibility and digestive tract usually suffer. Last time it took me a week to recover."

"Don't be too hard on Kalista. She thinks that she has to hit you over the head to get your full attention now and then. Believe me, it is all meant nicely, and it is nothing compared to some of the stuff she's pulled on me."

"Yeah. I've been on the receiving end of her well-intentioned efforts a time or two, Tresden. I think my nerves haven't returned to a normal state yet."

"You need to remember, Chuck; the only thing that matters is taking in the lesson. Your frayed nerves and burnt fingers will heal. The question is; will you remember not to touch the hot stove again?" Tresden was smiling mischievously.

Because of Tresden's gentle manner, I sensed that she was trying to prepare me for a difficult session. I had given up on trying to figure out how Kalista, Tresden and Geradl knew my every thought, what I felt, even before I arrived in the garden. I had long ago simply surrendered to that indisputable fact. I had also learned that, once they had selected a subject to explore together, particularly if it was likely to be stressful on me, that they prepared me by engaging in light discussion before we got too far into the subject matter. It was clear that Tresden was doing this now and I braced myself for what kind of shock to my system might be coming next.

"Why do I get the feeling this is going to be something that I'm not going to be very happy about?"

"Gee Chuck, she didn't even get to say anything yet. Why don't you wait until she clobbers you before getting all stressed out?" Tresden said with a wry grin.

Kalista had one of her sincere, yet almost devilish smiles working. I figured that it was her subtle way of letting me know that, I wouldn't be thrilled with whatever answers were coming. However, I'd be more enlightened when it was all over. One of Kalista's famed two-edged swords. But, like touching the hot stove, enlightenment is often accompanied by a certain degree of discomfort. It was a few years later, after I had logged a few hundred visits to the garden, that I began to really appreciate the compassionate, gentle and kind nature of both Tresden and Kalista. Their efforts were ostensibly designed to soften the impact of some of my more stressful lessons.

"O.K., O.K., I get the point. I assume that you already know why I'm here so, can you just answer my question without me actually having to ask it?"

"No. I think it's actually better if you can try to articulate it. That usually provides some clarity. Besides, Kalista and I have noticed that you have an amazing ability recently to answer your own questions when you're made to ask them."

"Fine. Look, I don't mean to be the one to say that the Universe isn't perfect. Or that Source isn't perfect. And I'm not because, it obviously is. But, I thought through what you had said about everyone in the world being involved in learning the lessons that they needed to learn no matter how painful and difficult the process might be at the time they're learning. But, even taking that into account, it seems to me like Source has allowed the process of Creation to run pretty much without compassion on Earth. That Source is either bored or doesn't care about it. Or, if we're 'all in the same school' as Kalista likes to put it, why aren't you upper classmen helping out us struggling children? It just seems to me that the advanced souls and God could get together and help the world out a little. We're in trouble if you haven't noticed."

Tresden and Kalista looked at each other for a moment. This was their usual routine when they were about to burst into laughter. As I braced myself for their playful mockery, Kalista slowly made her way over to me, put both her arms around me and gave me a gentle hug. When Kalista finally released me Tresden duplicated her actions. For a moment I wondered if this was a fast goodbye; whether I was about to be dismissed or reprimanded for asking what might have been considered by many to be a blasphemous question.

"You really do love the easy questions don't you?" Tresden said.

"I wouldn't be too hard on him, Tresden. As I recollect, you asked that very same question the first time you came around to this point of insight. In fact, I think you might have used Chuck's exact words."

From my perspective, if Tresden had arrived at a similar point of frustration along her learning pathway and, she had now made it to what was obviously a fairly advanced state of spiritual development, I'd hoped that this could be taken as encouragement for my prospects. I figured that if Tresden could make it from "here," eventually I could too.

"Is that true Tresden? Did you get to a place where you asked yourself these same questions?"

"Everyone does Chuck. That is, anyone who reacquaints themselves about the realities of Creation, Source and bothers to think about it at all. To tell you the truth, with the insights that you've had from your visits here so far I would have thought it a bit odd if you *didn't* have these questions."

"That makes me feel better on that account at least. So, does that mean that there is an answer? That there are reasons?"

"Boy, you've got to give it to him Tresden. He made it a whole two minutes without asking a question that's impossible for him to accept, or be deeply troubled by, any answer that you'll give him in return."

"What did I say?"

"Relax Chuck. She's just trying to give you a hard time. But you have to admit, your question had to do with a simple little subject like, "what's on God's mind?" Kalista said.

"What do you mean?"

"Well, you asked questions about Source's interest in Earth; doesn't Source 'care' anymore. Is God basically 'bored?' And then you asked about why the more advanced souls don't help out. There are different answers depending upon which part of your questions you want us to try to deal with. If you want to deal with what Source might be 'thinking' at any given time, you might find some of the answers we give you a bit...well, wanting I guess you could say." Kalista was answering from the posture of a compassionate, but stern teacher.

"But you're saying that there *are* answers. At least, some answers." I pressed on.

"Oh boy. Here we go." Tresden was beaming as she said this.

"What did I say this time?" I asked Kalista, defensively.

"You didn't say anything wrong. It's just that, well...it's just that... "

"I'm rapidly becoming an old man from this stuff. It's hard on me to absorb all of this. Why can't you guys just answer me when I ask a direct question?"

"First of all, the insights you want are very complex. They involve some pretty complicated concepts that you're not completely up to speed on. By the way you've stated your questions – you've obviously made some assumptions about the state of reality that are simply not accurate. More to the point though, the very answers that you seek you already have. You just haven't thought through everything that we've told you so far. These are things you've already learned and accepted long ago," Kalista explained.

"What the hell does that mean?" I asked.

"Chuck, we've told you this before. Everything that you, or anyone, wants to know – knowledge of all things, or what Geradl calls the true 'Resonance with the All' is, and always has been, available to everyone. The information; the answers that you seek, are imbedded within you. It's just that they're not in your heart and not in your brain where you'd probably be tempted to look for them."

"What do you mean?"

"What you have interpreted as Tresden and my affording you lessons is no more than Tresden and I reminding you of things that you already know. You just don't remember that you know them." Kalista said with some emphasis.

"Is that why so many of the things that you have gone over with me almost immediately and so completely resonate as being true? Because no matter how hard I might try to rationalize my way through these things and prove or disprove them through some theory, through thought process, that doing so is useless because all I have to do to learn is to have my spiritual memory jogged? In essence, when you're teaching me, all you're doing is reminding me of the truth of all things?"

"Exactly. But, instead of 'truth of all things' just substitute Geradl's 'Resonance with the All' and you'll have it. 'Truth' when you live in the world that you do right now, can get muddled in all kinds of subjective interpretations. You and your neighbor can honesty disagree over the 'truth' of whose grass is greener. Resonance, true Resonance, the kind that deals with the Reality of All Things can't be misinterpreted in such ways. Resonance is being there and taking it in directly. Bypassing the brain. It can't be talked about, only experienced. Truth is like hearing about Resonance from someone you trust. The trouble with truth is, it can be subject to the teller's interpretation

— how they *think* about what they've experienced. Resonance, can't be misinterpreted in such ways because, it can only be *experienced* directly through Source. Because of this, when you talk about Resonance you can do no better than to talk around it."

"But Kalista, it is very hard for me to believe that I know all those things."

"Does that give you any clue as to why it might be so hard for you to remember them?" I pulled to a sharp halt with what Kalista said. She was showing me that I was employing a kind of "Power of Positive Thinking" in reverse. That I was talking myself out of knowledge that I had, buried deep within my essence, by virtue of the fact that I was insisting that it wasn't there. This triggered a series of other questions in my mind.

"Wait a minute, Kalista. If that's all true, then why even have a River of Knowledge? What would be the point if we all knew everything but just couldn't remember?"

"See, you are brilliant. I told you that you're great at answering your own questions!" It was Kalista's turn to smile from ear-to-ear.

"What?" This wasn't funny to me.

"Think back to when Tresden and I took you to the River of Knowledge. When you were reviewing threads. Did it seem to you like the information — what you were learning — did it seem at some point as though the knowledge was already familiar to you?" Kalista was encouraging me with her eyes to reflect back on this.

I thought back to that session. It was draining to relive it, but it was also beautiful and inspiring. As I tried to replay the events of that day in my mind, a vague and nagging feeling of deep recognition began to creep over me. Kalista was right. As I had worked through absorbing the information contained within the various threads I remembered progressing to an awareness where I acknowledged an almost primordial familiarity with the material that I was examining on the threads. It was as though I was looking at my high school yearbook. I couldn't specifically remember the people's names but the faces were familiar. Looking at the names underneath the pictures was a device employed to remind me what I already knew but had temporarily forgotten. For me, The River of Knowledge, at some point in the experience, was exactly like that. I knew that material but, had no idea **how** I knew it. It was obvious that my connection with it was there – just like attaching the names to the faces in the yearbook – somewhere inside of me.

"O.K. Kalista, I can see that the general information on each thread was familiar to me. But the details, the finer points, were not."

"You mean, you didn't recall the details as well as you recognized the general subject?" Kalista asked with a mocked amusement.

"Yes, but... "

"Ever been to a movie?" she asked.

"Here we go. Every time you change the pace like that I just know I'm about to get clobbered. Won't be the last time I suppose. O.K., yes, Kalista, I've been to a movie."

"Name one."

"What?"

"Name one, pick a movie – any movie that you've seen."

"O.K., I'll bite. *Star Wars*."

"That's the one that has Princess Leah right?"

"Uh huh."

"How does she wear her hair in the movie?"

"How the heck would I know? I wasn't working makeup that day. What are you driving at?"

"Let me get this straight; you've seen the movie, right?"

"Sure, a few times."

"So, you know what it's about. You've got the essential story line. You know the characters and what happens as things move along through the movie, right?"

Within my mind's eye, I saw the trap door slamming shut behind me. I wanted to figure out some way to undo my error in tactics; the one that went back to the beginning of this short conversation. But it was too late. Besides, Kalista would never let me off that easily once I had committed such an obvious blunder. The opportunity to impart a lesson was simply too blatant. I braced myself for the good-natured onslaught that I knew was coming. I noted that Kalista's eyes were shining brilliantly in anticipation of being able to lower the boom on what I perceived to be her favorite class dunce.

"No. Well, I mean yes. But you see... "

"Never mind all that. You're telling me that you know all those things about the movie, that you'd recognize it immediately – at least the most crucial subject matter of it – even if you only watched a ten second clip of it. You know all these things about it but you don't know how Princess Leah wore her hair?"

It was game, set and match all in one sentence. Kalista was right, of course. As usual, she'd made her point in a way that left no doubt in my mind as to the truth of what she was saying. More importantly, she'd taught me the lesson in such a unique and entertaining manner that I'd never forget it. It left me with little doubt that we really do have all the information inside of us. But, there were still minor questions. The issues I was most concerned about had more to do with how to get *at* the information as opposed to challenging whether it was all actually there.

I still wanted to understand why Source seemingly abandoned her Creation, which was the question I'd meant to learn the answer to when I set out for the garden that day. Prior to going on to that though, I wanted to make sure I understood the full scope of what Kalista was saying on this particular topic.

"Let me make sure that I get this straight. Everything – without exception – all knowledge of all things is already within each and every person. It's all there. All we need to do is learn how to access it? Recollect it?"

"The answer to the first part of what you asked is an unqualified yes. As to the second part, I'd have to say no. Because, simply "learning the answers" as you suggested, isn't enough. You have to actualize them," Tresden said, taking over where Kalista had left off.

"Like the difference between book learning and street learning?" I asked.

"Sort of but, it goes beyond that. As an example, you might ponder the reality of Creation for your entire life. In so doing, you might conclude some day that, logically, all of Creation must have descended from one original source. One central point of energy. But, no matter how flawless your logic, your thought process, might be on that subject, no matter how completely you convince yourself that it "must be true," until you *actualize* that insight, as Kalista helped you do the last time you saw her – that knowledge does you little good in terms of increasing your Resonance. Knowing it helps the brain, but owning it goes to increased Resonance at the level of the soul. True knowledge, the kind of enlightenment that you set out to find when you sought us out, comes from actualized recollection. It is acquired and placed in service only by Resonating with the All."

"So are you saying that I could have sat in a room meditating about Creation for my whole life and never have learned anything?"

"I'm not saying anything of the sort. What I am saying is that, you can think about the topic of Creation or Reality or Source or anything like it until the cows come home but, until you remember – attain essential recollection of it – you won't increase your 'True Resonance' one iota. Whatever conclusions you reached about Reality through pure contemplation might have been interesting and, no doubt, intellectually stimulating, but they won't do a thing as far as moving your true enlightenment along. That can only occur when you tap through Resonance."

"Are you saying that thinking about all of this stuff does no good?" I asked incredulously.

"No. I'm saying that, eventually, if you want to move onward in any significant way, you need to go to a place that 'thinking' just can't take you. That is the place of recollection. Through recollection we reconnect with our origin. And the closer we get to our true origin, or what Geradl calls, The Original Center of All Things, the higher our Individual True Resonance becomes and the deeper our spiritual vibration gets. As the substance, the ostensible volume, of our Individual True Resonance increases, the greater and deeper our wisdom, compassion and connection to all things grows."

My head was swimming. I could feel that everything that Tresden was saying to me was boosting my enlightenment and awareness of reality to exponentially deeper levels. I'd understood all of these concepts to some degree before she clarified them, but somehow – maybe it was the way in which she described them – the impact was far greater than just her words.

I'd come to believe that enlightenment could only come about within us if we read enough, or meditated enough. The reality, as Tresden was explaining it, was at the same time, more simple and more complex than that. We need only to recollect that we already know all there is to know. Recollection of our origin and, our essence. It's innate. Now all I needed to do was to learn how to recollect all the things I needed to know.

"So why do we have such difficulty recollecting all of this if it is such an innate part of us? Is it because we are in human form?"

Tresden led me to the oak bench where we all sat down. "First of all, it is not only the human form that is an obstacle to recollection. As you move onward to higher Resonance levels, you in essence remember that you need to remember more clearly. The arena of what needs to be remembered is less vague at higher Resonance states. The answer to your other question is, subtlety. The information while you are in human form is always 'there.' Ever present. It's always 'available.' But relative to the noise and other distractions in your day-to-day world it tends to get drowned out."

"I'm not sure I get that."

"Here, let me show you." Tresden got up and walked me over to the edge of the stream that ran on both sides of Kalista's island garden. She picked up two stones from the ground, one about four or five times the size of the other. She walked up the shoreline until we came to a little backwash. It was a still part of the stream comprised of the amazing deep aquamarine blue water with the silverfish highlights. This small area though was virtually stagnant. She held up the smaller stone and prepared to toss it gently into the water.

"This stone represents True Resonance. When it hits the water, the waves that will flow outward from it will equate to the Resonance, the infinite information comprising the Totality, that pervades and surrounds all things at all times." With that, she gently tossed the small stone into the water. Almost immediately, small concentric circles began to flow outward from where the stone had landed. With almost no delay at all Tresden gently threw the larger stone into the water, fairly close to where the smaller one had landed.

"This stone represents the distractions, noise, suffering, pain, emotions and other things that constantly intrude upon, and overwhelm, your daily life. Watch what happens to the waves sent out by the first stone now," Tresden said.

The illustration was both immediate and shatteringly pronounced. Within a second of the larger stone – the one that was meant to represent all of the distractions in our lives – landing upon the water, the small circles that had been carried outward by the smaller stone were completely overwhelmed and covered up by the waves from the larger stone. The smaller waves were still there, within the larger ones. But they were difficult to discern from the larger waves. The point was clear; Resonance is overwhelmed by the noise and the sensory assault life imparts upon our lives much like the waves from the smaller stone were overrun by the waves from the larger stone.

The effect of Tresden's illustration was shockingly clear to me. I saw and understood almost immediately the nature of the challenge that we all face in sorting out the Resonance from the cacophony of our day-to-day existence. The point was made without any room for equivocation and I felt that I knew to some degree, where to begin to look for answers. What I was still a little lost on was how. How do we learn to recollect? And how do we know **what** to try to recollect in order to move toward greater Individual True Resonance?" I asked.

Kalista smiled broadly. "Finally, two questions worthy of my aspirations for you. Because at some point in our existence, once we make a determination that our objective will be to move onward and cease being distracted by the illusions that are the reality of temporal life, that becomes the sole focus of importance."

"Gee, thanks Kalista. So, is there an answer?"

"Yes. But, the answer can only be experienced. We'll show you as we move along in that direction."

"That hardly seems fair but, as usual, I have no choice. You spoke before about Individual True Resonance. Since that implies some degree of true genuine individuality of the soul does that mean that, even as we get closer to The Original Center of All Things that we retain our individual identities?"

"Wow Kalista, this guy must have been hitting the Gingko pretty hard this week. That's three really great questions in a row!"

I have no idea why Tresden's comment struck me as particularly funny. Maybe it was her reference to Gingko Biloba and the seeming incongruity that she would even know about it. Possibly it was just the strain of the moment attributable to the subject matter. Irrespective of the cause, I burst out laughing – something that I'd never done on my own in all of my visits to the garden. My doing so seemed to have caught Tresden and Kalista off-guard.

"The answer to that is going to sound like a sharp contradiction in terms. But, at some point, when your Individual True Resonance becomes great enough, it begins to meld in a way with The Original Center of All Things. For a while, you retain both your individual identity, although that undergoes a subtle transformation away from the customary definitions of individuality, while at the same time, the person that you think of as being 'you' will begin a kind of soft integration with The Original Center of All Things.

"Eventually, all remnants of the individual identity cease to be discernable to those that observe you from the perspective of a lower Resonance level. Since their perception is limited, from their point of view, you would have appeared to have been ostensibly absorbed into Source. At that point, what was, at one time, a spun-off part of Source – the thing you'd call an individual Soul in Transition, 'Chuck' – ceases to appear to be separate from Source. Eventually, the line of perception that denotes where 'Chuck' the individual, the identity that we would all agree was the unique 'you' starts, and The Original Center of All Things just blurs into nothingness. From any place outside of Source, you – the soul energy you represent, that is – would seem to have disappeared."

As Kalista's words echoed in my mind I found that I was swimming in a pool of frenetic confusion. It sounded to me like what she was saying was that, at some juncture along the pathway that is spiritual development, when we advance to a highly developed state that we are completely absorbed into Source.

Or was it back into Source? That we lose all remaining semblance of our individuality by returning from whence we came. I recognized the voice of my ego increasingly protesting – but loudly – at a fate such as this. But Kalista had also said something that seemed to suggest the possibility that this was more appearance than reality. Our being reabsorbed wasn't total. This would take some thought to sort out and, now wasn't the time for that.

I have no way of knowing where I got the idea to ask the next question. It simply came out before I really thought much about it. There was no thought as to the appropriateness of it nor how Kalista and Tresden might respond to such a question.

"Is that where Geradl is at this point? I mean, is Geradl basically at the place where he is beginning to lose some, or even most, of his individual identity in favor of Source? Or, is it that Geradl is Source?

Tresden and Kalista had genuinely shocked looks on their faces. They then stared at each other for a few moments. I was tempted to think of the expression they had as "mystified" save for the fact that, I didn't believe that anything I might come up with could possibly confuse or mystify them in any way. Their silence lasted for several minutes. When Kalista finally broke the quiet there was a near respectful tone to her communication.

"Why would you ask something like that?"

"I'm not sure Kalista. It's just a feeling that I get when I meet with him. I feel as though there is part of him that is as different from me as an ant is to a human. Almost as though he has to slow himself down artificially in order to even communicate with someone at my level. It is as though part of him is plugged in someplace else. Someplace completely unimaginable to me."

"Well, to that let's just say that your insight skills are a bit farther along than either Tresden or I suspected." Kalista was smiling in a way that appeared more like pride than anything else.

"So, that means I'm right?"

"In a manner of speaking, yes. Geradl resonates at a level where, his compassion and knowledge begin to approach just the outer edges of The Original Center of All Things. Just how much so, to what degree, Tresden and I don't know. Can't know in fact because, that experience exceeds anything that we are aware of remembering. Any attempt to actually talk about this defies any words we might try to employ. Geradl has only told us that the experience of attaining the deeper levels that approach the true outer-most edges of Source are so sublime that it defies even an advanced soul's imagination. The answer to your other question though is no, Geradl is not Source. Not the way you're thinking of it."

"But, Geradl still *does* have an individual personality."

"Maybe that is the personality of God, reflected in Geradl? Somehow, we retain our individuality in spite of 'blurring' in at the edges with Source. How about this; what if Geradl simply hadn't advanced yet to a stage where his individuality is lost. Maybe it is never lost. Take your pick. But neither Tresden nor I really know."

"Kalista, that isn't telling me much."

"We know how you feel. When it comes to this subject, we're genuinely not much better informed than you are."

"But what if we never lose our individuality? What if God is actually just a reflection of *all* the various spun-off pieces of itself? Always was and always will be."

Tresden smiled like the Cheshire Cat, "Yeah, what if?"

Tresden and Kalista's eyes were lit up like a million candlepower searchlights after I said this. In a moment of genuine arrogance, I allowed myself to believe that I had thought up something new. Something that had made the two of *them* think for a change. And then it hit me, they had already pondered this – or knew it for a fact. Probably longer ago than I had been a soul. If they knew what I was thinking at that moment, they never let on. I was about to delve deeper into this topic when Kalista broke in on my thoughts.

"We could talk about this for years and probably not get to a place of real understanding. It defies concepts that we can all understand at this point. Possibly at some time in the future, Geradl may choose to discuss this with you directly. Let's move on to the main question that you came here for today."

Before moving off of this subject I wanted to learn one more specific aspect about the status of the individual soul when it becomes very advanced and attains extremely high levels of Resonance. High enough so that their Resonance affords them a pass key approaching the outer edges of Source.

"Let me go back for just a second. At the point when a soul has acquired or achieved adequate Resonance where they begin to approach the edges of Source do they cease to exist?" I asked.

"Are you asking if they die?"

"Yes."

"No."

"Why not?"

"Because there's no such thing. You know that. That there **is** no death is a primary condition of the All. There is only transition from one state into another. Transformation from one level of Resonance to another level of Resonance. As an example, when people on Earth perceive that someone has "died" the fact is that the soul has done no such thing. All that has happened is that their awareness, their status as a perceiver, has shifted its target of focus from the incarnate plane to the discarnate plane. So when a soul attains this advanced level of Resonance and approaches Source, even though I cannot know specifically what happens to them, I know that it can only be a transformation of one sort or another. Some form of shift in perception at an enhanced level beyond what we can even begin to ponder."

"O.K., then what really ***does*** happen to them?"

"Obviously, I wouldn't know that."

"So it's not possible that you might have, just as one possibility, already attained that level of Resonance, sort of dipped a toe in the pool that is The Original Center of All Things and then returned to this level of Resonance?"

"I see what you're getting at. The answer to that is... I don't remember."

"What?"

"I don't know, really. It is not information or insight that is within my conscious recollection. I suspect though that, as we get closer to that level of Resonance where the line between us, as perceived 'individuals' and Source as 'The Original Center of All Things' is, that we probably find out. That's the only answer that I have for you."

As I thought more about this I concluded that it must be like a person who volunteers to travel, on behalf of a lost group of campers, far down into a canyon to see if there is any water there. But by the time the volunteer gets far enough so that they can see what's at the bottom of the canyon, they are too far away to be heard if they yell back up the mountain to the rest of the people standing at the top.

The fact that the volunteer has learned that there is water at the bottom helps only the volunteer, since the people at the top can't hear the person that made the trip down – equivalent in this analogy to those that have already relinquished their individuality to Source. One by one they each end up having to wander down to the bottom of the canyon on their own, at their own pace. When they do, they learn one at a time, that there is not only water at the bottom but food, shelter and everything else that could ever been needed to exist blissfully. Far beyond perfection.

"Chuck, if you try to go much farther down this pathway you're only going to get more frustrated. It is not only a very complicated affair but, some of the background material that you would need to understand, you simply have not remembered yet. Some of this falls into the category that Geradl calls 'the unknown' and possibly even 'the unknowable.' Maybe for now, you'd be better off moving on to something else."

Kalista never lied to me. It was obvious she had long ago gone beyond even contemplating such things. And no matter how frustrated I might have become at times that I couldn't get direct answers to some of my questions, I had no doubt that she always had my best interests at heart. She knew my objective was enlightenment. And I trusted her to move me along that pathway. I decided to take her advice and move on to something much simpler to sort out, like, why God chose to ignore her Creation.

"Sure, why not? But instead of trying to sort out these fuzzy issues that give me a headache, maybe you could just try one straight answer this time."

"Sure. What's the question?" Kalista asked with enthusiasm.

"Yes or no. Do you know why Source doesn't intervene and stop the evil that is destroying the world?"

Tresden was horrified. I could see it on her face. "Oh Chuck. Are you sure that's the way you want to ask her that?"

"What? What's wrong with it?"

"Well, to start with... "

"No, please Kalista, let me do it."

Kalista was tapping her foot, sternly. She seemed very impatient and she wasn't smiling this time. She had reverted back to the flat countenance that always mystified me as to what she was actually thinking. It also made me quite nervous.

"Fine. Go ahead Tresden."

"O.K., calm down Chuck. Try your question again but this time, be careful and think before you ask!"

No doubt, there was a lesson in all of this but I wasn't sure at this exact moment what it might be. The discomfort that I had been anticipating since I had arrived and seen Tresden and Kalista together was coming over me and at a significant pace. At that I took a few moments to try to think through carefully what I'd asked hoping to isolate the part of the question that she found offensive. After a few moments, I considered that, when I used the word "evil" in my question that it might have struck Kalista as both vague and inappropriate.

"Let me take a wild guess here. Was it that I used the word evil in my question?"

"I'm sure that was one of the words that struck a nerve." Tresden now had also adopted a flat demeanor.

"What else did I say?"

"Lots of stuff. But for one thing, you also said, 'destroying the world.'"

"Don't tell me that we don't have the capability to destroy the world."

"We who?" Kalista interjected.

"We us. The people that live there."

"That does it. Tresden, where's that dunce cap we used to keep around here?" I was grateful to see that Kalista wasn't genuinely upset with me. But I was still mystified about what, specifically, she was so sensitized to with regard to my question.

"Now what did I say? Surely, you're not going to tell me that, if the idiots running our world lost control someday and let loose with all of their nuclear, chemical and other weapons of mass stupidity that they couldn't destroy our world?"

"Who's world?"

"Oh. Sorry. I stand corrected. Our planet."

"Kalista, it's too painful watching him flop around like a fish on the deck of a boat. Maybe you should just help him out."

"Does that mean I can throw him back in the water when I'm done?" Kalista was smiling again. Now I knew that, if she could tease me in this way that my offences must not have been that great.

"All right. Listen carefully. First of all, you asked about 'evil.' There is no such thing. Not in the way that you mean it anyhow."

"Hold on. Murder isn't evil? Rape isn't evil? Abusing a child isn't... "

"If you'll let me finish, I think you'll understand. You remember what I showed you about all things deriving from Source. That traced to every beginning of everything that it all derives from The Original Center of All Things?"

"Yes, absolutely."

"Do you have any doubt about the perfection of that? Any at all? Is Source perfect?"

I closed my eyes and thought back to the feeling that I'd had when Kalista had shown me the cascade of magnificent events around Creation – The Original Center of All Things. I also went back in my mind to the session where Geradl had replayed for me the imagery and feelings derived from "The Totality of our Soul," he had called it. The immeasurable – and incomprehensible – depth, breadth and absolute expanse of the All. I recollected deep inside of my essence the feeling that I got when the conceptual curtain was opened only ever so slightly.

Either event on its own would have removed even any doubt that I might have had about the perfect and essential nature of Source. The two of them together overwhelmed me with such a sense of inner peace and confidence relating to our origin, that there wasn't even a possibility of doubt in my mind. There could be no doubt in *anyone's* mind that had experienced those things that, anything and everything that derived from Source was, by definition and process, the absolute embodiment of total perfection.

"No Kalista. Not even a little. No doubt at all."

"Are all people, all Souls in Transition, derived from – spun-off parts of – The Original Center of All Things?"

"Well, not directly. You said that... "

"Are they spun-off; yes or no?" She was feigning impatience with me.

"Well, sure. We're all spun-off parts of the Source. Derived from God or whatever words that might be chosen to express that."

"So you'd have to say that, by our nature, by virtue of our very composition, our very origin, that we have to be perfect because that's what we came from?"

"I get it Kalista. I understand. Since, at our origin, we came directly from Source and Source is absolute perfection, we therefore have to be perfect. The trouble is, if I use that logic then I have no choice other than to conclude that murder is therefore perfect as well since everything came from Source."

"I'll save her the aggravation of saying it; she hadn't finished yet." Tresden was smiling, but sparingly.

"Sorry."

"As part and parcel of the original bargain, when souls became spun-off, Source imbued them with the absolute will to do as they chose. The freedom to wander. Or not to wander. The ability and trans-mobility to act as they chose. Or not to act at all. The boundless freedom – or not – to do whatever that soul wanted and decided to do. And there were very few limitations or guidelines imparted upon those souls. As original spun-off parts of the Source little condition was required in exchange for those freedoms."

Now I was getting somewhere. This was the very information that I was anxious to learn. It would serve as part of the essential definitions for my tapestry of reality that I was attempting to outline. If Source really set out some original rules that had to be followed as conditions of our existence, those would be critical for me to understand in my effort to comprehend where some of the edges were on the tapestry.

"So, you're telling me that I'm basically stuck with reconciliation and balance for now? That karma is all that we can handle while we're still in the incarnate mode of existence in terms of guidelines?"

"You're kidding right?"

"What did I say, Tresden?"

"It often takes souls in the earlier states of Transition virtually an eternity before they learn and finally master, and reach a point where they have reconciled, what you call karma. Besides, you've been given far more than that to work with."

"Like what?"

"Did we teach you anything about compassion? Empathy? Love? I mean, if it takes most souls a hundred lifetimes to learn karma it can take them a thousand to master compassion. And along that pathway, some souls are so stubborn that they end up taking on some pretty terriblelifetimes – with inordinate volumes of suffering and pain – in order to drive home the need for compassion. They often can only learn to mete out compassion after having several lives where they received little or no compassion themselves. When you look around your world and see so much suffering you would do well to consider the possibility that those are souls that believe that they can master compassion only after having put themselves through extremely tortured lifetimes like those."

"So compassion, empathy and love are also essential guidelines?"

Tresden chuckled. "You say that as though you're saying 'so corn, broccoli and spinach are also vegetables?' Of course they are, but essential elements would be more accurate. And in the overall scheme of things, those guidelines are so essential that, without them mastered, no other meaningful movement along the pathway of enhanced Resonance can occur. The shift in Resonance that comes from those lessons being actualized is stunning. Without them, it is like trying to swim across a deep river with five hundred pounds of lead around your neck. You're just too weighted down to make any meaningful forward progress."

"But we fail at those essential lessons all the time, Tresden," I said.

"We?"

"Humans. Souls in Transition from the planet I currently reside on."

"Fail? Fail how?"

"Look. Here's what I'm asking; how is it we can be told these essential things over and over, yet still fail to master them? Why, after being presented with, or reminded of, these lessons between lifetimes

– and I suppose at other times through the very lessons we are challenged with in our daily lives – can't we get our act together and master tasks like compassion and empathy? And love? And karma?"

"I've told you before, Chuck. There is no such thing as failure. Only the failure to learn. And even that is impermanent. Eventually, everyone will learn what they must. Some students learn more quickly. Others, unfortunately, learn slowly. But eventually, everyone learns. I've also told you that, the Universe has forever for us to learn all these things."

"But Kalista, there has to be a better way. Look at the suffering – the needless pain – that occurs in the meantime. In the process of not learning very efficiently, the Souls in Transition on Earth are creating mountains of bad karma for themselves. If what you said about each of us in our own way reflecting Source, well, it seems to me that God must be getting drug down in our dirt. Sullied by virtue of her children's failures and from our accumulation of bad karma. You'd think that she would want to find a better way. If for no other reason than to show us how compassionate she is by reducing the suffering."

"I already told you this also. What you see as needless suffering is a device – a unique and perfect instrument for learning. And, a device of experience as well. It is a method – no, it is *the* method – for reconciling volumes of accumulated karma and, learning the essential lessons that are prerequisites to moving on through the more advanced spiritual planes. Remember your son and the hot stove?"

"So, the chosen method of the Universe is instruction by rape. By murder? Is that supposed to be Source's idea of compassion? Of empathy? Of love?"

Tresden remained compassionate with me. "You're picking on the extreme examples don't you think? And besides, how do you know that the murder victim wasn't the victimizer the last time around? Maybe enduring the murder is that soul's chosen path to total understanding that their doing the murder the first time wasn't a very compassionate and loving thing to do?"

"O.K., fine. Would you like to discuss some of the tamer examples of our failures as souls? Child abuse, spousal abuse, torture of unimaginable sorts. Famine that is within our ability to end, but we

252

choose not to for political reasons. Disease, same thing in many cases. Female children in parts of our world being drowned by the millions at birth solely because they are female. Stupid, thoughtless excuses for humans beings that amuse themselves by torturing animals. Do you really need me to go on?"

"It feels unfair to you? You think God is being unsympathetic. Non-compassionate. Unloving in every way imaginable." Tresden sounded sympathetic to my sensitivities in this area, almost as though she had walked this ground in her past as well.

"Not just God/Source or whatever people choose to call what they regard as the One. But what about the more advanced souls? Why can't you and Tresden help the world? What about Geradl? If the more advanced souls that are not incarnated in our world right now know about what is going on in our world why have they chosen not to do anything to help us? How advanced can they really be? How well could they have learned *their* lessons in compassion?"

"Chuck, do you really believe all that? Having met Geradl, do you really think that he is even vaguely capable of being dis-compassionate? Do Kalista and I seem the insensitive sort to you?"

Of course, Tresden was right. It was simply impossible to be in Geradl's, Kalista's or Tresden's presence without being consumed by the feeling of total peace and compassion that seemed to emanate everywhere around them. Still, the facts seemed to speak for themselves and, I felt as though I was entitled to some answers.

"Obviously not. But, the fact remains, our world – which according to you, is still part of the All – is in trouble. And it's getting worse all the time. It's not just murder, rape, and torture either. Most people just don't care anymore. Apathy has taken charge of the world. The only time when apathy isn't in the lead seems to be when selfishness has taken over. The average person in the street is out for what they can get and the world be damned, if they get in the way. Or if they do care, they stop short of actually doing anything about it. If we're supposed to be learning about the universal guidelines of reconciliation and balance, compassion, empathy and love, on the whole, we're not doing well. Not at all. It seems like half the world functions on vendettas; Northern Ireland, the Balkans, the Middle East. They bomb and then bomb in return as though that was the pathway to enlightenment. And some actually have come to believe that destruction of other souls is the pathway back to God. Strap a bomb to your back, kill a dozen people and go straight to heaven.

Heck Tresden, most of Europe can't stand the rest of Europe. And it's been that way for a couple thousand years now. Why doesn't God intervene? Or does all this compassion, karma and other stuff only work after you advance to a certain point? Do you really believe that, the way things are going now that it will somehow magically transform into a world where compassion is the main intent in people's hearts?"

Kalista had a look of great patience and understanding in her eyes. "What makes you think that some didn't try? Maybe what happened is that by virtue of some of the advanced souls' attempts to *try* to help the Souls in Transition on Earth move along the pathway toward enlightenment, that things actually ended up worse off. Not by design mind you. But because many of the souls on earth couldn't take in the message in a way that would work for them. Maybe they just weren't ready."

There was a deeper sadness in Kalista's words than I'd ever remembered hearing from her. Without her even saying it, I knew that what she was telling me had nothing to do with some non-specific intellectual theory or concept. There was a story here – a real one. Determined to find out the details of what she was inferring, I pressed on.

"Kalista, are you telling me that advanced souls have already tried to help us?"

"Of course they did."

"When? I mean, what are you talking about? How did this happen? What happened?"

"Slow down, Chuck. Everything you said was exactly what some of the advanced souls have observed for some time now. And these observations go back thousands of years. You have to remember though, we don't all sit around a spiritual television here and watch CNN. Souls in Transition are at broadly different levels of Resonance. Our awareness of what is going on here and there throughout the entire All at every single moment is not as universal as you probably think it is. Besides, as Tresden has told you and Geradl showed you, the All is a pretty vast thing. It would be ridiculous for you to think that yours are the only problems in the universe."

"But obviously, there **was** a level of awareness by some. The suffering. The absolute failure to conduct our pathways along a compassionate route. The progressively deeper and deeper levels of incredibly negative acts we commit against each other. The cycles of violence and hatred that are fast becoming the cornerstone of our existence. They had to have had an awareness of all that."

"There was. By some very advanced souls, yes."

"And they consciously chose to do **nothing?**"I was angry.

"At first, they chose to rely upon the essential guidelines that were imparted by Source. To the extent that they thought about it, which is approaching a contradiction in concept for advanced states of awareness, they concluded that those Souls in Transition would take longer to relearn reconciliation and balance, compassion, empathy and love before they resumed their pathway homeward.

They also saw that, since that form of awareness, what you call 'life,' is extremely transient, that no real damage would be done to the soul by virtue of those behaviors. No permanent damage that is."

"Something convinced them otherwise?"

"I don't think 'convinced' is the right word or even concept. What occurred is that some of these very advanced souls made an individual decision that it might be possible to help those souls on Earth by reminding them about the basic conditions of reality – to share with them the basic guidelines that Source had set forth as conditions of existence. And, to remind those earthbound souls of their essential nature."

"But I thought you said one of the basic 'laws' of the universe is that no soul can interfere or interrupt the pathway of another soul."

"That's true. But these advanced souls did nothing more than remind everyone what they already knew. Doing so in no way would be construed as interference in a soul's pathway." Kalista had an urgency to her explanation now.

Had someone handed me a mirror at that point in our exchange, I'm quite certain that my mouth would have been completely agape.

255

My assumption had been all along that, either because we weren't important enough or possibly, because we had failed so badly in our core mission as souls that God had decided to leave us alone. If we came around and straightened out, that would be great. If we didn't, then there would have been no time wasted on a corner of Creation that obviously wasn't worth paying attention to based upon how its citizens treated each other. Clearly, Kalista was sharing a version of events far different from what I had assumed.

"What happened then?"

"I think you're getting the wrong impression to some degree, Chuck. It wasn't as though nine advanced souls sat around a table in some alternate dimension, pointed to Earth and agreed how messed up it was. These were individual, advanced souls who, on their own, saw what was going on at various times in your history and effected their individual volition to assume an incarnation there in order to make some attempt at helping."

"Would I know of any of them? Anyone that world history took note of?"

"Well, how about Zarathustra, Gautama Siddhartha (Buddha), Jesus the Christ, Muhammad, Nanak, Lao Tzu, Moses. There are others. Should I continue?"

Of course, I knew many of the names and histories that Kalista was talking about. Some, I'd never even heard of. I tried to make a mental note that I wanted to remember those names so that, when I returned home, I could investigate them and learn who they were; what they supposedly said; where they fit into the historical scheme of things.

Beyond that, I was flabbergasted. Shocked. Of the people she had named that I was familiar with, there was little doubt at all that they were great visionaries. When you set aside the most likely scenario that, since it was human beings that had been responsible for passing down the stories of the lives of those individuals from generation to generation – in essence attempting to detail what they had said – the likelihood was that the great souls that Kalista was mentioning probably all had shared pretty much the same information and message with the world. The words might have been different. The context might have varied over the course of time. But I was willing to bet, not only because Kalista said it was true, but also due to my marginal understanding of the religions of the world and human history, that when distilled down, the underlying message that these advanced souls shared with the world was virtually universal when they first gave it. Consistent in every detail with everything that Geradl, Kalista and Tresden had been teaching me. Reminding me that I already knew since my very first visit.

I was just about to launch into an appeal for a much deeper understanding of all this when I felt my energy start to fade. It felt as though my very essence ran on electricity and that someone was starting to pull my electrical socket out of the wall. I felt a deep desperation to know the details relating to all of this; what happened to the message that the advanced souls came to Earth with? Where was Source in all of this? Before I could say another word, Kalista spoke up.

"Golly Tresden, he's looking a bit pale around the gills, don't you think?" She was mocking me.

"What do you figure it is?" Tresden was smiling broadly.

"I, well, I... " I had never been prone to stuttering but clearly, the insight that Kalista had surprised me with had completely overwhelmed me.

"It sounds like a severe case of over-enlightenment along with a slight touch of historical shock to me." Tresden was trying to suppress a giggling spree.

"What are we doing for that these days?"

Kalista smiled at me warmly, as did Tresden. In unison, they raised their left hands and began to gently wave goodbye to me as the garden rapidly began to fade into nothingness. I floated aimlessly in the void for some period of time. Overwhelmed by the shock that we'd been told all of this before and failed to benefit from the insight.

The common thread of literally all the world's major religions wove its way through these advanced souls. Could it have been more obvious?

This was the first time that I had departed the garden and not traversed the distance back to my study immediately. Looking back, I believe that Kalista "saw" the stunning impact that this information had on me and, in some way, held me in some in-between space while I became acclimated to what she and Tresden had shared with me.

After some indeterminate period of time had passed, I found my normal state of consciousness and noted the fuzzy edges of my study beginning to take form. Exhausted and almost unable to stand, I grabbed the notepad from my desk and began to scribble feverishly. More than anything, I urgently needed to understand precisely how messages of love, compassion, empathy and the irrefutable truth of karma could have resulted in outcomes such as the Crusades, racial, geographical, religious and spiritual intolerance and murder. Wars. Vendettas that carried on from generation to generation. Catholics and Protestants, Muslims and Jews at each other's throats. Not for a day or a week but virtually since the beginning of recorded time. People being tortured and murdered because they chose one particular way of believing in the core message over another. Thinking one messenger somehow superior, or different, than the other. Unimaginable. Unthinkable.

How could the essential spiritual messages carried to us through the efforts of these advanced souls – Jesus, Buddha, Mohammed and the others — get twisted from the simple beauty and perfection that they articulated so peacefully instead into anger, violence and vindictiveness? If none less than Jesus the Christ and Buddha had carried these messages to us and we so obviously failed to embrace those insights, where could we be going from here? What future pathway could there be for us if the remaining advanced souls, seeing how the messages of compassion and love had been so brutally distorted, simply chose to learn from history and simply leave us on our own? What hope could we grasp onto that would ultimately get us back on the course that might some day bring us home? Or, at a minimum, moving in the direction of home.

I spent an entire day pondering the irrefutable reality that Mohamed, Buddha, Jesus and so many others had come into our world to share the reality and essential messages of compassion and empathy. And love. Clearly, something had gone awry. And not now and then but in every case where these advanced souls came to share their knowledge with us. I was desperate to find out how, and why, this happened.

Unfortunately, my energy level was not great enough to make a return journey to explore this in the near term. I was far too depleted mentally, physically and emotionally. It was a kind of spiritual shock that I was experiencing, the same shock that Kalista had protected me from by holding me in some kind of mystical abeyance before allowing me to regain my normal state of consciousness the previous day.

When I was finally able to muster the energy needed to make the next journey to Kalista's garden two days later, I learned that my nightmares were not completely ill-founded. That without some kind of dramatic change to deter us from the course we were on, our future was likely to become far gloomier than it was now. Back in 1994, I found it difficult to believe that the world could possibly grow more violent. That hatred could increase; that greed could become more prevalent than it was; that neighbors could turn even more against their neighbors. Time would, sadly, prove me wrong.

I also learned during that follow-up visit to the garden that, despite all that we were enduring, irrespective of the underlying tone of pervasive non-compassion in the world – that there was hope. And, there was a plan. Of sorts. A pathway out of the incredible course deviation that we had all taken when we chose to hear the messages from these advanced souls but not to heed them. A way for everyone to make it "home," as Kalista called it. But it wasn't going to be easy. This time, it wasn't going to be just one person carrying the message.

As I took some time to heal my depleted state, I spent most of it wondering if we would listen this time?

CHAPTER TEN

Do not think of today's failures, but of the
success that may come tomorrow.
You have set yourselves a difficult task,
but you will succeed if you persevere;
and you will find a joy in overcoming obstacles.
Remember, no effort that we make
to attain something beautiful
is ever lost.

- Helen Keller

By summer 1994, almost a full year after I had stumbled upon the method to traverse the mysterious expanse that led to Kalista's garden, my life encountered a series of dramatic and exciting challenges. Tresden had taught me early on in my apprenticeship that, anything that is happening in one's life at any given time was either caused directly by us as a desired short-term outcome or, because of something that we had planned and agreed to long ago. In either case, according to what Tresden had told me, whatever was going on in my life I had to accept. I had either made it happen directly – as in orchestrated it unconsciously fairly recently – or, needed it to happen as part of my overall life plan. No matter what interpretation was chosen, any events that occurred could only be viewed as learning tools for me.

In this case, the lessons were harsh. Over the course of a few months, I had managed to skillfully orchestrate my early departure from a prestigious, secure, well-paying corporate job and to start the process of divorce. As if that wasn't enough, I managed to develop another fairly challenging health issue. Not the kind you can just pop a pill or two to solve, either.

Had all of these events occurred prior to the time when I had begun my visits to the garden, before I had the opportunity to benefit from the insights Kalista, Tresden and Geradl shared with me, I would have been in a deep state of panic. But with what most people would have considered their basic world collapsing around them, I found myself strangely and completely at peace. There were days when things seemed bleak; when I wondered aloud why I had chosen to take on so many challenges at the same time.

Looking back, I am able to see that the insight that afforded me the deepest grounding – and allowed me to traverse the pathway paved with great difficulty with complete serenity – was that we cause or agree to take on all the events that are occurring in our own lives. The only real issue left to resolve once this premise is accepted is why. Because, within why lies the answer to the purpose of the lessons that we have chosen to set up for our own higher educational theatre. All I needed to sort out was, what lessons did I intend to benefit from when I arranged for these near simultaneous life disasters to occur?

As Kalista had promised, once I became aware of the lesson as opposed to perceiving myself as a helpless victim swirling through some unseen tornado in life, the likelihood was that I would simply deal with the lessons and move on. As I went about my business and coped with the challenges inherent in those lessons, it became a much less frightening prospect. From there, all I needed to do was to ask myself why I chose to have all the walls that defined my security collapse around me at the same time.

Less than a year later, I had my answers. Having accepted that all occurrences in my life were simply lessons, it was only a matter of time until most everything began to turn to my favor. It wasn't just perception; things changed for me at a stunning rate. I met the woman I was meant to be with all along. I found myself earning far more money with much less aggravation than my previous job. And not insignificantly, had proven to myself that I had the fortitude and the strength to take on any medical challenge that might arise. This turned out to be a fortunate lesson as I would find out in the not too distant future, several times over.

Looking back, what enthused me the most was my state of confidence that everything would work out over time. Knowing that you are on the right path, even when that trail has many obstacles along it, provides a tremendous boost in confidence. No matter how complicated the crisis of the moment seemed, because of the lessons Tresden and Kalista had taught me, I had a calm, confident and peaceful knowing that these issues would ultimately end up as mere background challenges in my life. Fences to be jumped over. They were difficult lessons, but, once seen in that light, any questions that I might have had about how to proceed vanished into the wind.

My lighthouse in daily life became compassion. My primary touchstone was empathy. I dealt with everyone and everything – or did my best to – with fairness in mind and a deep understanding in my heart that we are all derived from the same Source. Once that is accepted genuinely, offending or harming another soul becomes unthinkable. I learned that if I held all of those touchstones in my heart, everything just seemed to take care of itself. I even managed to treat the lawyers I encountered even-handedly. Of course, it required a concerted effort on my part. Some people, I often mused in dealing with them, even God must have to work to love.

I considered this new-found psychological sure-footing to be a direct byproduct of the daily practices I had been employing designed to help me understand and improve my outcomes in reconciliation and balance; what I began to refer to as my "karma highway." Tresden had nearly exhausted herself instructing me in this area. Not just in the concept of it, but more importantly, she often patiently coached me in challenges that I came across in my day-to-day life. When she got near the point of frustration she resorted to her very advanced sense of humor in order to create illustrations for me. Her doing so kept things from becoming too serious and too somber, which was often just what I needed.

Having taken full measure of Tresden's guidance, I learned that, had I responded to my dilemmas with overt anger, resentment or hostility, things would have gone badly against me. Probably resulting in my having to repeat the same lesson, at least once, at some future time in my life. "Inevitability is inevitable," Tresden would tell me.

She went on with great care to explain to me the nuances of "immediate reconciliation" and "ultimate reconciliation." When I asked her to explain the difference, with a wry smile and a completely straight face she said that, "immediate reconciliation is when you speed past a cop and get pulled over a quarter of a kilometer down the road. Ultimate reconciliation is when it takes him seven kilometers to catch up to you. Either way, the ticket is yours."

Tresden also used her razor sharp sense of humor to illustrate the point for me that sooner or later, you have to deal head on with what you create. That assumed, any sensible person would attempt to create only positive things knowing that would dictate a like future for them. What amazed me was that after having the truth of this essential lesson driven home time and time again, so many people continue to repeat their negative patterns and behaviors over again with the same unfavorable outcomes. How could they not see that, the outcomes that were created were directly linked to their previous actions and behaviors? Yet they repeat those behaviors – often while they are complaining about the previous outcome. It would be comical were it not so painful to watch.

Years later, Tresden would explain to me that once we advance to a certain level it was possible to deal with certain negative karma that we created for ourselves in other ways. Ways other than coming back in another lifetime and having to endure what we gave out. She emphasized the word "possible" strongly; her way of telling me not to get my hopes up for an easy solution to a few of the unresolved issues in my past.

Even at the peak of the storm that was my daily life, my primary focus remained an intense interest in deepening and significantly expanding my spiritual knowledge. The events in my daily life, although deafening on some occasions, had sometime ago become not much more than background noise to me. Distractions. I heard it but, not really at a conscious level. What I really cared about was understanding everything I could possibly absorb about Resonance, The

Totality of our Souls, my tapestry, the pathway back home and, my most recent frustration, trying to comprehend why the more advanced souls in the Universe hadn't been able to help peace and civility prevail in our world.

In the mid-summer months of 1994, I set out to learn once and for all the details about our past as humankind. Kalista had only scratched the surface on my last visit. She had told me about several advanced souls coming to our world over a great period of time in an effort to reacquaint those that assume their incarnations here with the concepts of compassion, empathy and love. And of the truth of reconciliation and balance. Kalista called reconciliation "Source's radar gun." There to make certain that no one flies through any Resonance pathways without having balanced out their inner essences. I was constantly amazed at some of the analogies the two of them came up with, particularly considering that Kalista had told me that her last incarnation on earth was in the 1800s, just a *bit* before we even thought of radar guns.

How had the souls living on earth then taken the message delivered by these advanced souls and twisted it so completely? In the perspective of history, after Jesus the Christ delivered his message it took less than a few hundred years before the serious infighting began. The Council of Nicea, the various Ecumenical Councils, the Great Schism, the creation of divisions and splits that ultimately separated Protestants from Christians from Catholics. Other arguments and resentments. Anger. And yet deeper and more virulent schisms. People that had the same peaceful and loving point of origin, Jesus Christ, were rooted in the identical simple message. Now, they were at each other's throats. Literally. All within a few generations of when Christ lived. How?

It took barely a thousand years to turn the messages of loving and compassion that Jesus the Christ shared into the single most devastating carnage the world had ever seen; The Crusades. And those lasted for almost three hundred years. By some interpretations, they're still going on today. No one really knows how many were tortured, raped and killed in the name of a "holy war." Worse, it seemed that there was a near inexhaustible supply of similarly violent and incomprehensible tales throughout history. Protestants against Catholics. Muslims against Hindu. Hindus against Sheiks. Christians against Muslims. Jews against Christians. Muslims against Jews. It never seems to end. No one was truly innocent in all of this. Any objective reading of history seems to indicate that virtually all seem to be equally interpreting the original messages – no matter which soul was the original point of information – of love and tolerance into something quite different than it was obviously intended. As I read more and more about the history of these issues I was shocked to learn that even the Buddhists, those that evoke to mind the image of their adherents sitting blissfully in meditation, ended up with deep divisions. Fighting. Vicious violence. And sometimes worse.

How many millions had died so far, I wondered, in the name of love, compassion and empathy? I was struck at the time by one glaring historical fact though; Buddha, Jesus, Mohammed and the others Kalista had mentioned – all without exception – are said to have shared *only* the message. It was others, those that came later, that "organized" it. Turned it into something else. I tried closing my eyes and imagining Buddha or Jesus ordering a holy war. Telling those with whom they had shared the message of universal peace and brotherhood to ostracize those that wouldn't believe it. Or beat those that refused to repeat the message one particular way as opposed to another. No matter what scenario I tried to envision, I just couldn't see it.

Somehow though, these others had found it possible to hold in one hand what they considered to be the holy word of no less than God and in the other, a sword to cut off the head of an enemy. An enemy who, except for the minor detail of a few words here and there, would have agreed upon the same set of core beliefs almost identically as the person about to lop off their head. How was it possible that people could not see this? That all of these advanced souls were sharing the exact same message with the exception being the time it was given and particulars of how it was delivered?

As I thought back over the most recent few thousand years history of mankind, I saw a clear and heavily-littered trail. It was a course of progressively increasing religious, geographic, ethnic, cultural, racial and other intolerance and violence. A generalized ratcheting up of campaigns imparting ethnic, religious, racial and personal retributions. Cycles of inflicted offence and repayment for those offences. Or perceived offences. And it was everywhere. From the streets of Los Angeles to Africa, the entire Middle East, Europe, the Orient. China and Japan. Vietnam to the Philippines. There were no exceptions.

Clearly it wasn't all in the distant past. It wasn't as though this all happened before the dark ages and mankind had some kind of awakening to the errors of our ways. I began to wonder, as if looking into a historical rearview mirror at mankind, what future could possibly lie ahead with so much momentum along this particular pathway? I had great difficulty seeing where a shift in the road might come. On a few different occasions in the 1960s, we'd come within a day or two of blowing up the entire planet. So I wondered, what might cause man to make a change now? What catalyst might be on the horizon?

This put me in a state of mind where I began to ask myself; what would happen if a Buddha or a Mohammed or a Jesus came to Earth again in this day and age? Sharing the message of compassion and love but from the perspective and stature of a genuinely advanced soul not someone disguising the message within the hidden agendas of a TV talk show? Just send us your donation to be saved. Sadly, I concluded in less time than it takes to tie my shoes that in a world that fed upon cynicism and digested sincerity like sushi, it wouldn't take long for the media or the fanatics to crucify anyone bringing the message in this day and age. Either literally or figuratively. Probably both.

One had only to look back through history to gain perspective into this sad reality. Jesus, Mahatma Ghandi, Martin Luther King Jr. and a litany of others; anyone that attempted with sincerity to preach unity, compassion and a pathway of peace – whether advanced soul or not – is summarily put to death here. At least, over the last two thousand years or so. I tried to comfort myself with the reality that, advanced souls would see the likelihood of such an outcome before even coming here and probably, just go on to something else. Who could blame them? Our record as a species was consistent but not encouraging. It felt hopeless.

With this somewhat depressed state of mind, I set off to visit Kalista. Hoping that she would have answers. Any answers would do.

I needed to believe that, at a minimum, she would have explanations. I was hopeful that she could explain why it wasn't all as desperate as it seemed. Hopeful to some extent, I set out for the garden. As I arrived, Kalista was standing by the hanging baskets, smiling serenely and looking directly at me.

"Hi. I see you've brought your bags with you this time. Planning on staying a while?"

"Bags?"

"Oh, sorry. I should have said baggage."

"What are you talking about?"

"You're trying to carry around the weight of the entire world again, Chuck. That's baggage that simply exceeds your weight limit. If you want to get anywhere, you're going to have to learn to leave it behind and travel light."

"Uh huh. Look Kalista, this might all be a non-issue for you because you know all these answers already and have left them in your wake, but its pretty unsettling for me."

"Listen Chuck, this is important. You simply have to learn this – the history and the problems of the world aren't your responsibility. In fact, it's not really anyone's job. If you continue to try to take all of that on you're going to end up pretty unhappy and, completely distracted from dealing with the objectives and lessons that you set out to accomplish with your life."

"But Kalista, it can't be all right that all of this has happened. Is happening. If we all reflect the Source in our own way then it has to matter what happens to all of the souls that use the earth as a school. Eventually, if we keep sliding down the pipe like we are won't the sum total of all of our negativity make a difference on what Source is? What Source becomes?"

"Well, yes. You're right. It will, and does, make a difference. Source is, in reality, mostly the sum of its parts. So, when you commit an act that is not compassionate, the light of Source is diminished by that much."

"What if I commit a positive act of compassion?" I asked.

"Ah, great question. In that case, using the same analogy, the light of Source pretty much doubles by the amount of that act."

"Doubles?" I couldn't believe what she was saying.

"Absolutely! Pretty cool don't you think?"

"I was about to ask you how that could possibly be. But I know that you'll just tell me that The Original Center of All Things can do whatever she wants to. She made the rules."

"Thanks."

"Thanks?" I echoed.

"Yeah. For not making say something that obvious. You know how much I try to avoid such things."

"But why the skewed math?"

"You're a very smart guy, you tell me."

"I have no idea at all."

"Oh sure you do. Just think about it."

I tried to put myself into the shoes of Source. I smiled as I had the thought that, those shoes were just a *little* bit too big for me. As I tried to envision the rationale – assuming that Source even dealt at the level of rational thought – for creating a system of spiritual math that worked in such a disproportionate manner, I thought back to something that Kalista had said on a previous visit. Something about Source's "motivation" for Creation possibly being that she, Source, wanted to see if she could improve things beyond herself. That led me to a brief flash of an idea. Without even trying out my thoughts to the next logical steps I simply blurted out what I was thinking.

"Maybe it's so that Source has a better chance of having Creation end up turning into something even greater than Source itself! Maybe the offset math is a way to compensate for the fact that Source knew that it would be difficult for some portion of the spun-off parts to catch on at the beginning. That there would be remedial little corners of the Universe like Earth where we miraculously take the messages of love from the masters and turn them into wars instead of peace. A kind of spiritual dyslexia zone. Maybe this is just a way for Source to show us how vast her compassion actually is."

"I see. Hmm... so, I forgot, what was your question again?"

Kalista's eyes were gleaming. It was that mischievous kind of brilliance that made her eyes impossible to look at directly. But, after all this time I knew that this was also a kind of acknowledgement. It was about as close as Kalista came to expressing admiration. Her way to acknowledge that as a student, I hadn't disappointed her on this issue. She was a serious teacher as well as a compassionate one and would never allow me to bask for too long a period in her mysterious accolades. As I thought more about it though, I still had concerns that the pathway that humankind had taken was full of so many negative highlights that, even with the skewed math we might still be in trouble.

"Uh huh. O.K. But still, you'd have to admit that, on balance, and over the course of human history we've contributed a lot more negative acts than positive ones."

"And?"

"And nothing. I mean, are we close to blowing out the fuse?"

A knowing smile rose justbarely at the corner of her eyes, "Fuse? What fuse?"

"What I meant was, at some point, don't all of our cumulative negative acts – our failure to embrace the core message of compassion, empathy, love, karma – doesn't all that diminish the light of Source to some measurable degree?"

Kalista's smile broadened. "Like blowing out her fuse?" She was at the edge of one of her giggling fits. It was palpable.

From my perspective, I found my concern for Source and our collective disregard for the message that had been shared with us over and over again to be considerate. Even noble. Maybe the fuse analogy wasn't the greatest. But Kalista understood my point. Even if I hadn't said anything, she knew what I was thinking. What I meant by it. Why was she being so difficult?

"You know exactly what I mean Kalista."

"Yes, of course I do. Is it possible that you assumed things in forming your question that might be a little off the mark? Just a little presumptive?"

"Like what?"

"How many planets in your solar system?"

"What? How many... well, I guess nine... I think; there's been some debate about all of that lately. But nine I'm pretty sure. Why?"

"How many solar systems in all of the universes you can see from Earth?"

"Kalista, How would I know? A lot I guess."

"Thousands? Millions? Billions? More than billions?"

"More than billions I suppose. No, check that; probably more than billions."

"Probably. I haven't counted them either. How many do you figure there are that you can't see from that distant little corner of the your universe that you call home?"

"Uh oh. I hear a another trap door closing."

"Trillions? Granatillions? More than gazillions?"

"Well, I guess. I imagine that many at least."

"And Chuck, you saw for yourself that, the All makes all of just **that** look like a grain of sand on the biggest beach you can imagine."

"So you're saying that there are souls at other places."

"Other places. Other Universes. Other souls in different states of reality, other dimensions. Universes and realities that you and I haven't even begun to contemplate."

"And they're all part of Source – of the All?"

"You know that everything is."

"So, as long as they're doing better than we are – I mean better than we are as humankind in terms of making positive contributions – there's really nothing much to worry about? At least as far as Source being at risk is concerned?"

Kalista frowned. "Since you really don't know, can't know how they might be doing in terms of mastering their particular lessons, are you certain that you want to depend on them carrying the load for you? What if they did the same thing and depended upon the souls that incarnate on Earth to carry the weight for them? Besides, they most likely are working on completely different missions than we are in this part of Reality. What if the spiritual math that applied there was different?"

"Hmm, good point. So, is there some overall grand plan of sorts? Some objective that the Source has in mind?" I asked.

"Other than the one you already know about, other than to improve Creation, to improve Source itself?"

"Yes."

"How would I know?"

271

"Do you think Geradl knows?"

"Why don't you ask him next time you see him. I'll bet he'd get a real kick out of the notion that you think that he would know what Source was thinking."

"You're not helping Kalista."

"I am not willing to just make something up. I simply don't know."

"Guess."

"No. You guess." She folded her arms and smiled back at me.

"C'mon, you must have pondered this. What did you think when you thought about this?"

"I figured that Source must have been willing to allow whatever happened to just happen. But I also think that Source must have held enough of whatever makes Source pure unadulterated Source in reserve. That way if we all, meaning, the various spun-off parts of Source, didn't turn into more positive energy, that Source couldn't be drug down by all of us. But that is no more than wild speculation. You'd be surprised how often my guesses are not right."

In thinking through what Kalista had just said it all seemed to make sense to me. I had to constantly stop myself from trying to take our very simplistic equivalent of "thought" and impart that onto how the Original Center of All Things probably works. How ridiculous it was for me to even think of such things. That brief moment resulted in a small epiphany for me, I had the realization that Source probably doesn't even think at all. Doesn't need to. Not the way that we perceive thinking anyhow. Whatever processes Source uses to do whatever she wants I concluded, it must be so far ahead of what we can even imagine as to render what we do in that area equivalent to what an ant does in terms of intellect when compared to Einstein. And that example was probably an understatement as well. Vastly.

I didn't want to get too bogged down in this subject because I was worried that the specific topic I'd come to explore on this particular day might get left unanswered completely. I was just about to suggest to Kalista that I take some time to ponder what we had just discussed and move on to the next topic when she began communicating.

"Well, maybe you should think about all of that for a while. It is a very complicated prospect to contemplate. Maybe we should move on to what you came here for today."

"Show off! When are you going to teach me how to do that?"

She smiled, "I was just trying to move things along. Keep you on your silly schedule, as if there were one. I keep telling you, the Universe has an eternity. And, you're already learning how to perceive. You just don't recognize it because it is a very subtle skill at first."

"O.K., well, the last time I visited you and Tresden, you told me about all of these advanced souls that took an incarnation on earth to share the essential messages with us. But you didn't tell me why they all failed so miserably."

"Did they?"

"Did they what?"

"Fail?" She clearly gave the impression of being genuinely confused by my characterization.

This wasn't at all the way I thought Kalista might respond to this question. It took me by surprise. Instead of having her give me whatever answer was coming next, I took a few minutes to try to think through on my own what answer she might use to explain these events. A few of the ideas that passed through my mind in this regard seemed to have some merit at first but, upon closer examination, failed both the common-sense test as well as any objective recollection I had of history. After exhausting the possibilities that came to my mind, I decided to explore the issue directly with Kalista.

"I don't understand."

"Well, you said they failed. Did they really?"

"Oh. I see; it's that simple. It wasn't they that failed but those that twisted what they said made it seem like they failed."

"Pretty close. I don't believe it was as much twisting what they said as much as what certain people decided to do with what they said later on. Besides that of course, are the inevitable distortions that were imparted on the messages by people as they passed the essence of messages along over time. Still, I would maintain that, they did not fail."

"How can you say that Kalista?"

"Let's say that your objective is to grow a giant Redwood tree. You know that, if nurtured and all goes as planned that it can ultimately grow to be two hundred feet tall. Maybe more if it exceeds even your original aspirations. But you have to start somewhere. So, you patiently nurture a seedling along in your own back yard until it is mature enough to be planted in the environment in which it must grow to maturity. With absolute love and the greatest of care you make the trip into the woods – the location you intend to plant it in – pick the most opportune spot that you can think of and with the greatest of care, plant the seedling. Being the conscientious gardener soul that you are, you hang around for a while looking in on and further nurturing the magnificent seedling that you have planted. But one way or another, because of the axiomatic realities of the environment that you chose to plant the seedling, you end up dying first. And when you die the tree that you had such great aspirations for has only grown a little, to barely six feet tall. Barely a fraction of what you know the seedling can become. A small group of other souls that shared your dream of growing this tree into all that it could become, take up your well-intended mission. Maybe they don't all share your brilliant nurturing skills or methods. Maybe some do. Possibly the tree doesn't grow as fast or as quickly or even the same way as it would if you had been able to stay there for a few hundred years to help it grow. But it grows nonetheless. Probably not as you had intended. Maybe not exactly as you had hoped. But, you tell me, did you 'fail' in what you set out to do just because you weren't there when the tree finally made it to be two hundred feet tall?"

I was about to launch into a broad protest in an attempt to urge Kalista to explain some of the more subtle nuances of her analogy that were not immediately transparent to me. By the time I thought of the things I wanted to take issue with, all of the finer points that had been unclear to me simply evaporated into thin air. Kalista had, in a hundred words or so, managed to explain the initial missions of Buddha, Mohammed, Jesus the Christ and the other advanced souls – as well as the actions of all of their early apostles – and what went wrong from the outset as though she was reading a weather forecast. I made a mental note to never challenge her again in the analogy area.

"So, you're saying that, ultimately, the trees will grow into what they were meant to even though mankind has taken things fairly well off course for now."

"No. What I'm saying is that, once planted, by their very nature, these trees are hearty. I won't say that it is impossible to kill them, but, they can withstand an awful lot of abuse. The underlying tree is that strong. Once rooted firmly, it would take an inordinate amount of abuse to topple something that mighty. The message – the essence found within the seed – is resilient."

"So, the message – the original messages from the advanced souls like Buddha – survive even though people have twisted them over thousands of years. Distorted them so that in the most severe case, they are virtually unrecognizable from the original form. Even though the messages have been exploited and used to accomplish incredibly vicious, vindictive, selfish and even violent things?"

"If we go back to the tree analogy for a moment; if some people are acting in a discompassionate, unloving manner and they decide to use that tree to toss a rope with a noose over a branch and hang someone, is the tree itself in any way part of what you would call the 'evil' act?"

"Of course not. But it gives other similarly-minded people the idea to use the tree for similarly evil acts – things completely opposite the original purpose," I said.

"Maybe. But the tree is still the pristine tree it always was. Just because someone might choose to use, or even purposely abuse it for purposes other than what it was originally intended, that in no way changes, detracts or sullies the perfection and beauty of the Redwood. The original message remains perfect therefore, no matter what color paint some might try to gloss over it, or ropes that might be used to conduct hangings on it, the tree remains a perfect tree. The only issues still in doubt are; how many people are able to see the perfection within the tree, what it can still become if nurtured and, do souls still see the opportunities for learning in spite of the fact the tree might have undergone some abuse and misuse over its early development?"

Everything that Kalista was saying was true. Brilliant, in fact. At least as far as my intellect could take in at the time. The fact remained, it still seemed to me that religion had, and continued to so terribly distort the original messages from the advanced souls, and so often, to genuinely terrible outcomes, that it seemed very difficult to believe that the underlying message could ever be restored. Reclaimed in its original perfect and unadulterated form. To be used as Mohammed, Jesus, Buddha and the others probably hoped that it would. To foster universal compassion. Love, Empathy. Peace.

As nervous as this made me, I needed to pursue this further with Kalista to learn what she knew about what choices mankind had going forward to restore and reclaim the original message. Had the messages been twisted and abused so badly as to render them useless at this point? Were we destined to ultimately fail despite having been given the very insight that we required in order to move beyond this simple and often unhappy plane of existence? This arcane and primitive school. Where suffering is virtually guaranteed. It was only a matter of how much suffering one took on in any given lifetime. Not *if* they would suffer. Almost desperate to know our future – or what Kalista knew of it – I pressed on.

"But the tree has been pretty abused at this point Kalista. I mean, the people left in charge of – or should I say, that took control of – nurturing that tree haven't done a wonderful job of nurturing the original vision, the message, that those advanced souls that originally planted it seem to have intended."

"Them."

"Them?"

"Well, you made it sound like there was only one tree. I think the Redwoods are actually a fairly substantial forest."

"Forest? Oh sure. A whole forest. What was I thinking? But still, are you saying that... "

"It's true that some of the trees have been mistreated. Some have even had entire limbs loped off. As though those limbs were not even parts of what the tree was intended really to be. Others, despite the abuse and failure to nurture have somehow managed to survive and grow. They've grown somewhat differently than the original vision but, since everything in the Universe changes, some amount of adaptation is not a problem. In fact, you could say it's necessary. If the adaptation is consistent with what nature intended for the tree in the first place. Nevertheless, it's still a Redwood underneath all of the clothes, flags and other things people have hung from the branches over time. But, you have to look past all of the decorations and debris that in some cases has partially obscured some of the trees."

"So, some parts of the tree, if they're still intact might be enough for the message to survive?"

"You're doing it again. You told me to tell you when you're doing it and, you are."

"Doing what?"

"How many trees in the Redwoods? How many different Redwood forests?"

"Oh. So, are you saying that, between all of the trees there are that one way or another the message is still pretty much intact. I mean, the original message."

"If you take the time to look at the whole forest and, disregard certain damage that has been done to some of the trees over the course of time."

"But how do you know? How do you know what to keep and what to disregard?"

"Any tree that looks like it is about compassion, empathy and peace warrants your attention. One that obviously gives you the immediate impression of the immensity of the All. Any one that conveys the unconditional love of Source. One that, upon looking at it, through following the perfection of its branch structure makes it completely clear to you that – no matter how circuitous a pathway it illustrates – that all things derive from one Source. And finally, any that convey, by their very structure, balance. Perfect, absolute, awe inspiring balance of and in all things."

"That's magnificent Kalista. So that would be how to tell if a certain religion has kept the original lesson pretty much as it was?"

"Religion? I was talking about trees," she smiled, her eyes lit like two gigantic searchlights with amusement.

"WHAT?"

"You know this already, Chuck. Source did not invent religion. Man did. Source has no need for religion and has no need for souls to practice religion unless doing so helps them in their learning. Rites. Practices. Chants and services are all devices invented by man to instruct others as to the specifics of their perception of the ***only*** way home. And Tresden, Geradl and I have told you many times, there is no such thing as limiting the pathway that leads home. In the final determination you need only to contemplate and experience the various lessons offered through the spun-off parts of Source itself to garner joy, bliss, happiness, love and the perfection of Creation.

You are clearly free to do this in your own way, subject to your own developed individuality. Dependant upon how and when you choose to experience the Universe and its lessons. To select and carve out your own, unique and individualized pathway. To ride the trails that you choose on your own. And having done that, you need only to focus on the parts of the message that will return you home. To The Original Center of All Things. And in so doing, further your mission to contribute openly and freely ***your*** experiences, your learning, the love you gave, the love you felt, the compassion you afforded, the empathy that you granted to others and, to Source. To add your increment to the sum of the All. To fulfill every soul's primary mission; to enhance The Original Center of All Things in every way imaginable – to whatever extent they can, in any way possible."

"Wow Kalista. I never... I guess I never thought that I could or would, that every individual single soul would, have the responsibility for making their own individual contribution to Source. But are you saying that there is anything wrong with religion?"

"Obviously there is and just as obviously, there isn't. Any device that helps raise the awareness in people that, without practicing compassion and empathy that they can not possibly move onward in the Universe is a very positive endeavor. That part of religion is O.K. But as you know, some religions have gone well past that – have been used and are used by others – to exploit the purpose and created a purpose of their own. Purposes that have nothing whatever to do with the original messages or, helping to articulate the highest mission of every spun-off part of Source.

"What do you mean?"

"Some have turned the message of mission into a need to worship the messenges themselves. Did Jesus the Christ, Buddha, Mohammed – any of them – or any that proceeded or followed them, did they ever say "you have to worship me and only me in order to be saved? To move onward as a soul. To fulfill your mission to Source?"

"I don't think so."

"I don't either. What they said was; "listen, love your fellow man, don't hurt anything or anyone. Be compassionate. Help others. I very much doubt any of them said, *do all of that and, bring me all your gold and build statues of me everywhere to worship. And by the way, anyone that tells you that they have 'the' message is lying. Make sure you kill them or ostracize them. I, and only I, am the messenger for the Universe. All others are false.* If any worship was to be done I suspect those advanced souls would have wanted it to be limited to the ideas, beauty and ideals contained within the message."

I thought just then of something that had occurred just the weekend before I'd made this particular visit. In driving down one of the local streets on Sunday morning, I went past a church just as it was letting out. A car driven by a middle-aged man with his family was just beginning to pull out of the parking lot when an elderly woman drove by in front of them and cut off their exit. In actuality, the older woman was completely in the right. What shocked me was the obscene gesture that the man made at the elderly woman and the man's wife rolling down her window and letting out a barrage of profanity that would have embarrassed an army sergeant. So much for turning the other cheek, respecting your elders and showing compassion to all those that you come across in life.

As I drove off, I wondered aloud what the sermon might have been about on that particular day. I was doubtful that it suggested road rage as a pathway to heaven. I wondered what impression the two children in the back seat of the car might come away with after watching their parents' tirade on the way home from church, of all places.

The explanations and the analogy about trees that Kalista had shared with me covered the first part of the main question I had. What remained unanswered was where do we – as humankind, those incarnating on Earth – go now? What future lay ahead for us with this violent, angry, murderous history as our past? Had we done irreparable damage to far too many trees in the forest at this juncture in time? Even with all of the various versions of the original messages still contained within the abundant volumes of trees, might it just be that the messages were no longer viable as the basis for our enlightenment? Had greed and ego applied without restraint effected terminal damage to the forest, thus limiting our ability through the remnant religions of the world to afford us the basis of a pathway home? Hoping that I might discover if there were answers to these questions I pressed onward with Kalista.

"Kalista, it sounds to me like we've wandered an awful long way off course. Worse than that, if feels to me like we drift further and further away from embracing those essential concepts every single day the way the world is going."

"We?"

"I was speaking collectively. Giving my impression of the world on the whole."

"Well, that's a difficult question. Let's take a walk and talk about it." Before I could say another word, Kalista stood-up and took off at a brisk pace across the bridge. Without giving it a thought, I followed after her. I managed to catch up to her just as she reached the far side of the bridge. The only other time I had ever crossed this bridge was when Kalista and Tresden had taken me to the River of Knowledge several months ago. I assumed that this was where she was taking me today. But as Kalista reached the far end of the bridge she turned sharply to the left – the exact opposite way we had proceeded the day we traveled to the River of Knowledge. This surprised me and, at the same time, raised my curiosity to a level approaching concerned nervousness.

"I take it we're not going to the River of Knowledge?"

"No."

"No? Just no? That's all you're going to say?"

"We are going to another place of learning. A far different kind of learning. A much different kind of place."

"What do you mean? Will Tresden be there?"

"If I had tried to describe the River of Knowledge to you before we arrived there, would you ever have understood?"

"No. I guess not," I said, nervously.

"Don't worry. Tresden will meet us there to hold your hand in case you get too excited," she smiled.

In spite of the teasing way in which Kalista had made this last remark, it made me aware of something that I had not fully realized yet. Tresden had the effect, whenever I was in her presence, of offsetting any nervousness or discomfort I had because of whatever experience I was enduring at Kalista's garden or, what Tresden playfully called "the surrounding vicinity." Some time after this when I mentioned this to them, they showed their sly smiles. When I asked them if the effect Tresden had on me when compared to the nervousness that Kalista often instilled was their equivalent of good cop/bad cop roles, they laughed so hard that had they been in human form, I suspected they might have done damage to themselves. As usual, they provided no insight beyond that on the subject, leaving another mystery fully intact.

"Is it... I mean, is it far?"

As I let this question slip from my mind outward in open communication, I immediately wished that I could take it back. After almost a full year to think about just where I was while visiting Kalista's garden I had concluded that everything I perceived was simply another form of advanced imagery – much like the imagery Geradl played for me demonstrating the unfolding of Creation – that was somehow manufactured by Kalista. Just how she managed to insert me, Tresden and on rare occasions Geradl into the imagery I had no idea. This was the notion I had decided upon because my rational mind could not create any other viable explanation.

When I had confronted Kalista and Tresden for the third time on this subject just recently, they would only say that the garden and the vicinity around it, was a "collaborative effort in which everyone in the garden at the time participated in creating and maintaining." When I pressed them further and asked about the "walks" we all took and what was actually happening to me when I perceived things such as movement within that arena, they said that my belief that everything I was experiencing was solely perceptional was ill-founded."

Frustrated by this, and looking for a logical answer that I could wrap my arms around, I asked them what someone would see if they walked into my study while I was in this deep meditative state.

Without hesitation, Kalista answered "not much" and applied every effort she could muster at the time to not bursting out in one of her giggling fits. Because I had never attained any real satisfaction on this topic, I chose to adopt my initial assumption that this was all some sort of advanced perceptional state and left it at that. By no means was I satisfied with this assumption. Nor did I intend to leave it unresolved indefinitely. My intention was to continue pressing Kalista and Tresden until I had a deeper understanding on this topic. But not now.

Kalista suppressed another Cheshire grin. "Far? Sure, it's quite a hike, Chuck."

"Sorry, my zealousness got the best of me for a moment. Will it take us long to get there?"

"Long? Long... sorry, I couldn't resist," she smiled.

"I know, it's one of the perks in having a protégé that's a dunce."

"When did you get promoted to protégé?"

I caught on immediately this time that Kalista was once again engaging in the good-natured banter that she and Tresden did when I was about to take on some difficult experience or learning.

"You gave me those stripes two months ago, Kalista. I'm just not as egotistical as you and Tresden are so I don't wear them for everyone to see. I assumed that you could see – being the deeply advanced soul that you are – that my Resonance was that much greater when I got the promotion."

"Ever wonder what it would be like to get hit by a lightening bolt?"

"Very funny. So, does that mean I'm not your protégé?"

"More like pain in the..."

"Don't even **think** about saying that about my favorite earthling!" Tresden shouted.

I hadn't seen Tresden standing along the pathway we had been walking on since we had crossed the bridge. I was so involved in my conversation with Kalista that I wasn't even looking where I was going.

"Tresden, I've asked you a hundred times not to do that to me," I shouted.

"Sorry, I just felt that I had to jump in before Kalista started in on you again."

This time it was Tresden's eyes that were shining brilliantly. It was though some billion-log bonfire was burning inside of her and was pouring solely out of the area that was defined by her eyes. My intuition told me, Tresden, Geradl, Kalista and God knew who else, might well just pop up out of the bushes to this place at will.

In this form of reality – no matter what that was – souls were not limited to location as I would think of it in my normal state of perception. Or movement. Being somewhere or going anywhere was probably only a matter of thinking of that place and wham, there you were. If you knew how to do it, it was all pretty handy. If you didn't, you were subject to getting the living daylights scared out of you. Tresden, knowing what I had been thinking at that moment lit up all the more because of it.

"He's getting smarter, don't you think Kalista?"

"Don't flatter him Tresden, he won't be able to get his head through the doorway to the garden."

"I'm not going to engage in all this silliness. Can't you just tell me where we are going?"

"You asked a question. We're going someplace that you can see the answers."

"But it's not the River?"

"No. The River of Knowledge can only enhance your recollection of things that already are. You are asking about something that does not yet exist within the collective records of what 'is' in the history of your Earth. At least not in the way you're asking about it."

"Whoa Tresden. You're taking me to someplace that I can see things that haven't happened yet?" I asked, somewhat amazed at the prospect.

"There is no such place. But we can take you to a place where you can observe visions of what may occur. Possibilities or even likely probabilities. Where assumptions dissolve into the background and likelihood's slide ever so gently into the foreground. In this place the range of what might occur in the future is significantly narrowed by making assumptions of the present," Tresden explained.

"Is it... I mean, is it accurate? I can learn what's going to happen?"

"No. As you know, there is no knowing for certain what will happen. That is one of the original gifts from Source. The most you can attain is eliminating some of the more extreme possibilities of what won't happen."

"Oh, I think I get it. So, going there won't tell me if the world comes to an end within a hundred years but it will tell me if we destroy ourselves with nuclear weapons?"

"Well, it might give you some insight about the likelihood of the latter. Remember, nothing is absolute. One of the only absolutes that exist in the All is that absolutely nothing in the future is absolutely certain."

We continued up a narrow pathway through what appeared to be a small glen. We could have easily been hiking through some of the more colorful deep green valleys in Ireland. The surrounding foliage was not at all like the pathway that had led to the River of Knowledge. All of the trees, bushes and flowers that I saw, while definitely awe inspiring in color and textural richness seemed completely consistent with what could have been located almost anywhere at home that had a lush forest.

The main difference that made it clear that we were walking through this part of the otherworldly vicinity as opposed to an Irish glen was the brilliantly intense depth and texture in everything that could be observed. The grass and trees were of an emerald green that imparted a sense of being alive in ways that defied description. Every flower and the enormous volume of flowering shrubs gave the impression of being plugged in to a high voltage power source that internally lit each growth in the image with an eerie intense brilliance. The effect was completely mesmerizing.

After a short time, we came to a distinct three-way fork in the path that we had been walking. For reasons that I don't understand, since I happened to be in the lead of our small group at the time, I took the far right-hand path. After taking maybe a dozen steps, I noticed that Kalista and Tresden had stopped at the fork and were not following me. My immediate assumption was that I had turned the wrong way. I turned around and walked back to where the two of them were standing. "What? Did I go the wrong way?"

"Actually, no. You went the right way. We're just trying to understand how you knew to take that particular pathway."

"I didn't know. Not for certain. It just felt like it was the right way to go."

Kalista and Tresden were smiling broadly. Kalista could barely contain herself. From my perspective, I had simply guessed about which pathway to take. They had a completely different interpretation of what had just occurred.

"His memory is coming back."

"I should think so. Remarkable really, don't you think?"

"What are you two talking about?"

"You've been here before. That's how you knew which way to go."

"No I haven't. This is another one of your tricks, right?"

"Not at all."

"So what's the big deal?"

"The big deal is that, once your True Spiritual Memory starts to return, other parts of your memory will begin to function as well. It is much like what happens to an amnesia patient when something triggers their recollection of their past. Their memory often cascades to them from that point like floodgates have been opened. In the same manner you will now accelerate your spiritual development exponentially – as anyone would – once they reach the point where their essential memory begins to return and they increase their connection to their True Resonance."

"How do you know that is what's happening?"

"You had no hesitation. None at all. You didn't even think about which way to go as you approached the fork in the path. It was like watching a person walk up the pathway to their own home every night."

Tresden was right. At least in that regard. As I noticed the fork in the pathway we had been approaching, without any thought at all I clearly "knew" that we needed to go right to get to the place Tresden and Kalista had talked about. But I had no recollection at all of ever having been there before or, of going to the place they had been speaking of. Their insistence that I did only heightened my confusion and nervousness.

"If I've been here before why don't I remember it at all?"

"It's not within the scope of that part of your memory. You're thinking of remembering this as though it were part of your temporal, everyday mind. The recollections we are talking about are within your Spiritual Memory. Part of your Individual Resonance."

"You're saying that the information about which way to go as I'm walking up a pathway is available to me through someplace within my essence – someplace that is not part of my physical being?"

"You're making it much more complicated by the words you're using. We've both told you; everything there is to know is available to everyone at all times by accessing their True Resonance."

"But is it inside of me?"

"It *is* you. It is the very stuff that you are made out of. It is the construct of every cell in your being and, in excess of every cell in your being. Both inside and outside of any limitation of the physical. You know that. You just have to remember it by accessing Resonance," Tresden insisted.

"You're making me dizzy."

"That's because you insist upon looking at all of this as though everything is limited to only the physical. The physical is a minute part of the All. You have to lose your attachment to the notion that things are either inside or outside of you. The essence of what you 'are,' in reality, is much more than just that. In fact, as we've told you, you, me, Kalista, Geradl, everyone you know, ever have known or ever might know is everything. Is made of everything," Tresden explained.

"And that part is what I used to recollect the way that I needed to go on this path."

"Your connecting to that part of you, yes. Beginning to. And if you get out of the way, that part of you will help you recollect a lot more than just which way to take along a certain spiritual pathway that you're walking down at a given time. In the recollection of those other things lies more than you can ever dream of."

It must have been the inflection or urgency Tresden availed herself of when she said this. Because at that instant, I realized that the pathway we had been walking down, although real in appearance, might well have been a metaphor that Tresden and Kalista had created for me solely for that day. Literally out of thin air. What I liked to call a conception of perception.

More than that, the imagery device – whether it was metaphor or something else well beyond my ability to understand – accomplished two simultaneous purposes. It not only distracted me from my becoming overly anxious about the destination we were heading for, but it also showed me that, along the spiritual pathway that every soul walks along, that we reach a fork where we have a distinct choice to make; to recollect, or not to recollect, which is the pathway home. My taking the far right-hand pathway without even consciously thinking about it was a signal to them – but more to myself – that I instinctively knew the way home. That I was somehow already in touch with my True Resonance to a much deeper degree than I was even vaguely consciously aware of. The brilliance of their device and the boost that it afforded my realization were about to send me spinning out of control when Kalista stopped me from falling into the perceptional abyss that most likely would have conveyed me directly back to my study.

"Hold on, Chuck. Calm down. Breathe."

"Sorry. I think I understand now. What you're telling me is that all of us know these things about Reality, the nature of the All and whatever else we want to know. Anything really and everything specifically. We 'know' all of that because it is essentially part of us – or maybe, we're part of it. But until we remember that we actually know, truly believe that, we can't gain access to the insights. It is in the very confidence of 'knowing that we know' at the level of our essence, not in our mind, that opens the door for us."

"That's right," Kalista said.

"That's absolutely right. Brilliant!" Tresden echoed.

"So having recognized that, I automatically know all those things?" I asked.

"Nope. That's wrong," Kalista responded.

"That's absolutely wrong," Tresden said.

"What did I miss?" I asked.

"Not much but, what you skipped over is a pretty important detail of Reality. Arriving at the realization of knowing is like walking into the photo store with an exposed roll of film in your hand. All the pictures are there. Well, they're sort of there. The images, the very definitions of the All and everything about it, are all there. Complete. But they need to be developed, picked up and then reviewed by you. In order to appreciate the content and the context of those photographs, some of which are very complicated. Because of that, you need to study them carefully. One at a time as it were. Even with that, it has probably been a very long time since you saw these pictures and you will have difficulty recollecting what you are looking at and, in some cases, not even remember the context that the picture was originally taken in.

Some of the images might even require that you pull out a magnifying glass and study them very carefully in order to understand all of the detail and nuances within the images. While it would be true to say that, when you arrived at the photo store to drop off the film that everything was contained in your own hand, it is also true that without allowing the images to develop and then taking the time to understand them in context that the roll of exposed film in your hand may as well have been blank. In the example I just gave you, recollecting is equivalent to remembering that you dropped the roll of film off and, at what photo shop. Now, you need to go pick up the pictures and start looking at them. Only then will your recollection allow you to unfold the imagery. To recollect the reality of the All, and do you any good in your objective of enlightenment."

Everything that Kalista said made sense to me. This was surprising on its own as, her explanation and analogy were very complex. It reminded me of what I had thought about while looking at the high school yearbook not that long ago. It was as though there was a familiarity to many of the faces. In fact, once I looked at the names directly underneath the photographs I immediately identified that I knew that's who the person was. Began remembering all sorts of details about them that I would never have been able to bring into my mind spontaneously without some form of prompting device. The information was definitely in me somewhere, it was only a matter of figuring out how to recollect it. Once I began remembering, information just began to tumble out like water over a waterfall; at that point, the memories just flow and cannot be stopped.

What Kalista was telling me was that reconnecting with our True Resonance, the valve we needed to open up in order to access our deepest knowledge about God, Reality, Creation and everything else about the All, was a very similar matter. We only needed to figure out the best way to awaken ourselves to the reality that the information is, in fact, part of us. Kalista and Tresden had devised a brilliant scheme designed to prove to me that the knowledge was part of me. Well, I assumed it was a scheme. Somehow, I wasn't sure how, I knew immediately that what they had shown me was irrefutably true.

As I was about to engage them in further conversation Kalista began to communicate again.

"O.K., here we are,"

I was completely caught off guard by Kalista's pronouncement that we had arrived at our destination. Having been so completely engaged in the conversation we were having about recollection I had totally lost focus on the fact that we had continued to negotiate our way through the magnificent Irish glen. When I looked up and focused on where we actually were at that point, the setting was so completely and totally inconsistent with the Irish glen setting that the incongruity sent me spiraling out of control. I tried desperately to hold onto the imagery around us with the desperation of a man falling over a cliff would clutch for a rope as he slid further and further down. The last thing that I remember with any clarity is Tresden reaching out trying to grab my arm and Kalista urging me to "hold on."

The shock of what I had seen and my perception that the environment around us had changed so dramatically had jolted my senses to such a degree that I was no longer able to grasp that reality firmly enough to remain there. Before I had an opportunity to even think about it, I was on the floor of my study, pounding my fist on the side of my desk in absolute frustration that I had lost control and been unable to hold on as Kalista had urged me to.

In the hazy, partially disoriented daze that remained in my head I began to write several notes and ended that day drawing a picture of a very odd structure of an archway. No matter what effort I applied though, I couldn't remember where in the day's events I had actually seen that archway. Something in my mind told me that it was possibly just as I exited, but the vision wasn't clear enough for me to be certain. I just intuitively knew that the answers I was seeking must have something to do with that structure. As much as I knew that though, I also recognized that I just couldn't imagine how that could be.

My energy had been depleted to a level far too low for me to make another visit to the garden right away. I stared at my notes for close to an hour trying to add incremental cogency to them but for some reason, couldn't do so. Whatever had occurred that hastened my departure from the archway area had clouded my clarity to a point where I wasn't really functioning well anymore.

Determined to complete the journey I had set out on that day, I concluded rest was the only pathway for me in the near term. I planned to complete this next part of my journey and learn more about the mysterious archway in the morning. Looking back, there was no way for me to know just then that, within that fog that surrounded the mysterious vague image of the archway, many of the answers I had been searching for over my entire adult life would be revealed.

CHAPTER ELEVEN

All that we are is the result of
what we have thought.
The mind is everything.
What we think, we become.

- Buddha

My focus was so intense and my need to learn more about the arched structure, the images of which were echoing around urgently in some vague portion of my memory, that I was barely able to sleep. Frustrated and mystified at the same time, I arose in the middle of the night and made my way down the stairs to my study. Determined to put the issues concerning the advanced soul's message – the teachings of Buddha, Jesus, Mohammed and others – not being embraced by the world and the mysterious archways to rest, I set out for Kalista's garden.

I had tried on previous occasions to visit the garden when my energy was not completely restored and had not done well. In spite of not sleeping and having not fully restored my energy, I was able to make the early morning journey without encountering any obstacles or delays.

Upon arrival, I found Kalista sitting on her bench under the giant weeping willow tree, alone. She appeared to be meditating or concentrating intensely on something. I considered an immediate return to my study because I didn't want to disturb her. Just then, she opened her eyes slowly and motioned with a subtle movement of her head that

I was welcome.

"Hi. Feeling any better?" Kalista asked.

"I'm fine, thanks. Sorry about the other time there. I guess that I just got overwhelmed," I admitted.

"Don't worry about that. Lessons, remember – it's all lessons. All of it. No matter what happens, make certain that you learn from it," she said.

"I've been trying to Kalista. Really I have. But sometimes, I just can't see any lesson in certain things that happen in my life. Often, I have even less insight about what lessons could possibly come from certain events in the world around me even after I have the experience."

"Don't worry about that either. But remember, what you call life is a fairly dense form of existence relative to the other possibilities along the pathway that spans your existence. Many of the lessons there have to do with learning patience. Forbearance. Shifting your intent not just your actions. Sometimes the lesson is as simple as applying compassion and patience to your own mistakes. Your own faults. For most people, that's the hardest of all."

"What happened to compassion, empathy and love for others? Learning the reality of reconciliation and balance?"

"Patience, forbearance and other components are essential parts of compassion. Compassion is part of empathy. And in mastering both of those, only love – and a loving pathway – must follow. More than that, you need to understand that the immutable truth of reconciliation and balance is so deeply implanted within the very fiber of all souls that our recognition of it follows naturally once we have begun the journey on the road homeward. And that journey is inevitable once a commitment is made and pursued with sincerity to walk a path paved with compassion and empathy. It all follows. All of it comes together as a naturally elegant and perfect process. Momentum impels you along once you have committed at the level of your essence, in your very soul, to adopt a compassionate way."

Her description evoked a mental image in my mind of those moving walkways at the airport. The volitional decision to get onto the walkway was tantamount to effecting a conscious decision to shift one's life intent in the direction of compassion and empathy. Once on the moving walkway, there was a certain amount of forward movement that was bound to occur solely by virtue of having made the decision and commitment to practice compassion and empathy. Of course, there was nothing that would stop a person from walking faster while traveling on the moving walkway if they chose to. All that happens is that you arrive at your chosen destination earlier. Just as I was about to become lost in this train of thought Kalista began her communication again.

"You know all of this already. Why don't we return to the desert again and finish what you were pursuing last time?"

"Desert? What desert? What are you talking about?"

"You don't remember anything?"

"I remember that we were walking through a beautiful emerald green place, I thought I was in an Irish glen. But nothing about it looked like a desert to me."

"O.K. We'll do the whole thing again from the start. It will be good experience for you."

"And Tresden?"

"Oh, I suspect that she'll meet us along the way."

Kalista and I set out across the bridge and as before, made a sharp left turn as we reached the shoreline. Before long, I noticed that we had entered the pristine Irish glen that had made such an impression on me the last time we had traversed this pathway. Oddly, it felt as though it was much longer ago than just the day before.

About half the way up a gentle slope ahead of us, I noticed that Tresden was sitting by the side of the pathway. She appeared to be playing a woodwind instrument of some kind. As we approached her the eerie sound of the music she was playing created a haunting effect in me. The music was not familiar, but was enchanting beyond words. I thought it was Gaelic, almost like something Enya would come up with, but its mystical charm went far beyond that. It was enchanting, hypnotically luring. As we arrived at the place she had chosen for this musical serenade she stood up in one swift motion and placed the instrument into a soft, Kelly green backpack she was wearing. She greeted me warmly with an enthusiastic smile.

"Good day, Chuck. How are you?"

"I'm fine, Tresden. What was that music you were playing?"

"Oh, nothing in particular. Just something in the back of my mind bouncing around."

"Really? It almost sounded familiar to me but I couldn't place it."

"Can't say that I'm surprised to hear that. I suspect that certain tunes are familiar to us, even if we can't quite remember where we heard them before."

I started to answer, but she silenced me with a look that I felt was meant to induce me to think carefully about what she'd just said. We started walking up the pathway again, but as I glanced over my shoulder I noticed Tresden was still looking at me intently. As the words she had just said to me echoed around in my mind, I thought about the likelihood that she meant what she had said both literally and, as an analogy for me to think about as we continued our walk up the gentle rise ahead.

"You didn't mean that literally did you?"

"I didn't?" Tresden smiled mischievously at me.

"I know you didn't. You were telling me – no, reminding me – that if we hear something and it seems familiar to us it is because all things are actually within our recollection. That recollection is only a process of dialing into that portion of our Resonance that holds that particular memory. And then you were going to say that it applies to recollecting a song that we might know in exactly the same way."

Tresden didn't say a word. I noticed as I was talking that she had reached into her backpack, pulled out her musical instrument and began playing the same tune she had been playing when Kalista and I approached her on the pathway. I had enough experience with Tresden and Kalista at to recognize that this repeat musical interlude was her clever way of answering my question. If I had any doubts remaining, Kalista's slight, lilting giggle in the background in retort to my question was all that was needed.

Somewhere along the pathway I lost my awareness that we had continued to walk the entire time we were discussing these things as we bantered back and forth playfully over Tresden's educational methods. As I looked up I noticed that we had arrived at a clearing. The surroundings were completely unlike the Irish glen we had come through to get to this place only the day before. The area we were now in looked more like a quiet desert chaparral. What struck me as particularly odd was that I was completely unaware of going through any area where the scenery made a transition to this new environment. From my perspective, we were making our way through the Irish glen and then my next awareness was that we had arrived in some magnificently unusual desert clearing.

The chaparral itself was stark. There was no flora of any kind that I could see. The only feature that was recognizable was an odd looking archway directly in front of us, about twenty feet away. Although this same image had haunted me only the day before, I was having difficulty recognizing the image. What appeared in front of us now was what had been the vague memory that I failed to connect with only the day before.

At first blush the span appeared to be made of some unusual type of stone. As I studied it more closely though, I concluded that its construction was more consistent with something like a twenty-first, or even twenty-second century metal. Not aluminum and not titanium. Something with a softer appearance while at the same time giving the impression of resolute indestructibility. It afforded an impression of timelessness carved into and made an intrinsic part of this place. The arch was half-moon shaped and was no more than twenty feet wide and as much as fifteen feet high at the apex of the archway. Both ends of the archway span connected directly to the ground. There were no stands holding it up or connections to equipment – at least that I could see, of any kind. Just as I was thinking that it reminded me of the famous arch in St. Louis, only much smaller, I noticed to that there were three other arches of identical construct in the area around us.

As I slowly turned completely around, I became aware that we were actually standing in the middle of an area that was perfectly round, probably one hundred feet but not more, in diameter. There were four of the unusual archways spaced equally on the outside perimeter of the circle that we were standing inside of. This afforded us an unobstructed access to all four arches if we either turned around or, craned our necks enough to see the archway directly behind us no matter which direction we were facing. I was preparing to ask Tresden about the place we were now standing in, when I heard a vague, non-descript low-pitched sound. I was stunned to see that all four archways, which had been completely see-through only a moment before, now had images flickering within and projecting outward around them. The archways gave the impression of being multidimensional projectors. The three-dimensional images were enhanced with some other-worldly technology that allowed me to sense the feelings – and I believe, even the thoughts, that were experienced by people within the imagery. I hoped to learn more about the arches and their uses as things progressed.

I looked at Tresden and then at Kalista for some indication of what would come next in this odd series of events. My impression was that they were in the mode where they would willingly answer questions, but only if I asked them directly. I had seen them in this state on a couple of occasions previously. Sensing this, I thought about how I could best form my first question as it was evident that it was the experience – and not our interaction – that was the major reason we were all here. If I had questions, I felt, those were secondary to whatever events were to take place.

"What is this place Kalista?"

"It is a place for viewing future possibilities. Or probabilities. Depends on the level of detail and how complex the issue is that you are examining," she said.

"I don't understand."

"Let me show you. It will be easier that way. Just hold a subject in your mind for a few seconds. Focus solely on that subject and nothing else. Then observe the archway directly in front of you."

Kalista's instructions were precise and when compared with her usual intonation, very direct. What she had just conveyed to me came across in the form of an order but yet, was just short of that. She was urging me and at the same time teaching me how to access the mechanism of arches that we were now standing within. I didn't understand why but being in this area, evoked an odd nervousness – almost reverence – within me. I felt at the time as though I had snuck into a theatre for a movie that I probably wasn't really supposed to see.

"What kind of subject? I still don't understand," I communicated, in a whisper.

"Start with something simple. Anything that you know the history of with some level of detail. That will help give you perspective."

Kalista's instruction created for me a contradiction of sorts. I believed everything that Kalista said without the slightest margin for doubt. I had attained this level of absolute trust in her dating back to the second visit that I'd made to the garden more than a year ago. But what she was inferring now – if I understood her correctly – was that this place was a kind of enormous crystal ball. That I could pick a topic and it would show me the future. Before I could articulate the question Tresden broke in on my thoughts.

"Not the future, Chuck. Possibilities or probabilities of future outcomes based upon the momentum of what is given. What is assumed."

"How does it work?" I asked.

"What differences does it make? Besides, we're not certain ourselves. Geradl showed this to us some time ago."

"Is this a place? I mean... well, you know what I mean."

"From your perspective consider it a specific locality of focused perception."

In my spiritual reading explorations many years back, I'd remembered reading about the Akashic records. These were supposed to be a repository of some sort that included all human experience; past, present and future, a record of all events within the Universe and are purportedly an integral part of the Cosmic Mind. It is suggested that they are a record of every thought and event that has ever occurred, will occur or could occur. What Kalista was talking about sounded much like a viewing chamber designed specifically to access records of this kind.

"Is this a place to view the 'Akashic records'?"

"It is far more than that. Besides, you need to resist getting too tied down in placing labels on things. Remember – always focus on the lesson. Forget about the experience."

"So I can pick anything I want."

"Start with something very simple at first."

I thought for a minute or two of things that I would have wanted to know the outcome of in my current sphere of life. I was tempted for a moment to try to get a leg up on the future of the stock market, but knew that Kalista and Tresden wouldn't see any humor in those attempts. My next thought was of a very wonderful woman that I'd met a few weeks earlier, and of whom I had grown very fond in a short period of time. I held those images in mind to the exclusion of all other thoughts for maybe five seconds. To my shock, the imagery of this woman and I having dinner – not coincidentally the image I had just held in mind – took three-dimensional form in an area that extended ten feet on either side of the archway directly in front of me. This afforded me the impression of true depth and a sense of total reality from the imagery. The images were even more vivid and detailed than the life review process that Kalista had played out for me previously.

Since this particular scenario was one in which I was both a participant and a viewer of events, it was a bit difficult at first to sort out the various emotions and feelings playing themselves out in the scene before me. It took some effort to sort out the feelings emanating from the images and, from my own feelings as projected within the imagery. As the scene continued to play out I was fascinated at the prospect of learning how to gain access to the possible future outcomes of what I was watching.

"Kalista, how do I learn what possible futures will come from this?"

"In your mind, start to add in assumptions. Developments. Things that you think about when you ponder your future with this woman. Where you might go next. What you might do next. Posit questions as you factor in the assumptions. Hold those questions in the front of your mind as you continue to watch the front archway."

At first, I didn't do very well in my efforts to interact with the mechanism. Finally, I thought about this woman and I taking some kind of vacation together. Wondered about the possibility of a meaningful life together. After a brief period of failed experimentation along this line of thought, and some guidance from Tresden, I learned that through the subtlety of my mind, I could ostensibly ask questions of the mechanism by adding in or taking away certain assumptions about the scenario unfolding on the front archway. As I brought the specific issues or questions to mind, the archway in front of me immediately moved to imagery that would reflect those assumptions. Simultaneous with the front archway changing, the arches on both sides would begin to reflect the possible outcomes given those changes. It was a overwhelming and extremely disorienting experience. It evoked in me the usual list of questions that were bound to send Tresden into fits.

"This is amazing! What is the archway directly behind us used for?"

"That one will show the immediate past factoring in the assumptions you just added. Of course, just as with the life review, you can rewind it, play it forward in slow motion or any other viewing possibility that you could imagine by directing the mechanism with your mind. Since it allows you to feel everything that all of the participants in the images feel, if you go back and forth around the images you can gain some deep insight into many of your interpersonal relationships. You can also get a grasp on what feelings might result from certain decisions that you might consider making that concern other people in your life."

"Why do you say that what appears within the arches on each side is only a possibility. Why can't the device actually say with certainty what is going to happen?"

"First of all, no future, no outcome of any kind is assured. Ever. Not within the known portions of the All at least. Obviously, I don't know about the unknowable or the unknown. Nevertheless, this is one of the basic guidelines that Source imparted on the All at the point of Creation. No outcome is absolutely guaranteed until it happens. In a way, that is a by-product of free will because, if any future was guaranteed it would preempt free will.

Next, if futures were assured there would be no point to having the participants play out their various life roles. They would be limited in what they could learn to the extent that their script was indelibly and inflexibly written for them. People, souls, would be doing no more than walking through their parts with no possibility of having any outcome other than the one already written for them. No real learning would take place. That would be pointless. You have to remember that, above all else, Source set in motion Creation with the objective of improving Source itself. In essence, determining what was possible. The only way that could possibly occur would be if the various spun-off parts of Source, the individual souls, had the absolute freedom to make their own choices and to experience the outcomes of those choices. To learn whatever they chose to and then to return someday back to The Original Center of All Things. If any part of that pathway was controlled, in any manner at all – if the outcomes were already known – Source would have 'rigged' the end point. Source wanted only an authentic, uncontrolled outcome – uncontrolled within certain guidelines. Because of this truth, future events can be at best, only a likelihood. Sometimes even that is a long shot."

"So you're saying that I really control my own complete pathway? It is not as though God or some heavenly angel is ever controlling my course, my actions, ever? Even a little bit? How about watching out for me; making sure I don't fall into a ditch?"

"Not at all. And trying to assign blame in that direction, for painful events like that, is where a lot of people really fall astray and get muddled down for lifetime after lifetime of frustrations."

"Meaning?"

"Some people feel that they need to have an explanation or an excuse or to find someone that is responsible for every bad thing that happens in their lives. A villain – besides themselves – to assume the blame for every bad thing that they do. They look for villains in their lives as whipping posts. 'Officer, I'm speeding because my wife made me late this morning.' 'Boss, my report is late because Givens was using the copy machine.' And, if they can't find a temporal target, in essence, an earthly explanation to blame, they'll reach higher thinking that somehow doing so adds that much more credibility to the story. They'll try everything from 'God hates me' to 'the devil made me do it' to explain what they think of as problems they are experiencing in their lives," Kalista said.

"Like blaming the manufacturer of a hammer when you hit your finger with it?"

As Tresden interjected this I pondered how many times in my life I had said "stupid hammer" after missing the nail head and slamming my thumb into a two by four.

"Exactly! But the reality is much simpler than that. And far more elegant. All outcomes are neither guaranteed nor even necessarily likely. At the individual level, you have a choice to make in every single thing you do. Those choices control your own outcomes.

Every outcome that you experience is a direct product of a decision that *you* made. Now, some experiences might mystify you in this regard because you can't remember what specific decision you have made that would cause such an outcome. But that doesn't in any manner change the reality that your outcomes match up exactly with your decisions and actions. This is why I have said to you that no matter what is going on in your life at any given moment you – and only you – are responsible for it. The truth of that is absolute as well as immutable as you expand the example and look at larger pictures. Because, if your family makes a choice as a family, the entire family then has to live with whatever the outcomes might be of that choice. If you and your wife sign for a loan and things go amiss, both of you share the responsibility for finding a way to pay it back. In that particular case, both of the individual members – you and your wife – have to live with it individually as well.

The same goes for your community. Your state. Your country. Your world. Ad infinitum. All of it, absolutely everything that comprises the All, are outcomes based upon the collective choices, actions and experiences of everything within the All. In fact, if you want it reduced to the least common denominator; the All is literally defined by the sum total of the decisions and actions of each of its constituents added together."

The manner in which Tresden had explained this to me had devastating consequences on my sense of emotional equilibrium. At the same time there was absolutely no question at all that everything she was saying was precisely accurate. God didn't have her hands on the levers and dials of each and every thing in our individual lives or even the Universe as we have all pretty much been instructed to believe as children. We do.

As I pondered this it all tumbled down to the realization that, whatever happens to us at every possible level of experience, from our lives as individuals to our families and our communities, it is completely dictated by our actions. Whether that action was yesterday, tcn ears ago or ten lifetimes ago. The lesson was as overwhelming as it was simple: we are responsible for everything going on in our lives and whatever portion of the world we choose to interact with around us. Actions equal future outcomes. Individually. Communally. Globally. Universally. And beyond. And because it is in our nature to attempt to sidestep responsibility, we often try to avoid facing this sometimes difficult fact. In no way does that invalidate the truth of the matter.

The good news that went along with this reality was that, we – and only we – are also directly able to change our own outcomes. If you don't like what is going on in your life the only person you need to go see about changing all of it is right there in the mirror staring back at you. If your community is insensitive to environmental issues then the "we" that comprises the community can change that. If the world doesn't want starving children or wars then the "we" that comprises the world – and only that we – can change that. From my perspective, the obvious truth of this example extended into and beyond the horizon. A genuine gift from God; if the citizens of the Universe don't like the way the Universe was, they have the absolute power to change it. If there was a better definition of freedom I couldn't think of it.

All of this reminded me that I had returned to the garden that day with the hope of increasing my understanding of where we had gone astray as mankind. Our little endeavor with absolute freedom hadn't worked out too well so far. In fact, we'd surrendered to that freedom in exchange for the right to act recklessly and irresponsibly long ago. I needed to learn how we had taken what must have been a clear and concise message of peaceful loving of all mankind from advanced souls such as Buddha, Jesus the Christ, Mohammed and others like them and turned it into something far less productive – even destructive – than it was originally meant to be? Pondering this for a few moments, I made a conscious decision to forego the topic we had been exploring more deeply and move on to my primary objective for the day. I could always come back and learn more about the dynamics of personal of responsibility or how this place of future probabilities actually worked.

"Can this place be used to help me understand where we might be going as mankind? What I mean to say is, can I gain any insight about our likely future from here? Or does it work only as it relates to an individual's pathway and possible future?"

Kalista hesitated for a moment before answering. "That's a difficult question. Let me answer it in this way. The greater the number of souls involved in any issue in question the outcome would be close to proportionately less certain. Therefore, when you start to ask questions as broad as 'the possible future of your world or of mankind or of the Universe' the reliability of the insight diminishes greatly as compared to examining possible outcomes concerning just one soul, one person."

"But it is possible."

"It is possible to get broad insights and inferences. And it's going to be better than even a very advanced rational mind might be able to speculate."

"So, if I wanted to understand where mankind was going in the future taking into account what man had done with the messages brought to our world from Mohammed, Jesus, Buddha and the others you mentioned how would I do that?"

"I see that, once more, you're after the easy answers again," Tresden said, smiling warmly.

"You're sure you don't want to try something a little less... well, a bit less daunting? First time I brought Tresden here she asked about some silly soccer match."

"No, I really want to know this."

Kalista explained to me that in order to accomplish what I was asking that she and Tresden would be taking the context of my question and serving as a kind of conduit for controlling the array of possibilities that manifested its output onto the multidimensional projection mechanism that we stood in the center of.

As I was about to ask her some of the details about the place we were standing, she interrupted my thoughts and explained to me that Geradl had called this place "The Hallway of Possibilities." I started to object to Kalista's comment because, from my perception, even though I was unable to identify even vaguely where we actually were, I knew that we were most assuredly not in a hallway of any kind. I caught myself just in time and decided instead to focus on the issue at hand. I did so with the knowledge that I could always ask about any perceptional issue on my part at some later date.

A few moments after Kalista finished her explanation to me I noticed that the archway directly behind where we were standing began to project a sequence of complex images, emotions and sounds. It took me several moments to discern that, what was playing out within the multidimensional imagery was some of our earliest history of human civilization on earth. I had never been astute in my studies on the history of world civilization. However, I got the impression from the raw imagery and the equally frayed emotions that I sensed from the people passing by within the image that the period being shown must have been at least 1,000 years B.C. Possibly even earlier.

What struck me most was the overbearing suffering and barbarism – the direct raw emotional and physical reads that I received from the unique attributes of the system that allowed me, as a viewer, to empathize with participants in the scenes. The sense of reality was so vivid that I had to fight off nausea several times as the harshness of life – the struggle for day-to-day existence – was conveyed directly into my senses. I had a moment or two where I questioned whether these were in fact, human ancestors, as their psychological and emotional construction felt somehow sub-prehistoric to me. Their makeup and what they projected simply felt that raw to my perception.

Then the archway directly in front of us began to flicker and project outwardly in a circular span around the archway with a sequence of new images. The device was now showing us the introduction of one specific possible outcome, no doubt factored into the system by Kalista or Tresden. Somehow, I perceived that Kalista and Tresden were able to feed their assumption directly into the mechanism as though they were the actual events unfolding on the Earth at that early time in civilization.

In matter of a few moments, I observed imagery that I imagined was ancient China or possibly India. It was difficult to tell the period other than to say that it was clearly ancient history, at least a few thousand years ago was my initial guess. As the imagery gained speed and the scenes began to play out very quickly, a character was introduced that I intuitively knew had to be Siddhartha Gautama, who would later become known to the world as Buddha – The Enlightened One. Having read the history of Buddha's life many times I was familiar with the miraculous pathway that he followed; from Prince of a great kingdom to starving ascetic. How he attained enlightenment at Bodh Gaya, India and went on to share that knowledge with thousands of seekers in that part of the world.

As the imagery of Buddha's life continued to play out, I became far less focused on the details of his pathway and how it matched – or failed to match up – to the history of the life of The Buddha as reported in the various texts I had read. Instead, my attention was now shifting to the scenes beginning to unfold around the archways on either side of where we were standing. At this juncture, the rear archway was now showing events as they passed into history – in essence events would flow from the front archway to the back archway. The events displayed in the archways on either side, were mere possibilities based on assumptions. They did not pass onto the back archway unless, of course, it happened to coincide with events as they actually transpired in our history.

The side archways, Kalista explained, were meant to display the possibilities of the future based upon what was being introduced on the front archway at the time. Change the assumptions factored into the front archway and the resultant possibilities would immediately be reflected in the content of the archways on both sides. These two side archways were now showing what might have happened in our world based upon Buddha having carried the message. The true meaning of the essential realities of compassion, empathy, karma and so forth passed to us along with the assumption that the messages remained pure over the first few hundred years after his death. Untouched by egos and human agendas. This was the main assumption that I had suggested to Kalista.

305

At first, it was difficult to follow the events on all four archways. But Tresden showed me that the back archway was really only a point of reference and needed very little attention except for intermittent context updates. A glance now and then sufficed. In a similar fashion, the front archway, once I had taken in the basic thrust of developments there, became less and less important as long as I held in mind the assumptions that had been factored in. As such, it didn't require much attention either.

Tresden explained to me that the archway to the left would play out, in this case, the possibility that would equate with man rising to the most optimistic likelihood possible. While the archway to the right of us displayed the most likely outcome, assuming mankind performed in a far more mediocre manner. It wasn't absolute Tresden explained, but for the issue I had chosen it was probably a fairly reliable baseline upon which I could rely. At least for today. Tresden reminded me no future is assured. No outcome guaranteed until it actually occurs.

I watched in a kind of mystified absolute awe as the magnificent insights that Buddha had recollected were passed on directly by him to his disciples and then to others. But that awe quickly shifted to horror as the years passed by on the front archway and turned from possibilities into what I saw on the rear archway; history. It showed the transformation of Buddha's realizations and messages into an organized religion. Soon there were divisions, sects, counter-sects and worse. By the time Jesus the Christ alit on Earth millenniums later, the images played on the front archway shifted. Now illustrated with painful clarity was that the essential message originally shared by Buddha around 550 B.C. had suffered at the hands and minds of mankind and those that insisted that it be organized almost as a condition of being perpetuated.

My sense was that, in the interests of bringing the answers that I sought to bear more quickly that Tresden and Kalista were using a kind of fast-forward application to jump though to other major intersections and important developments in our history. Providing for me past as prologue to the future possibilities that I had come seeking that day. I watched how the incredibly loving, sensitive and gentle teachings of Jesus ended up pushed to the side and barely remnant fodder for the creation of division after division, sect after sect, church after church of the same belief system. There was more time spent talking and arguing about the issues that divided the various sects than of the essential truths that they all had in common. Truths that served as the foundation for Christ's original message.

The real trouble began around 1100 A.D. as the first Crusades were launched. The imagery was more than I could bear to take in as I watched several hundred years of Spaniards against the Moors; Prussians, Lithuanians; seemingly everyone aligned against the Mohammedans. In spite of knowing the basic historical context of events, I shuddered as I used the empathy feature of the device and felt the sword brutally inserted into a defenseless woman whose only offence was her belief system being slightly different than the Crusaders. The images illustrated in horrific detail a religiously spon-sored several hundred year ceaseless course of rape, pillage, torture and murder by those proudly wearing the symbol of the cross upon their uniform. History would validate no favorites in such actions as even-tually, I noted from taking in the events played out on the archways, one way or another violence followed not far behind almost every belief system.

Kalista was about to move on to the next major event in this his-torical thread when I asked her to skip over any more of this kind of detail. I had believed up until that day that my rudimentary under-standing of the events of history was more than enough to grasp the incredible hypocrisy of those involved. But watching the events play out in this other-worldly viewing chamber impacted me. Shattered me. The images were not only in multiple dimensions but each per-son's feelings could be felt merely by me mentally placing myself in their place for a moment afforded me a more realistic perspective on the genuinely unbridled, blind, an absolute hatred of the day than I wanted. Or could stand.

I observed that many of those swinging swords and wreaking havoc on their neighbors never even slowed for a moment to think about the possibility that the core message of their enemy was the same as their own. Never once considered what the original carrier of the message – Mohamed, Buddha, Jesus – would have thought of their sword swinging barbarism. At the time I tried to emotionally compensate for what I had just experienced as being long ago and ideally, forgotten to the past. Ancient history. It was a lie and, I knew it. If anything, man is equally as vicious as he used to be. Unfortunately, the weaponry has become more efficient. Our skills in brutality have been honed to a fine edge over time. Religious agendas have moved even more center-stage as justifications for violence over the course of history.

Kalista sensed that I had endured more than enough of this horrific brand of barbarism and man's inhumanity toward his fellow man and moved us on to another era. As if to emphasize my assumptions about man's record over time, Kalista stopped by a scene on the front archway that gave the impression of fifteenth or maybe sixteenth century Europe. Since I had started out in my younger days aspiring to be a physicist, I recognized almost immediately two of the scientific world's genuine heroes appearing there; Copernicus and Galileo.

Kalista slowed down the images just enough for me to take in some of the blustering highlights of the Inquisition which at the time was rampaging its way through France, Italy, Germany and Spain. Punishing all so called heretics through torture, murder and most often, fates worse than death itself. I saw just the highlights of the Catholic Church placing Galileo under house arrest for daring to sign on to the Copernican theory that the earth circled the sun and not the other way around. It took *three hundred and sixty years, until 1992,* for the Catholic Church to admit that it had made a mistake in their prosecution of Galileo. Just how events like these interrelated to the peaceful and loving messages of tolerance and compassion preached by Jesus the Christ when he first shared that word only 1,500 years earlier remained a bit fuzzy to me.

By the time we caught up to what was current time, 1994, I was emotionally spent. I breathed a guarded deep sigh of relief with the foolish assumption that the worst was definitely behind us. Man would never revert to that level of animalistic, irrational behavior. Religions must have learned their lessons from the incredibly thoughtless insensitivity and brutality of the past. Kalista looked at me with a sincere gaze of compassion and picked up the conversation as though we had only been engaged in this viewing process for a moment or two. She had the antiseptic tone of a surgeon asking the nurse for the next instrument in the procedure.

"O.K., what assumptions would you like to make going forward?" Kalista asked.

"Me? What do I know? I thought you guys would have some ideas. Maybe something that would help me sleep a little better at night. Something to give us all a little hope that its not all hopeless."

"Sorry. We have barely more insight in this area than you do," Tresden said.

"Barely. I heard you say barely. What does that mean?" I asked.

"Just what I said."

Kalista was disguising a faint hint of a smile. Tresden also had a vaguely mischievous look to her but I couldn't really qualify why I felt that way. They obviously had something in mind and I sensed that I was being baited.

"I sense another trap door closing behind me."

"Not at all. This is far too serious a subject to take lightly," Tresden said.

"But there is something. Something that might make it all seem less hopeless."

"Sort of. As long as you don't think of 'something' as being some kind of magic wand that is waved and wham, it solves all the problems of the world just like that."

"Hmm, that's pretty non-descript. Can you tell me about it?" I asked.

"It would be better if we showed you," Kalista said.

"O.K., but go easy Kalista, I'm not as resilient as I used to be. All these visits here have taken their toll on me."

"Don't worry about it. Before we begin though, a little background is appropriate. During the period that would have roughly equated with very early in World War II on Earth a number of souls that had recently incarnated there and returned to spirit form formed a loosely associated informal spiritual pact of sorts. These souls independently agreed to take on incarnations with a very dedicated, spiritual mission on Earth for their next life. Their objective was to deliver the essential message again but on a far broader scale than had been attempted previously by just one ascended master at a time."

"Did they all incarnate in one geographical area? India? Tibet?" I wasn't sure if I necessarily believed what Kalista was saying but I was fascinated.

"No. They individually effected conscious decisions to incarnate pretty much everywhere so that when they, themselves consciously recollected the essential message that they would be able to share those messages with the greatest number of people over the broadest possible area."

"When was all this?" I was stunned.

"As I said, the individual began incarnating around the beginning of the time of World War II. They continued – and reached a peak – several years after the end of that war, probably in a period that would equate in your terms with the 1960s although, apparently in an effort to maintain some degree of continuity, there are still some incarnating with that basic mission even now. The last grouping alit with the advent of the atomic bomb and other destructive tools of warfare and most importantly, a generalized downturn in 'Recollection' by souls incarnated at that time. They perceived that an entirely new and potentially cataclysmic outcome was possible for the souls incarnating there unless some form of spiritual intervention took place."

"Do they... I mean, would all of these souls recognize each other if they, for example, met on the street? Is it one clan of related souls that decided to do this?"

"Not particularly. They wouldn't recognize each other on sight. But they would recognize each other's enhanced Resonance level below the line of conscious awareness. That the person they were talking to, if they were part of the Original Group, was deeply invested in the project to awaken others – to remind other souls of their essential nature. They would intuitively identify with something in the others without necessarily knowing what it was at first. Sort of like when you are introduced to someone that you feel you've met before but, you can't quite remember the circumstances of the original meeting."

I was stunned. My thoughts barely processing. Although completely unimportant in the scheme of overall events I now recognized why Kalista had been smiling a few moments before. Recognizing my sense of hopelessness over the state of affairs in the world she knew that she was about to deliver the sustenance of hope that I needed to carry on with at least some measure of enthusiasm. Hope. Knowing me as she did, she saw that affording me just that might help me carry forward for at least a while.

"You're not teasing me. This isn't one of those 'wouldn't it be nice if... ?'"

"Not at all. This is how do you like to say it? Oh, 'in progress.' Those souls have already assumed those incarnations and have been – and will continue to be – in various states of awakening themselves. As more of them recollect the primary purpose for which they took on this particular lifetime, they are hoping that the momentum will build and even more – beyond those in the Original Group – will become awakened." Kalista had a tone of real encouragement in her communication.

I had a thousand questions pouring through my mind all at once. I felt like the proverbial deer frozen in the headlights, though, as I racked my thought process trying to prioritize which questions were most important.

"How many? I mean, how many are in the group, or is it groups?" I asked.

"Ah, my mistake. I've given you the impression that this is some sort of army – in spite of the fact that the cause is totally peaceful – and that there are generals, sergeants and an organized infrastructure behind the effort. It's not like that at all."

"O.K. How is it then?"

"The souls that came to Earth in this effort are all parts of individual, non-related soul groups. Most, but not all are relatively more advanced in their learning compared with others still taking on physical incarnations. Enough so that, had they not decided to be part of an effort to help they might have decided not to take another physical incarnation at this time. But it was not as though there was some town hall meeting in the after-life dimension and people just raised their hands and volunteered. As souls, they made individual observa-

311

tions of what was occurring on earth and decided of their own volition – in consultation with each of their soul counsels – to attempt a
mission where they would carry the message. Others in their direct
soul group might have known what they planned to do, but each soul
that went, did so on their own," Kalista explained.

"But, the master souls – or whatever you call them – that sit on
the soul counsels must have seen that there were a number of these
types of souls deciding to take on these missions during that time
frame," I said.

Kalista gave me a look a great compassion. "They did. But again,
it would be a misconception to think of the inter-life experience as run
by a formal organization – a hierarchy in the way you think of say, a
corporate structure. The universe is organized but we are not an organization. That doesn't mean that some of the advanced souls didn't
perceive what was going on and might have even appreciated the idea
in their own way."

"Could those advanced souls have stopped it if they thought it
was a bad idea?"

"You know they would never do that. Couldn't do that. In this
case though, considering the previous fates and ultimate outcomes
that resulted from those that had tried previously to deliver this essential message into a fairly hostile world, the more advanced master souls
saw the effort as fairly noble. An act of true and genuine selfless compassion. Particularly considering that the last several times that it was
attempted those efforts were carried forth by very, very advanced spiritual masters. The souls going this time were not nearly as advanced."

"I know that you know Kalista. So why won't you tell me; how
many went? Ten, a hundred, a thousand, more? How many?"

"I don't know but I suspect it is at least tens of thousands of souls
over the 20 years or so since that all began. Probably more. I keep
telling you that we don't need to meet here to discuss things like this.
But you might be missing the point; every soul recognizes the essential message for what it is. Some need to hear it over and over again
before they begin the process of attaining basic Resonance. Of awakening. These *particular* souls, already advanced in their learning, had
some solid Resonance working for them when they took on their cur-

rent incarnations. Because of this, it will be easier for them to recollect. And once the souls that comprise this group awaken individually, their actions should facilitate a cascade of awakening in others from the Original Group. Hopefully, many of the other souls currently incarnated that were not part of the Original Group will also begin to be awakened as the message is spread," Kalista explained.

"Like an avalanche?"

"Sort of. But, I believe most that alit in the Original Group were thinking if they, on their own could trigger some basic recollection in a handful of people, and that handful triggered a hundred and so on, that over the course of a few lifetimes their original efforts would add up cumulatively and make a real difference. Their objective was to raise the overall world Resonance up several notches but over a period of time."

"And what starts the whole awakening process? I mean, are all of these souls on their mission waiting for some kind of sign?" I asked.

"Again, you're implying a broadly organized effort under one fixed set of organizational guidelines. It isn't anything like that. All I know concerns only those few souls who were in one of my groups that made the individual decision to go. Beyond that, I can only go from my perception – it would be a guess at best," Kalista said.

Kalista's words landed on me like a bale of hay. She had the inside story on this the whole time we were standing here talking about it. Why didn't she just say so? My experience with Kalista had taught me that when she was unwilling to volunteer her insights at the outset that there was likely to be some detail in the offing that wasn't going to make me very happy. I was about to complain to Kalista that she was toying with me, but decided to pursue the main thread of this conversation instead.

"And those that were in one of your soul groups? What were they counting on for impetus that would trigger their recollection?"

"Many forms actually. How did you do it?"

"What, How did I... WHAT," I tried to contain my emotions as I began pacing wildly in between the archways.

"You've obviously answered some sort of call. You *are* here, after all. You can not deny that you have begun to walk a definitive and serious pathway of compassion. And empathy. It is obvious that you have gone beyond the intellectual acceptance of reconciliation and balance and applied intent toward embracing that as a code of conduct for your life. For your very soul. You've told Tresden and me that you've shared these insights with others. What do you need, a neon sign?"

"But you always said that I had a ways to go until I got my 'promotion.' You said that… "

"And you mistakenly assumed that the promotion was from spiritual moron to spiritual buck private. I never said any such thing and wouldn't because in your case, it isn't true. Maybe that's something you need to think about." Kalista was forceful in her comment, in essence prodding me to search for greater self-confidence in my life.

"Personally, I think you just slipped though when Kalista wasn't looking. Last I heard you were taking that lifetime in Venice, cleaning the streets and pushing around the gondolas as a night job," Tresden chided me.

"Very funny Tresden. Look, this is serious. So, are you telling me that this is how those in the Original Group are supposed to begin the process of recollection? Meditation. Reading books by Carlos Casteneda, watching videos of the Dalai Lama speak about karma? That they… "

"Each soul will choose their own pathway. They must find their own individualized trigger for recollection. But I believe that their hope is that, as greater numbers of the various souls from the Original Group awaken and begin on their own to share the essential message with others that their doing so will trigger an awakening in greater numbers from the Original Group. It doesn't matter how they are triggered, only that they are triggered to recollect," Tresden said.

"Will it work?"

"It can work. Maybe not over the course of just one lifetime though. Those in the Original Group might have to take on several incarnations until enough souls have their Resonance raised to the point where there is a palpable shift in the demeanor and intent of a significant enough number of souls incarnating on earth to make a difference. Even so, even if it began to approach a majority of souls it won't assure the significant level of change that you might like to see. But it would be a meaningful start. Any basic shift in momentum might well be enough, over time, to create real change."

"Very well said Tresden." Kalista was acknowledging the progress of Tresden as an understudy.

"So, you really don't know how it will turn out... what happens?"

"We can show you what some of the most likely possibilities are," Kalista said.

With that, all four archways burst into activity at the same time. The archway behind us picked up in the Middle Ages. The side archways were still showing various future possibilities based upon the last developments and assumptions that Kalista had factored in. As the imagery sped up again I noted some of the horrific events of human history playing themselves out on the back archway. Civil wars. Unthinkable atrocities. The second world war. The Holocaust.

Viewed from this unique perspective, I saw the history of mankind since the time when several advanced souls had come to Earth to share the messages of compassion, empathy, love and peaceful existence had done nothing to stop us. Not from a seeming non-stop millennia-long cascade of hatred, bigotry, greed, violence, wars, murder and other unthinkable events. As sensitive compassionate beings I empathized how difficult it must be for those in the Original Group to watch as the world went through such a reality.

With great relief I noted from the images on the back archway that we were approaching current time. Foolishly, I had envisioned this to be a period of respite from the millennia of barbarism that had been passing by through the rear archway. Kalista indicated with a subtle movement of her head that she wanted me to shift my attention to the front archway. I perceived that she intended to show me something about the Original Group of souls coming to Earth.

My first awareness of a change was that the imagery slowed significantly concurrent with events and personalities that I identified with World War II. Goose-stepping Nazis. Hitler. Fascism. Suffering and violence on a scale almost unimaginable and certainly indefensible from a supposedly compassionate race of beings. At the time I was thinking through the impacts of this era on future world events as the images on the front archway changed completely in perspective. It was as though the viewing mechanism for that archway had been launched on the space shuttle to an altitude well above the Earth. From this view none of the violence was directly visible. Of great relief to me was that none of the emotions could be sensed any more either. As I was about to comment on the shelter granted by this higher view, Tresden motioned to the image of the Earth and instructed me with her eyes to pay close attention.

At first, I was unable to discern what I was supposed to be looking for. But in a matter of a few moments, I noticed that there was a faint and brief flickering of lights seemingly striking the surface of the Earth. The lights were very intermittent when I first noticed them. Over the course of a few minutes though, the speed at which these light bursts were hitting the earth and the sheer number had increased to the point where the effect gave the impression of a substantial meteor shower. My initial impression was that these were bombs exploding. But I immediately caught my mistaken assumption when I remembered that there was obviously no such broad scale attack in world history. As I was pondering how to interpret the images Tresden communicated in a very quiet, almost sullen manner.

"These are the souls of the Original Group assuming incarnations throughout the Earth."

I was shocked. "This is... this is what it looks like?"

Tresden smiled. "No. This is merely a representation of those events."

"They appear to be everywhere," I said.

"As Kalista said, they are," Tresden acknowledged.

"Tresden, how did the individual souls decide where they would go, the specifics of their incarnations?"

"Almost always, that process of assuming an incarnation is a very careful, well thought-out product of the individual soul contemplating and reviewing their immediately previous life, their other previous incarnations and deciding what they need to learn next. This is always done in consultation with their soul counsel and, often, members of their immediate soul group as well.

From that point, the individual soul goes to an area where they can begin to view a variety of incarnation forms that they could assume in their next life. Lives that might facilitate their particular need for specific lessons. You must remember, this planning is a complicated affair because, the individual soul, in addition to having specific lessons that *they* need to learn, also have karma to work out with others in their soul circle. Possibly even some souls outside of their direct soul group. There is a period where the individual soul considers different incarnation opportunities. But the soul also has to think through, on the basis of the incarnations that others in their soul clusters are contemplating, whether the combination will allow them the best opportunities to reconcile their karma and to learn essential lessons specific to their needs. Since there are many souls involved, it can be a fairly complicated process to set up the next lifetime. To create opportunities for many souls to reconcile their issues with others with whom they have issues to resolve. The soul advisors are there to help advise souls about these decisions."

"So, the souls in the Original Group had to cope with the assignment of recollecting, figuring out how they might be able to help other souls recollect as well as their normal life assignments like sorting out past karma and other lessons?"

"In most cases, yes. But some in the Original Group were so focused upon the mission to help others awaken that they assumed whatever incarnation was available to them at the time. Think of it as though the train was pulling away from the station. Some souls were so driven by their sense of mission to help others attain some level of awakening they said. 'I'll take any seat as long as I get there,'" Tresden explained.

"I don't understand."

"In the process of planning one's next lifetime, there are all sorts of arrangements and agreements with other souls who are integral to the process. All that can take time to arrange. Maybe one member of your soul group that you have critical karma to work out with is still incarnated while you are already present in the inter-life experience. That means either you waiting for them or, waiting for them to catch up to you if you opt to incarnate earlier as opposed to later. In the case of the Original Group, their desire to help rescue others was so great that some of them took whatever incarnate form was available," Tresden said.

"Wouldn't that mean that they would be sort of lost though? Cut off from their soul clusters for that lifetime?"

"Kalista?"

This was the first time I had ever observed Tresden actually need Kalista's help to answer a question. The other times Tresden had asked Kalista to intervene it was because she wanted another way of explaining something. I was surprised because I didn't think that she would acknowledge that while I was present. I also assumed that if Tresden didn't know the answer, the subject matter must have been fairly complex.

Kalista took over the explanation. "You need to consider a couple of things in that case. First is that, none of the souls in the Original Group were novice souls. In fact, I suspect, if my soul circle was any indication, that most of them were in the moderately-advanced stage - relative to other souls still taking on physical incarnations – when they assumed this particular life. That gives them an edge in a way. Because moderately-advanced souls – and even those that have not quite accomplished everything the moderately-advanced have – intuitively know their way around the incarnate world better than most souls that still take physical incarnations. They've had substantial life experience a good number of times already. That familiarity with the venue helps them negotiate their way about.

Those skills would allow most of those souls to find one or more members of their soul circle on their own if they needed to. If they really needed help, they'd find a way to locate at least one other soul in their circle. It wouldn't matter if they were on the other side of the world or next door; the skills these souls command would support their efforts. More importantly though is the focus of mission that these souls had when they assumed this particular incarnation. They knew they might be on their own and possibly separated from others in their soul group when they agreed to take on that particular life."

"Why would they do that Kalista?"

"Their very nature – the level of Resonance that they had attained – left them very few true alternatives. Once a soul attains a certain level of Resonance, compassion pretty much takes over their momentum and acts as a supporting pillar for their intent. When incarnated, identifying these souls with some degree of consistency is not that difficult. They are completely intolerant of other soul's suffering, they are almost always engaged in activities that are overtly and obviously designed to help others – if not as their work then as a primary activity outside of their work. They are driven to extend their spiritual knowledge and, where possible, spiritual awareness to those around them. Those souls in the Original Group, as they reached their own inter-life experience during this difficult period in Earth history, were no more able to resist doing what they could to try to help the other souls – without regard to their own pathway for the time being – than you would be able to pass a starving child on the street without taking immediate action."

Everything that Kalista was saying had an eerie effect on me. It was almost as though I could have finished her sentences for her. I identified with what she was saying.

Resonated with it completely. Somewhere inside of me, I not only knew this was true but felt as though I had heard all of this at some time in my past. I was so wrapped up in this contemplation that I almost missed the fact that Kalista had continued on with what she was explaining to me.

"If you think about all of this very carefully, within that place that equates with Resonance you will know that this is also very much about you. Specifically you and others that comprised the Original Group who no doubt have very similar life experience touchstones as you do."

"How do you mean that?"

"Think back throughout your entire conscious memory of this particular lifetime. As far back as you can remember you knew that you were on Earth for some mission. Some purpose. You *never* even had a doubt about that. To do something worthwhile not just to pass through and go through the motions of living. For as long as you can remember you knew that you couldn't quite recollect what that mission was. That gnawing deep inside of you that you didn't understand was your core Resonance knocking on the door of your conscious self.

Trying to remind you exactly why you agreed to the life you are living now.

At times, it almost drove you crazy as you tried so desperately to recollect the specific reasons that you took on this particular life. 'Why am I living?' you would ask yourself. You were driven to the spiritual but determined not to be limited by the strictures and failures of the organized religions. No matter how frustrated you might have become at your inability to identify your mission, you never gave up. And if you did, it never lasted for long. You always returned to your searching. Almost as though drawn back to course by some magnet. Your Resonance ceaselessly coaxing your soul even when your conscious mind fought off the idea of anything that couldn't be understood by its limited perception. You recognized on your own that, all the things that you were working yourself into exhaustion to acquire would be gone in a matter of years.

Fortunately, you recollected that there was more than that. In your case, you needed to get to the point where your rational mind finally capitulated to what your Resonance had been telling you all along: you are far more than what you see when you gaze into the mirror. And you **do** have a purpose other than acquiring assets and paying taxes. You began meditating to seek shelter from dissatisfaction with your day-to-day life. You became more and more frustrated at your inability to remember why you were living at all. The form of novel mediation that you stumbled upon quieted your mind and allowed your Resonance to shine just brightly enough for me to reach out and grasp your perception and bring you the rest of the way into the garden where Tresden and I decided to help you. When Geradl made an appearance and told us to accelerate your learning, we knew that we had done the right thing. Such was the pathway that you followed to recollection. Others from the Original Group may take similar pathways or, find other ways."

"So others from the Original Group would feel the same way? Have the same frustrations, feel that life was more or less empty? Wonder why they were here, why the world was so violent and seemingly alien to them? That they had somehow possibly incarnated in wrong world? That they didn't belong?"

"They may feel other things beyond this. Have different factors that frustrate or motivate them to finally set aside the illusions of their day-to-day life and finally seek answers. Just how they ultimately end up recollecting their Resonance and remembering their mission is completely unpredictable. And it makes no difference how it happens only that it *does* happen. Any trigger that works in this case is a good trigger," Kalista said.

"I wish you could get that message spread around on Earth. There are some folks there that can get pretty testy when you suggest that there is anything but their way – one way, the only way – to return home. In fact, some say that anyone that doesn't choose *their* pathway is going to hell."

"They can believe that if they want to. Eventually, they'll arrive at the awareness that believing that there is only one pathway to accomplish anything is solely a product of personal and in some cases, religious insecurity. Programming. A fear that someone other than you might have another way and that the inflexible one, the fervent true believer, doesn't. There are endless numbers of pathways that will trigger recollection. Ceaseless alternatives to find your way home. It's one of the basic assurances, a literal guarantee, from Source," Tresden explained.

"Can we get back to the Original Group for a moment; in the end, does all this work out? I mean, does the world make it... survive and prosper in every sense?" I asked.

"You know that at best, we can only illustrate for you the range of possibilities. Maybe even probabilities. Let me show you."

The archways immediately sprung into action again as Kalista indicated she wanted me to focus on the forward archway. At first I didn't understand the context of what the imagery was illustrating. The scenes playing themselves out were in current time, circa 1994 as near as I could surmise and very much indicative of everyday life in a variety of settings. Large cities. Rural small towns. Geography ranging from Japan to Canada; Iceland to Chile. The United States to Australia. And everyplace in between.

As I concentrated intently on the characters and related imagery within the scenes though I began to sense every now and then that, what I would perceive as one of the everyday people that I noted in the imagery seemed to have almost a faint glow about them. They were somehow just a bit more defined in some vague manner than those around them. I effected the subtle transformation into the empathy mode of the device. As I did so, it became very clear to me that those people must have all been from what Kalista had called the Original Group. I sensed a genuine and deep feeling of heightened compassion and sensitivity seemingly emitting from their very core essences.

There wasn't a tremendous number of them. For a few minutes, I engaged in a pointless exercise wherein I tried to determine how many out of a hundred might have given me the impression that they gave off this effect. Then I realized that it would be more like one out of a thousand. The test I was attempting to perform was too difficult for me to reach any real firm determination on numbers. But the point was not lost on me; these souls were everywhere. And it was just as clear that they were all in various jobs, doing various things in life and, in differing states of awakening themselves. Most of them, I sensed, had a ways to go until they reached a point where they would actively begin sharing their message overtly and broadly with others. At least on a larger scale. It was going to be a while, I perceived, until they managed to convey the message to those outside their own inner circles.

But they *were* there. Or should I say, *are* here. More than I ever imagined. I also sensed an incredibly deep sense of commitment from these souls to their mission. It afforded me a deeply reassuring sense of comfort.

Not lost on me were the events that were playing out on the side archways. My impression from these images was not as comforting. In 1994, I had believed that things were about as disjointed, violent and uneven as the world might be able to tolerate. That self-dealing and greed couldn't possibly go further than it already had without severely testing the limits of society in general. But the imagery beginning to play itself out on the right-hand archway – the one that illustrated potential futures if we did not, as a community of souls sharing one planet raise our collective practices in compassion, empathy and love

– illustrated an even more violent and far less tolerable world.

Many of the images had marginal context for me. I noted severe cataclysm in Africa on a broad scale. But the detail was not discernable from viewing images in the archway. They were either moving by too quickly or my perception was not up to the complexity of the imagery. Of course, the fullness of time would afford me an all too clear look into the realities of those events; the AIDS pandemic, famine, more brutally violent civil wars than anyone could ever reasonably contemplate and inter-tribal and ethnic violence and murder on a near wholesale basis. From my perspective outside the archway, all I noted was disaster on top of disaster. I noted violence but not the individual faces of those killed. Disease, but not the cries of those without medicine. Or hope.

The imagery that represented the rest of the world was not as primitive or overtly out of control but was equally as disheartening. Fifteen or so years after the millennium my impression was that the world had fallen into a state that looked more like one of those futuristic movies where everyone has a weapon and is barricaded in compounds more than anything else. Unable to tolerate any more visions of this as our future I shifted my attentions to the left archway.

The future as illustrated on the left archway – indicative, according to Kalista, of mankind attaining a more favorable overall demeanor – was far more encouraging to me. My first and most lasting impression in this sequence was that souls from the Original Group assumed a far higher profile. In this version of future events in a time horizon that I envisioned as starting what looked like five to ten years after the millennium, these slightly more advanced souls had become broadly awakened themselves and were actively sharing the messages of karma, compassion, empathy and love with others. Many others. Not just in monasteries, ashrams, temples and churches. The clear vision afforded me by the imagery was that the message was being adopted on a broad scale by people in virtually every walk of life.

And the result was just shy of dramatic. Changing the world overnight was likely impossible. More than reasonable to even hope for. But these images showed a palpable shift in the overall tenor of some meaningful number of souls here. There was a clear difference in the overall sense and "feel" of the world that I got when I compared these images to those projected within the other archway. There was not only greater peace in the world but an underlying desire by far more people to have peace. And to seek peace. To pursue a peaceful way of living. To set aside the obsession with the accumulation of personal wealth in favor of considering the merit in accumulating spiritual insights. And merit.

Secular, religious, ethnic, geographical, economic and political intolerance were on the wane as well. Greed was down a bit. Compassion, although by no means universal, was a flicker of light in many who had not been overly conscious of its value just a few short years earlier. There were still problems. There was still violence. There were still murders. Most significant of all though, there was a definitive shift in the intent of substantial numbers of people.

Far greater numbers of people stopped themselves for a few seconds before saying something. Before responding to someone. They actually thought about what they were going to do or say – considered the potential impact on others – and quite often caught themselves just in time. Most of the time they ended up saying far less than they would have under the future vision illustrated on the opposite archway where people would have been as likely to respond with a gun. Or maybe saying nothing at all. Those few seconds of hesitation before speaking had resulted in a broad ratcheting down of negative feelings that had been so pervasive in the world under the other scenario.

There was also a broad-based and ever-increasing inquisitiveness and momentum toward enlightenment. People took the time to think about why they were here. What lessons they were meant to learn. How they individually, might go about mastering the essential practices of compassion and empathy. How they could craft their own pathway home. People began to dedicate time to these issues. Real time. Not just for an hour on Sunday. Maybe only the time when they were driving off to work each day. Before long this became the dominant focus in many people's daily life. Not the majority, but there was momentum in that direction. The numbers were building every day as more souls from the Original Group attained heightened awareness and shared that message selflessly with others.

As I watched this version of the future unfold before my eyes, a blissful peace began to envelop every part of me. I was floating in a sea of absolute comfort and peace, basking in images of a world gone sane as opposed to crazy for a change. Just about the time that I was about to comment to Kalista and Tresden that I preferred, by far, this version of the future of the world the images from the left archway flickered once or twice and then the entire archway went completely black. Not hazy fog. Not partially opaque. Not blurry images. Black. Just black.

I was so shaken by the rapid change in environment and shattering of the peaceful state that I had been immersed in that I lost my perceptional balance completely. It was as though I had been laying out on a blanket on a perfect, lazy summer afternoon and suddenly, someone had come along and thrown one hundred gallons of ice-cold water on me.

My next awareness was that I was sitting on the floor of my study. I noted that it was still dark outside. Or had I been at Kalista's garden all day and returned during the late evening hours? I managed to get to my feet and grab my notepad as I steadied myself and sat down at my desk. I wanted to write my notes so that I could try to capture the essence of what had just transpired in as detailed a manner as possible.

Most of all though, I really needed to know what happened. What did all of that mean? I pondered for a time a world gone totally dark and a sinking feeling jolted me into considering a melancholy possibility. Maybe we're not going to make it. Maybe those in the Original Group doesn't succeed. I needed to get back. I needed to understand. And I desperately needed to know what that blackness meant for our future.

CHAPTER TWELVE

I can not conceive of a personal God who would directly influence the actions of individuals, or would sit in judgment on creatures of his own creation.... My religiosity consists of a humble admiration of the infinitely superior spirit that reveals itself in the little that we, with our weak and transitory understanding, can comprehend of reality.

- From, The Human Side, 1954, Albert Einstein

The events surrounding my visit to the "Hallway of Possibilities" left me in a kind of spiritual and psychological catatonia. On a few previous visits to Kalista's realm, the insights or sensory assaults that I had taken in so overwhelmed me that my perceptional handhold was lost and I found myself mysteriously back in my study pondering what had happened. This most recent displacement wasn't like that. The impact on me of watching the events revealed within the archway go black, and at a time when the images appeared to be illustrating so much encouragement for our future left me feeling as though I had run into a spiritual and perceptional brick wall while going 1,000 miles an hour.

When I finally regained my bearings in my study, it was impossible for me to write any notes or comments about the session. A broad and seemingly systemic numbness held me virtually hostage. I just sat there, unable to move and barely able to breathe, for a long time. All of these were remnants from the shock of what I had just experienced. On earlier occasions when I had become overwhelmed by some

327

experience that Kalista, Tresden or Geradl had guided me through I was usually able to recover quickly. At least initially.

For whatever reasons, this time it was much different. Something had happened to me. And whatever it was, I knew that it wasn't good. I had lost something that I had spent two years acquiring; my firm grasp on much of the knowledge I had absorbed. I was also deeply saddened and depressed by what the images seemed to indicate was our future.

I tried in vain for nine weeks to engineer another visit to the garden. It was the first time in almost two years that I was literally unable to make the connection. My objective for a visit was simple and direct; I needed a clarification and deeper insight from Kalista as to the meaning and import of what I had experienced at the Hallway of Possibilities. More paralyzing than anything, I was carrying around a near all-consuming fear that what I had seen somehow indicated that mankind might not survive the technological adolescence it had exploded into a half-century ago. I'd find some temporary relief in the fact that the imagery I'd experienced coming from the archways didn't conclude with a large mushroom cloud. But that relief was always short-lived as I recollected Kalista's words that the Hallway of Possibilities often illustrated its insights symbolically or inferentially. Cataclysmic nightmares invaded my sleep. I began to make mistakes in my everyday life; some were failures in concentration, others were errors in judgment relative to what Tresden and Kalista had worked so hard to teach me.

Each time I attempted to make a connection to the garden my mind became a total blank. The blackness that pervaded the archways now invaded my concentration to the point where I simply couldn't make the transition to the garden. The process of making my way to Kalista's garden that seemed so simple and almost automatic only two months earlier now seemed completely foreign to me. In a measure of near desperation I began sifting through the hundreds of scraps of paper that bore the notes I had made after two years of sessions. I'd begun making session notes almost reflexively when I had the very first experience with Kalista. I had continued making these notes as a form of grounding for my sanity.

As I stared aimlessly at drawings I had fashioned, notes both extensive and brief, it was as though someone else had written them in some code with which I was almost completely unfamiliar. There was familiarity to the content but I couldn't connect the critical elements of the puzzle. More than anything I felt as though I was a castaway adrift on a raft; the notes were equivalent to an oar and a sail, but I had little idea how best to use them or, in which direction I should go. I remember thinking at the time; castaways usually end up loosing their minds, and now I know why.

Just where the breakthrough came from I'll never really know. In retrospect, I've always been tempted to believe that it was Kalista in some mysterious spiritual way whispering to my just-under-the consciousness awareness. Providing both instruction and encouragement to me. Irrespective of where the epiphany arose. It began in late October 1994, in my study. I found myself placing the notes and drawings I had made in a sequence of sorts, although at the time, the sequence didn't mean much to me. My hands were arranging the various scraps of paper far faster than my mind was providing instructions. It was as close to an out-of-body experience as I've ever had besides, of course, the trips to Kalista's garden. In less than an hour, the pile had undergone a transformation from cacophony to coherence. From mystery to mysteriously insightful.

As I leafed through the now well-organized, assemblage of notes and drawings, a cascade of insights began returning to me. It was not as though I had forgotten the concepts that Kalista, Tresden and Geradl had shared with me during my past two years with them. The raw information was still within me. Somehow the emotion of it all – the true emotional-spiritual connection to the All and the profound sense of being one with all things – had been deeply compromised by whatever had happened to me at the archways. I didn't understand the details of it. Not at all.

Sitting on the floor of my study I began making my way back through the pages in front of me, my spiritual connection with everything that I had taken in from Kalista's insights began mysteriously reconstituting itself within me. In the matter of moments I traversed from a place where I understood, but only in loose concept, that we

329

are all derived from one source back to the irrefutable place of true *knowing* at the level of my soul that we all, are all, in fact, Source. Not only in essence but in total. One by one the insights began returning to me like a series of firecrackers programmed to explode one after another. At one specific moment during this process I finally grasped with true comprehension what Kalista meant when she urged me over and over again to take in and embrace fully the concept of 'recollection.' I thought back to the time when she said to me "everything is there, inside of you. It always has been and it always will be. You just need to get to the point of accepting that and master the process of recollecting it."

I spent nearly the entire day basking in the warmth and spiritual security that recollecting our attachment with these universal truths brings us to. And then, with barely a nudge on my volition, I recalled the warm blanket feeling that I had used countless times to push me across the barrier to Kalista's garden. With no more than the effort we all expend to breathe, I found myself standing on the pathway in the rose garden. Tears were rolling down my face as I celebrated my return. My learning. My success as an erstwhile student under Kalista and Tresden had paid off. Kalista was clipping rosebuds a few feet up the pathway and smiled from ear to ear as the incredibly lush scenery took form around us. Kalista noted my tears but ignored them.

"Hi! Did you... "

"Kalista! I made it! I actually made it! I thought I'd never figure out how to get back here. I'm so... "

"What? Why not? What happened?"

Over the time I'd been coming to visit Kalista, I had learned a thing or two about how she used various teaching devices to instruct me as a student. One of those realizations was that Kalista loved to tease me, particularly when I had either forgotten something that she considered essentially unforgettable or when I bungled some basic maneuver like how to find my way to the garden. It was obvious that she knew all about the difficulties I had been having recently, probably long before I even arrived that day.

"Kalista, you can't fool me with that stuff anymore. You know full well what I've been going through."

"I suppose I do. I just thought I'd try to cut you off from indulging yourself in all that silliness."

"Silliness?" I was taken back, "I was really stuck Kalista. Lost is more like it. There was the possibility that I'd have never made it back."

"Never? Never? No, not really. Actually, you just forgot for a moment the most important thing that Tresden, Geradl and I have taught you."

"I thought that all of it was important?"

"Have I ever showed you what it feels like to be struck by a bolt of lightening?"

"Sorry. It's just that I never thought that from all the insights that I've learned here that there was any kind of hierarchy to their importance."

"Not more important. Think of it as everything that you have learned here exists inside a house. In order to gain access to the information within that house you need the key to the front door. By the way, its also quite helpful if you remember what street you live on." Kalista was still taking her shots at me because I'd forgotten my way to the garden.

"And now you're going to say that I don't have to remember all of the information that's in the house. I only need to remember where the key is. It's like a library, if I know where the building is, there's no need for me to memorize all of the information in all the books there. I can just go look up what I need."

"Very good. So in that analogy, tell me; where is the library?"

"I don't know; in my mind I guess."

"That does it Tresden. Oh, Tresden!"

Kalista was back in her mock anger mode. She was disappointed in my response. I suspected from my long experience with Tresden and Kalista that setbacks of this nature were not completely unprecedented from souls that were attempting to traverse this difficult pathway of knowledge. That she invoked Tresden was my clue that she was neither disappointed nor angry. Not that I have ever seen – or would expect to see – Kalista actually angry. In this case it was apparent that she was looking for a different way to explain a way past my current short-sightedness, something that Tresden had proven to be quite masterful at on many occasions.

Tresden, cued in through some silent communiqué from Kalista, came skipping in from the far side of the garden whistling the theme from *Man of La Mancha,* "To Dream the Impossible Dream." The effect of Tresden entering the garden while skipping and whistling this song was too comical for me to resist laughing. It was Tresden's brilliant way to let me know that I was again, being my own worse enemy in my quest for knowledge while at the same time, not allowing me to become overly-morose that I had reached a stumbling block. Her humor as always, kept me from falling over a cliff at my short-term failures in learning. But even Kalista, a fairly stern teacher, appreciated the mock humor Tresden was employing. In a matter of a few moments, we all regained our composure but only by applying a serious dose of self-control in my case.

"You called Kalista?" Tresden pretended to be out of breath which only served to emphasize the comedy.

"Yes. Your protégé here is having some difficulties with the core concept."

"Not possible."

"Oh yes it is. Just ask him."

"I will. Hi Chuck. Where's the library?" Tresden's direct assumption of the analogy that Kalista had been using before Tresden arrived threw me for a second. I was learning that Kalista and Tresden were in some form of near total communication at all times – at a level far beyond my ability to comprehend. I had also begun to contemplate the possibility that Kalista and Tresden had used many of their teaching scenarios before; to throw off balance the student while concurrently instructing them in some basic spiritual lesson. It only felt new to me because I had never seen it before.

"I told her Tresden, it's in my mind," I said.

"You're joking right? I mean, no offense meant but, there's nothing in your mind. Not really."

"What does that mean?"

"Well, you think of your mind as being your brain right?"

"I guess so. Isn't it?"

"Doesn't matter. What *does* matter though is your need to understand where the gateway to all knowledge resides. And that isn't in your mind. It's within your recollection."

"Tresden, are you saying that I don't recollect with my mind?"

"Sure you do; you recollect where you left your car, what isle the apples are at in the grocery store, what the names of people you work with are. But the true recollection, the kind that affords genuine insight into the nature of reality and our pathway home, *that* recollection is performed only by the Essence of your Soul. Your 'mind' can only stand in the way of processing information of that nature."

"So are you telling me that the 'library' is located within my essence?"

"I'm telling you, and more importantly you already know, always have known and always will know, just like everyone else, that all knowledge is inherent within the essence of what you are. You remember what we showed you about Source; that at Origination, Source was one thing and that everything within the All derived from Source?"

"Yes."

"That is the level then that you must access – the *only* level to access – if you want spiritual knowledge and understanding. Truth, all truth, the only viable and meaningful truth, derives from that connection."

"But how do I know if what I perceive as truth is flowing to me from my mind or from my essential self?"

"Very good question. In fact, one of your best ever. Do you remember all the times that Geradl, Tresden and me have instructed you to forget the experience and retain the lesson? Kalista seemed very focused all of a sudden.

"Yes, and I've tried to do that Kalista."

"As confusing as this might be for you, the reality is that the only way we can know for certain – at least for the level you have attained right now – that the knowledge you are absorbing is directly from the essential self, is that it has come to you solely from the experience. Only through recollection outside of the mind can we avail ourselves of knowledge that is pure. That is genuinely derived from recollection of the All."

"So the address of the library is recollection with the essential self?"

"Very close Chuck. Try it this way: true knowledge flows to us *only* through the essential self and only by the process of recollection."

"I think I understand. So how do we know that we are actually hearing the essential self and not some deep portion of our mind?"

"Another very excellent question!" Geradl said.

I had no idea that Geradl had quietly made his way up the pathway from the rose garden and taken up a position directly beside me. I made a conscious decision not to show any outward signs of the shock Geradl caused to my system in spite of the fact that I knew that all of them could see right through me. Hoping to impress Geradl that I had progressed in some ways, I responded to his comment with no break in the cadence of the conversation.

"But, is there an answer that a soul at my level can really grasp at this point Geradl?"

"Do you remember when I showed you the events around Origination?"

"Yes. Quite vividly."

"Ponder for a moment the range of experiences you had when you attained true recognition that everything within the All derives from one, and only one, Source." Geradl was studying me intently as he communicated both the thought and imparted the recollection of the event to me.

It took me a few moments to shift my focus and spiritual awareness back to those specific events. As I began to revisit that experience I was again overwhelmed by the images and sense of absolute vastness that consumed me back then. At about the fifth intersection where the All was about to unfold yet again – the point where I had become fully overwhelmed previously – Geradl shook me out of my awed state with urgency.

"The vastness which you experience at this moment, that is pure experience of the essential self. That is purified recollection of Totality of the Soul. Remember that experience always and you will forever know the difference between the true essential self and that which your transient mind creates to distract you – that which your ego invents to perpetuate the illusion of itself."

Geradl's words landed on me one at a time and in what felt like some mystical rain shower where each drop lands several seconds away from the next. It felt as though each word permeated every cell of my being and as I absorbed each word, the next one would begin processing its meaning within me. I concluded that it had to have been some far-advanced spiritual technique that Geradl was using. Designed to indelibly etch into the target soul some essentially specific spiritual knowledge, crucial learning, that they must never, ever forget. What had overwhelmed me, the question that seemed so impossible to me only a moment before; just how we are to know the difference between insights created by our everyday mind as opposed to true insights from Source, the essential self, seemed child's play after Geradl's instruction. I took a moment to ponder the incredible power and sheer vastness of responsibility that must be implicit in Geradl's ability to impart knowledge of this nature. Geradl again interrupted my thinking.

"All of that knowledge, including the explicit ability to comprehend the subtlety between ruminations of one's own mind and knowledge flowing from the true Source has always been within you Chuck. Always. It is sometimes the case that when we hear confirmation of these concepts from a soul that we perceive to be more learned, more accomplished in knowledge, that we are more open to the prospect that this soul has somehow imparted that learning to us. It is not the case. As with all true learning about the essential self, it is all only a process of recollection. Once the reality of recollection is accepted, once we identify completely and without qualification with the truth that we all derived from and are inexorably a part of Source, that insight creates both impetus and momentum of its own. From there, our journey homeward on the wings of recollection is both inevitable and accelerated."

"So are you saying that it's instantaneous? That once we recognize and accept at some level inside of us that recollection is the key, we soar to a place of understanding?"

"No. As much as anything a prospect like that would overwhelm an individual soul to the point of confusion. It would be like pulsing 10 trillion volts through an extension cord all at once. The insights have to be absorbed over time."

I was fascinated by the analogy that Geradl used and thought about pursuing his knowledge of something as banal as electricity and extension cords, but thought better of it. I appreciated his willingness to provide clarification.

"I see the analogy Geradl but I'm not sure about the detail of it."

"Maybe we should reduce it to something simple like Prokofiev's 5th piano sonata?"

Geradl's statement floored me. I wasn't sure whether I should be more shocked that he even knew of one of my favorite classical composers, Sergei Prokofiev, or that he knew my affinity for the 5th piano sonata.

"Prokofiev, sure. Why not. What about it?"

"Here's a record of Prokofiev's 5th piano sonata." Geradl said this as though he was saying "isn't it a nice day outside?" I hadn't seen him move from where he was standing or even reach anywhere for the recording he held out to me. One second it didn't exist and the next it was in his hand. A standard, twelve inch, old-style vinyl record. In a moment of self-amusement, I thought about why he hadn't simply handed me a CD, but knew that wouldn't be an acceptable subject to pursue.

"O.K. Now what do I do with it?"

"Exactly! I think you finally have it!" Geradl didn't get excited. He was the most sedate, even-tempered and competent soul I'd ever met. There was no need for him to use voice inflection or emphasize his points in other ways because the content and style of his communication left no room for doubt that, whatever he was saying, was crucial information. The trouble in this case was, I had no idea at all what he was talking about.

"I don't understand."

"Yes you do," Geradl responded, almost smiling.

"Yes you do," Tresden echoed.

"Yes you do," Kalista chimed in.

"No really, I don't get it. What am I missing?"

"You know how inherently beautiful and perfect the music on this record is don't you?" Kalista asked me.

"Of course I do."

"How?" She urged me along.

"Because I've heard it before."

"*How* did you hear it?"

"Well Kalista, I've heard it lots of ways. I have several copies of the CD, a few copies of the tape and I've heard it performed live at concerts. It's beyond magnificent."

"And?"

"And what?"

Geradl was standing there once again extending his hand out and holding the record for me to take. Not wanting to appear ungrateful or rude I reached out and took the record from him and thanked him at the same time.

"Now what do I do with it?"

"Exactly! You're right Geradl, I think he finally does have it," Kalista said.

"What are you *talking* about? I don't have anything. I'm standing here like a fool holding a record in one hand with no way to play it. If I want to hear the music I'll need a record player and some time to experience it."

"And? C'mon, you're almost there now," Tresden encouraged.

As I heard the echo of my own words the foolhardiness of my density became clear to me. In a blistering bolt of true insight, I began to see what Geradl, Kalista and Tresden were trying to say to me. "Wait a minute, wait a minute. You're going to say that the record in my hand is the same as all of the information available to me through recollection. And that all I need to do is to find a record player, well, the equivalent of a record player, and then take the time to hear the music."

"And revel in it. Enjoy it. Drink it in. Bask in its glory. Experience the vast range of all the feelings and insights that derive from it. And far more than that," Kalista said enthusiastically.

"And the record player? Where do I find one of those in all this?"

"You tell me since you're moving along so quickly now?"

"Hmm, I'm not certain. Is it the volition, the innate desire within my soul to reacquire that knowledge? Some deep 'programming' to return back home to Source and report on what we learned, what we experienced?"

Geradl didn't say a word. But he almost smiled. Almost. It was subtle. At first I thought I might have been just hopeful; just kidding myself. My imagination giving way to anticipation of what I wanted. But it was there. I could see it. With that, Geradl turned around for all of a half-second and produced an antique style record player, probably circa 1935 or so. He then gently took the record from my hand and placed it on the record player. Then ever so gently he cranked the spring and then placed the needle on the record.

I've never been a stereo buff. But I do know that the music that resulted from Geradl's antique record player far exceeded any technology we might ever see at our electronics retailers. The simple record player created an impact of sounds that was equivalent to hearing 500 symphonies all in perfect harmony playing the most exquisite music all at the same time. It created a feeling of absolute bliss inside of me that was almost more than my senses could handle. I was transported to a place where I would have been happy to stay for eternity. Or so I thought for the first few seconds. Geradl interrupted my joyful state with his communication.

"I want to give you a gift. It's a very special gift, unique in all the universe. It will forever serve as a touchstone for you to recollect the most important awareness that any soul can command and will serve as both your motivation and an reminder of how to return home. This particular gift will afford you unfettered permanent access to the insight of where you are, where you have been and, most important for where you have progressed to at this time, where you are going. The mystery for you to unravel for now is that all three are exactly the same place."

"But I... "

Geradl cut me off with a brief, but powerful look. It was clear once again that this was one of those occasions when the lesson was in the experience and not the content of any kind of overt communication. I had a few moments to ponder the riddle within Geradl's words. How could it be possible that where I was, where I am and where I am going could all, be the same place? Before I could gain any real momentum of thought on this enigma Geradl continued.

"Once before when I showed you the Origination I cracked open the curtain so that you could obtain a brief glimpse of Source. The time has come for you to take in a greater exposure to Source. Doing so will permanently convey to your essence a reminder. A beacon that will signal to you the nature of your true self – of your origin… of your true construct. Once done, any question that might have existed within you about your immutable connection and relation to Source will be forever erased. It will serve as a touchstone for all eternity should you ever lose your way home. It will not give you answers to your questions but will crack the door so that you may push it open just enough to walk through it and seek your own answers and insights by recollecting what you experienced during this moment."

I was about to appeal to Geradl that I needed time to prepare for what sounded like more than an awe-inspiring rite of passage. Doing so would have been a waste of effort and I knew that. Geradl knew what I was capable of handling and what I was not. Probably far better than I did. If Geradl believed I was ready then I had better find a way to make myself ready. It took all that I had within me to fight off the fear and trepidation that was starting to consume me. I was cognizant of the fact that the last time Geradl exposed me to this I passed out.

Geradl took a half-step toward me. The look on his face was one of total serenity and absolute peace. I recall clearly hearing the music still paying in the background and sought a form of shelter within it. In a brief movement of his hand Geradl reached up and touched the left side of my head, around the temple. In an instant, I was again transported back to the enormity of the empty vast space where Geradl had shown me the unfolding of reality; what he had called The Origination. It was also the place where he had performed the cracking of the curtain and exposed me for a barely an instant to what he had referred to as true Source.

Oddly, I found that I was quite interested to learn more about our immediate surroundings. Our generalized environment. As I glanced around to see where we were standing I was shocked to learn that we were literally suspended within the vastness that spanned all eternity around us. I attempted to say something to Geradl but found that I was unable even to communicate to him through my mind. Fortunately, Geradl was not impaired and the last thing I recall him saying to me was "remember this always." It sounded as much like a friendly command as anything else. The way he said it gave me a brief moment to brace myself for what came next.

As Geradl reached out into the vastness he once again cracked the curtain behind which was what he referred to as pure Source. The essence and Origination of all things. This time it was clear that Geradl intended to go beyond opening the curtain just a crack. Spaces and measurements have no frame of reference at all in this environment. My perception was that a small distance in that state of awareness is probably measured in terms of light years. Geradl slid the curtain open marginally beyond where he had the last time and as he did so I found myself once again completely consumed by the experience.

The first recollection I had of the experience was that every thought that I'd ever had or idea I had ever contemplated about individuality being important simply vanished. I recognized without equivocation and immediately that our insistence that we, as individuals, are "real" is as farcical as an actor in movie claiming that they are actually the character that they are playing in that movie. The indisputable reality of that is when the movie is over, so is the character that was played.

In a similar manner I saw clearly that, when any life is concluded, so is the "individuality" of the person living it. The soul – the actual actor – remains, but they go on to play different characters and different roles in different lives. And have different experiences. I saw that where we go astray in this life is our attachment to the character that we play at any one time. Because it is that very belief that we *are* that character that blinds us to the fact that we are, in reality, the actor behind the character. And that actor is something else completely. Something that never dies even when the film has run its last reel. When the character we had played has long left the sound stage.

I also saw with clarity that the charade we play at every day, what we call life, is really a gift from God, from the Source of all things. It is no more than a very sophisticated stage stocked with other souls playing out other roles and learning varying lessons. It is maintained and fully animated solely for us. For our learning. For our practice. To improve and enhance our skills in compassion, empathy and love of other souls. I saw that there are an endless number of settings in the Universe, courtesy of Source, that we can avail ourselves of to learn our essential lessons. To hone our skills.

More than anything, this particular vista illustrated for me with clarity that death is the largest illusion of all. Imagine the entire cast of a movie bursting into tears because one of the actors had finished their particular part in the movie and had gone on to another set, to a different part, in a different movie – to a separate sound stage located elsewhere in the movie studio. It was clear beyond equivocation to me at this moment that we can always reacquaint ourselves with those souls that we have known in other lives. We just need to be cognizant of the fact that they may be playing a different part when we see them again. They might or might not take off their then current mask to reveal for us in what context we knew them previously. It was also apparent that we tend to incarnate as groups of actors over and over again. Playing out different roles in different plays and wearing different masks. Learning and relearning our various lessons.

Once this is understood and accepted we can recognize those with whom we have millennia-long relationships. If we are interacting intensively with someone in our daily lives the likelihood is very high that we have a long history with that person going back many lifetimes. What we need to sort out is, what can we do to help that person? And if we find ourselves locked in a negative cycle with that person, we must search for a solution as to what can be done to bring that cycle to a close. Because it is inevitable that if we do *not* do so that we are destined to have to come back and play out those issues and learn those lessons over and over and over again.

These insights were flowing to me, to some essentially unknown part of me, directly. They were not in any way thoughts that I was processing consciously at the time. Many years later, Kalista told me that these were recognitions. True Recognitions. A way in which we, as spiritual beings, acknowledge our identification of reality as it is, not as we might have erroneously perceived it to be.

The last recognition that I recall being aware of is an understanding that God is not a puppeteer. Our strings us are not pulled by gods or angels. Nor devils for those that are tempted to assign blame for their misfortunes and actions on others. I saw that everything that Kalista had shown me in this regard was absolutely true. Whatever we're experiencing we brought to our own vista. And if we didn't set it up that way for a specific learning then we are experiencing it because we need to learn something that we were not aware of. As Tresden used to remind me over and over again: if you've got a speeding ticket in your hand, the chances are better than average that *you* were the one speeding. Yelling at the cop doesn't take away from the fact that you were speeding.

It became clear to me that no real forward movement as a soul really can occur until we understand the absolute truth of, 'that which we experience we created.' And until we understand that, and take responsibility for that immutable truth, we sentence ourselves to an endless cycle of life after life after life of unhappiness and mystification of why we are suffering. In the throes of this experience I was suddenly jolted out of my blissful state by an instruction that I heard clearly from Geradl to "come back."

"Hold on Chuck, you almost sunk in too far for us to pull you out," Kalista said.

"What? What are you talking about? Sunk in?"

"It's complicated to explain. Reuniting with Source can be pretty addictive as well as informative."

As Geradl communicated this thought to me, I became conscious of the fact that wherever I had just been was far in excess of being just a comfortable place. In fact, being pulled back from wherever that was created an acute feeling of unhappiness and displacement within me. I was about to protest when Geradl read my thoughts and answered me before I could think to communicate anything.

"It's just a matter of being ready. Nothing more than that. You've made tremendous progress recently. This specific exposure to Source will provide you a great repository of knowledge and experiences upon which you can recollect and perform recognitions of reality. If you try to take in too much too soon you wouldn't be able to hold onto what you learned. You'd have the blissful experience of it, the exposure to pure Source, but the actual recollections would leave you after a while. You are ready to move onto a place where you can retain that learning and, if you choose, pass it on to others."

"But what I want to understand is... "

Geradl smiled at me for a brief second and surprised me by reaching out to shake my hand. I was panicked by the thought that in some way this was goodbye. But I knew from what I had just experienced that there are no goodbyes. Not really. At worst there are so longs. But even the thought that I might not see Geradl for a while sent me into an anxious state. I was about to ask Geradl to stay for a while and tell me that everything would work out but realized that anything I said would sound childish and unconvincing.

"Don't worry, Chuck. When you are ready, I will see you again. And it will seem as though barely a moment has passed. Kalista and Tresden will help you always, as well. You will never be lost again, believe me."

With that, Geradl, as he had done the last time I had seen him, used his left hand to sort of half wave goodbye to me. He turned and before I could even really focus on him, he was gone. Before I could begin to lament Geradl's departure, Tresden picked up the conversation as though nothing significant had even happened.

"Bollocks! That guy sure knows how to make an exit doesn't he? I wish he'd teach me that someday," Tresden said gleefully.

"Very funny, Tresden. I wish you'd tell me who he is in the overall scheme."

"We already told you all that we can about that. Besides, it doesn't matter. You'll understand more when you are able to comprehend more. For now, there are other things you need to take in," Kalista insisted.

"Like what?"

"For one thing, your focus. Your tendency to wander off and get muddled down in the issues and problems of what you call daily life."

"As opposed to resist what you're saying and put up a battle – which I know I'd lose anyhow – why don't you just tell me what you mean?"

"See, I told you he's getting smarter all the time," Tresden said.

"Maybe a little. O.K. Listen, if you really want to make spiritual forward progress you need to alter a few things. Adopt a few stylistic changes," Kalista said.

"Like what?"

"I'll give them all to you at once. Then you can think about them and come back when you want to," Kalista said.

"O.K. but... "

"That should be the first one; you never learn anything when you're talking."

"But I do if I ask a question and get it answered."

"Should I go get the boxing gloves for you guys or... "

Kalista and I broke into a hearty laughter. As always, Tresden's humor was the perfect break with exquisite timing. It was neither the first nor last time that Kalista and I would go toe-to-toe over some issue. It was always good-natured and from my perspective, done with total respect. Fortunately, Tresden could always be counted upon to step in and play referee. It was many years later that Tresden explained to me that Kalista actually had great respect for the fact that I stood up for myself now and then and that she thought of me as a worthy student. The compliment went well over my head for many years.

"O.K. I'll shut up," I said with a smile.

"I wish I could find some clever way to arrange all of this advice. Some rhyme that might help you learn and retain it. I have no such arrangement of this guidance. I will though, impart it to you in a way that will allow you to remember it. If it will help you, write it down and put it somewhere that you'll be reminded of it everyday. Some of this may sound familiar because Tresden and I have attempted to convey these things before. That I'm reiterating it now means that you haven't embraced those ideas enough to make a difference, yet. Here we go."

Don't waste energy. The only way to grow spiritually is to conserve your energy and focus it on spiritual learning. There are several activities that drain energy. They are useless endeavors and should be avoided. Anger, hatred, resentment, retaliation, retribution and all things like them are totally negative. They weigh the spirit down and are absolute impediments to moving onward. Each time you indulge in any of these feelings imagine placing a ten-pound weight around your neck. That weight – and all the other weights that you add on by virtue of indulging in similar feelings – stay with you twenty-four hours a day, seven days a week. Forever, even into the next lifetime, until you let go of those feelings.

Practice at compassion constantly. If there is a sure pathway to God, a highway back to Source, that road would be paved with compassion. The act of laying that pavement is equivalent to integrating a compassionate lifestyle in your daily living. Start out with a reminder note to take on one act of compassion on the first day you begin your commitment to grow. Each day, add one more act of compassion to your commitment. Any act large or small will do. When you have arrived at twenty-five acts of compassion in one day you will have integrated compassion as a crucial element of your personal style. From there, the pathway homeward will be evident to you.

Practice forgiveness actively. This is one of the simpler and most productive spiritual practices that people have the most difficulty with. Everyone living an incarnate life is there to learn. Learning involves making mistakes. And even if someone harmed you purposefully, maliciously, thoughtlessly – that too is a mistake and needs to be treated that way. Each time you recognize that you are carrying a grudge or have refused to forgive someone for a perceived wrong, add yet another ten pound weight around your neck. Plan on carrying it with you always, until you afford that person complete and unqualified forgiveness for being human. For making mistakes during their learning as you too have made mistakes. For every person you forgive you can take two ten pound weights off. When you forgive yourself for something you have done, take four weights off. Take a look around you at the people that are really unhappy in their lives. Chances are, if you really look, you'll "see" that they've probably got a few hundred pounds of extra weights around their necks. Learn from this because they have a choice to drag those weights around or free themselves of them forever.

Release completely your fascination and any obsession with "things" especially money. There is nothing wrong, at all, with having money or things. Only in the foolish belief that they matter. Remember, you're not leaving this life with those things and there are no ATM machines in the reality that comes after this one. There are, however, reconciliations and reflections upon the actions you took and the lessons you either learned or failed to learn. When this life is over, that is the only "bankbook" that you will carry with you. And it is that bankbook that will determine what life you lead next time and what "assets" you will go forward with. Therefore, learn lessons, be compassionate and recognize material things for what they are: props in God's play that are leased not owned. All that you will ever truly own is what you learn and what you have done.

Remember always that everyone you know, see, hear of, think about or even imagine is, was and always will be part of the same Source from which you also derived. That Source is pure, perfect and constructed of absolute love and incomprehensible light energy. That means that every person is so constructed as well. This being the case, you have to accept that there are no evil people. There are no bad people. Only people acting badly. People acting evilly. At one time or another we all have done things that we regret. Therefore, look beyond the overt actions of people that offend you and accept that deep within them they too are inexorably connected to God in the identical way in which you are. They will need to face their actions and reconcile them in the same format that all souls do. For that, we should have compassion for what they have done and wish for them as speedy a path to enlightenment as possible.

Source created all things – and imparted awareness to individual souls – with the objective of improving Source itself. Each one of us then is both a delegate of God/Source as well as a child of God. Respect that. Ponder how you want to return home someday; a compassionate, loving soul that has accumulated thousands of entries in their "bankbook" of love, empathy and improving the All or someone that did otherwise? Source/God will – and always has – loved us no matter what we do. That is one of God's essential gifts to us. But our lives, our freedom to pursue our own course is another gift. How will you respond to that? When you return home, and along the pathway toward home — will you embrace and act in a way that contributes to the betterment of the All or will you indulge in acting selfishly?

Kalista's words hung in the air long enough for me to somehow absorb and remember virtually everything she had said. Almost a miracle considering the sheer profoundness of what she had conveyed to me. As with many things that I had learned in Kalista's realm, some of this was partially a reiteration of essential concepts that had been conveyed to me previously and some was a more impact full and concise way of explaining some core idea. It was clear to me that if I could manage to get these down in writing and plot a course to fully embracing them I would be well along the way to walking the pathway of true enlightenment. I was about to comment to Kalista on the beauty and incredible wisdom of the things she had just told me when she began communicating again.

"These assignments would be more than enough for most people to absorb in ten or twenty lifetimes, probably many more. Considering the accomplishments you have made thus far we are hopeful that you will take far less time than that to master these."

"I don't understand Kalista; I thought you always said that the Universe has an eternity for us to learn these things?"

As I said this, I had a panicked recollection of what happened the last time I had visited. The images of the archway at the Hall of Possibilities going black flashed across my mind. Taken with what Kalista had just said to me my mind began to consider the possibilities that maybe the Universe didn't, in fact, have an eternity. Maybe something was or was about to go terribly wrong, and there was now a reason to accelerate my education.

"Well... "

"Kalista, I'm getting the impression that there's something that you're not telling me. That there's some disaster coming our way. You know, the Bible has stories about Armageddon. Just tell me. Please."

"Relax, Chuck. The universe isn't coming to an end. And I doubt that your world is either. You have to understand though, those in the Original Group that came to Earth are all at or near a very critical point right now. They will either awaken in significant enough numbers and begin their efforts to awaken others in larger numbers or they won't.

That leaves the future pathway of your world in some doubt at this point. The concepts I just told you about – the guidance for daily living as it were – are embraced less and less every day. Because of that, many souls incarnated on earth have simply drifted too far away from their recognition of the essential self to find their way home without some help.

"But what does that have to do with me?"

"We told you. Look at your level of awareness. See how far you have come in your determination to attain deeper and more meaningful levels of enlightenment. Like it or not, you are part of the Original Group. The good news is there are others. Many others in that group. Some of them have begun their awakening. Others will require some catalyst. Help of some kind. Something to trigger the basic recollection deep within their awareness."

"Same question, Tresden; what does that have to do with me?"

"You're going to abandon your commitment? Abrogate your mission?"

"I'm not a quitter Tresden. You know that. But what can I do?"

"Well, for one thing, all these trips here aren't helping."

"WHAT? They're helping me a great deal. I mean I'm... "

"Time to use that learning to help others, don't you think Chuck?"

"Are you... I mean, are you telling me that I can't come back?"

"You're always welcome here Chuck, you know that. That will never change. Not as long as you have a need for us to be here. But remember, like everyone else living an incarnate life right now, you are there for a reason. To learn certain lessons. To reconcile past events. And to show compassion, empathy and love for others through practice. In your case though, you have a greater purpose right now," Kalista said empathetically.

Now I was panicking. Geradl's departure felt more like a goodbye than it did a few moments earlier. Now it sounded as if Kalista and Tresden weren't going to be far behind him. In an instant of true recognition I began to see just how dependant I had become on Kalista, Tresden and to a lesser extent, Geradl. They were my solace. My shelter from a cruel, harsh and foreign world where I felt more like a visitor than a resident. Nearly at the same time, I had the recognition that this was most likely exactly Kalista's point. I had become too dependant upon my interactions with Kalista. I wasn't truly living my life in my world; the one where my lessons and mission really were. Somewhat sad and partially resigned I sought out a few more brief clarifications.

"Why can't my learning just take place here?"

"Because Chuck, you took on the mission that you are engaged in now on Earth. Everyone there has done the same. For now, your learning and your contribution must be made there. The fact that you are there is the greatest testament to that."

"You know Kalista, I could just walk out in front of a bus. I'd be back here by this afternoon and you'd be stuck with me."

"Don't even go there Chuck. She'd send you back as a turtle in the Mojave Desert just for thinking about it. Besides, you have a great mission. I'd give anything at this point to take on a challenge like that," Tresden replied.

"O.K., what about the archways going black? I suppose you're going to tell me that bodes well for our future."

"No, I'm going to tell you that unless a substantial number of souls wake up and begin working together to share the word that things are pretty much up in the air there. That blackness that you saw was the archway telling you that blackness is a possibility, maybe a probability, unless some spiritual momentum is applied to counter the current muddiness there."

"It's too big, Kalista. I can't take on the problems of the world. No one can."

"No one is asking you to. But what would happen if you found a way to wake up just one hundred of the Original Group? And what if they all woke up another thousand. And that thousand awakened ten thousand? How long would it take until the essential message was making a meaningful impact on Earth?"

"Well, I guess I don't know that. Can't know that."

"Any possibility that you'll find that out talking to us here?" Tresden answered sharply.

"No. I guess not. But I can come back; I mean, if I need insight. Encouragement. I can come back and find you? You'll still help me?"

Kalista smiled, "You don't need us anymore right now. Everything that you require is inside of you. It always has been. For now, our job was to help you see that you need only look beyond your basic human form, what you perceive as a broken gate, to understand that everything is already within you. Is an innate part of you. All we have really given you is the confidence to see that and the insight to hold on to that understanding. It is time for you to share that with others."

"Kalista, I don't... "

Before I could get anything else out she and Tresden waved goodbye to me. I reached out for both of them, believing that if I could get a hold of them that I could somehow stay just a bit longer. Reap just that much more confidence to take on what I had wondered but now understood clearly as my reason for living this particular life.

Many complex spiritual mysteries and questions remained. Over the course of the next seven years I continued my visits to Kalista's garden, but with far less frequency. Their point about my mission being here, in this world, was not lost on me. The details of how I should accomplish it were though. Now and then I would ask Kalista and Tresden about how *they* would go about accomplishing my mission; what would they do if their mission was awakening one hundred or more of those from the Original Group. People I didn't know and wouldn't vaguely recognize. But they were silent on that account. They smiled at me compassionately. But they remained silent.

Mystified. Frustrated and suffering from self-doubt about how to accomplish that which I had set out to do, I sat down at my computer one day to work and thought I heard the most gentle whisper speaking elegantly to my soul. I believe it was Kalista. I could have sworn that I heard her say: write it; why not just write it all down?

THE JOURNEY CONTINUES

The believer in God must explain one thing;
the existence of suffering.
The non-believer, however,
must explain the existence of everything else.

- Dennis Pragerland/Joseph Telushkin

These days, I lead a life unrecognizable from where I began my search for answers. Looking back, I realize that, at one point, I actually believed that this journey began in August 1993, when my frustration, my inability to comprehend what I was doing in this life at all seemed the greatest. A fool's assumption.

After thinking about it for barely a moment, it became clear to me that the reality is that my journey actually began eons and many life-times ago. Just like everyone else's did. No matter what we might think, or have been indoctrinated to believe when we were children, we're all derived from one Source. One beginning. And since that time when we originally separated from that Source, we've all taken our own individualized journeys. Thus far, they've brought us here. To this place. To this time. Into this form of reality. We intuitively know that we've lost our way, we just can't easily reconnect with the details about how to get back. Along my journey, I learned above all else that we will – all of us – make it back home eventually. But it's our choice how long that will take and how much we choose to suffer until that time.

Still, there's no shame at all that we find ourselves left in school – no mater what grade we might be in as individual souls. Because the truth is, we all separated from the Source-God and came stumbling more or less into this world. Into this form of awareness. At first out of simple and innocent curiosity. Then we made a few mistakes. And then, a few more. When we arrived here, at first, the purity of our souls – what Geradl called "our spiritual naiveté" – left us unprepared to deal with the primitive emotions that we had to adopt as a condition of our souls teaming up with our human forms.

Hate, greed, anger, jealously, fear, the concept of revenge and retribution, and many things far worse, became the bars of the prison that we sealed ourselves inside of with each act that we committed against other souls. We've been beating up on ourselves – and each other – ever since. And to understand whether that pathway, whether the way we do things in our world is working for humanity and the individual souls that reside here or not, you need only look at the morning newspaper, or watch the nightly news or pick up any history book.

As a species, we might be accomplishing all sorts of amazing things technologically. As Albert Einstein said, "it has become appallingly clear that our technology has surpassed our humanity." It is a sad reality that, as mankind, an aggregate of souls occupying this planet for the last several thousand years – purporting to be a civilization – that we're failing spiritually. Failing badly. We strike bargains every day where we mortgage our soul for a few dollars, drachmas, lira, pesos or deutchmarks. Money that will be gone from our grasp in a flash of a lightening bolt in the grand scheme of the Universe. But the things we do – the people we might have run over to get that money – well, those acts stay with us. And for a lot longer than a lightening bolt. We've been doing it this way for a long time and, on the whole, we're not getting much smarter about it.

It was my frustration with this reality and a desperate need to try to find some of the answers that we all long for deep inside our souls – why we even bother to come here in the first place, among them – and the other questions we ask ourselves that we often can't always articulate – that launched me on my journey in the first place.

That boundless emptiness that you can't quite put a name on but feel more often than every now and then; that's exactly the feeling that

I had when I set out. Most people will do anything to make that empty feeling go away or even just subside for a while. That emptiness is our soul trying desperately to scream to our sensibilities over the noise that is our daily world and the titanium wall that is our ego that we're far more than we think we are.

Of the few absolute truths that I can share at this particular point in my spiritual development there is this among them; our true nature, what we really are, is not what you see when you look in the mirror. We are far more than that. That's no more than the masquerade ball mask that we try on for one life at a time. And we'll use all sorts of desperate devices – food, sex, drugs, alcohol, buying new clothes, distracting ourselves with relationships good and bad – absolutely anything to fill in that emptiness we suffer from, even for just an hour. A day. But it never lasts.

The problem is that next week or next month or even the next day comes around and that new car or new dress you bought or the high that the drugs or the alcohol has given you for a few hours aren't satisfying that emptiness anymore. And you find yourself in spiritual pain. Feeling incredibly empty again. Needing to find something else this time to make it go away. Even if it's just for a day. What I learned along the pathway that was my journey was, there is a way to satisfy that emptiness and for a lot more than an hour, a month or even a year at a time.

The fact is, you can obtain relief from that emptiness for all eternity if you want it. But you can't use cash, a credit card or anything that you can touch with your five senses to experience the fullness, completeness, joy, peace and absolute bliss that is the Totality of Your Soul. The boundlessness of your being. The connection that manifests as unconditional love that we all have with the Source-God if only we will reach out for it and remember that it is essentially what we already are. What Gerdal called "aligning with our True Resonance."

My journey has not been perfect and certainly not painless. True learning rarely is. I've made, and continue to make, mistakes and missteps all the time. Not as many as I used to though. Still, there are times that I am not as happy or blissful as you might expect from someone that has been given some of the shattering insights that provide true meaning and comprehension to the purpose of this life and deep perspective on the true dimensions of our souls.

For someone that chose such a painful pathway to learn many of the essential lessons about the realities of the universe and what we need to do in order to make it back home, I am incredibly happy, and most of the time, at peace. It's a very deep and meaningful peace too. The tears I shed now flow almost exclusively from the sheer joy of dancing in the direction of enlightenment as opposed to tears derived solely from pain and suffering.

Not a day goes by that I am not completely awed by what I have learned. Not an hour passes that I am not immensely grateful for my path no matter how much discomfort it has resulted in for me personally. I began this particular lifetime as a badly abused and literally tortured soul. An orphan beaten so badly that the Police had to intervene numerous times to remove me from my environment with stops at the hospital along the way. The temptation to give in to those circumstances and lash out at the world was a battle that required every ounce of will that I could muster. Many, I'm told, would have simply given into the hatred that derives from such histories and struck out at the entire world. I made a choice not to. My choice was to learn from the pain and suffering that I endured and forego having to endure those lessons again.

Sometimes I become frustrated that I have temporarily slid back a notch, or lost my temper at someone going out of their way to make my life or someone else's difficult. Then I take a deep breath and resonate with the truth of what Kalista told me: "there is no failure, only the failure to learn from whatever challenge that we might be facing or enduring at the moment." She's right of course.

The only true losses in this world are when we suffer or endure pain in some way and walk away without learning one of the essential lessons that such opportunities always offer us. We have to remember; we either set that lesson up on our own – ostensibly wrote the script – or, at a minimum, agreed to play our part in it as a tool for our own spiritual learning. Tresden always uses the expression that, "it wasn't God or the Devil that made you hit your own thumb with that hammer." I know what she means is that it's my own thumb and that it is

me who is swinging the hammer. Ultimately, we are responsible for everything in our own lives no matter how much we might not want to own some of what we have created for ourselves. And sadly, sometimes what we have created for others around us that we love.

In this regard I have learned most that, no matter how difficult the lesson might be, if I fail to learn it, I am destined to have to repeat it and the suffering that went along with it. I've learned that it is by far easier to simply accept that, not touching the hot stove the second time is obvious. We all have to understand that touching it in the first place was the lesson. Cursing God or the Devil or whatever your favorite target for misfortune is, won't ever enhance your learning. In fact, it is a sure pathway to failure if your objectives are to eliminate problems from your life and move onward.

The stunning insights that Kalista, Tresden and Geradl shared with me over the first several years of my interactions with them haven't changed the world as much as my perception of what this reality that we call life actually is. More importantly, what we are meant to do here. Had I learned only that in this lifetime it would have been a pretty satisfying outcome for me. I now know that, when I set out on this particular life, I made a conscious choice to take on certain painful difficulties and tremendous challenges so that I could have an opportunity to go beyond understanding just why we're here. It has been my privilege after lifetimes of pursuit, to finally be exposed to some of the insights that go beyond just why and into the *how* we get out of this mess. How we can break the cycles that force us into lifetime after lifetime of frustrating, painful and unhappy circumstances. Whether we're currently playing the victim or the victimizer. The objective must always be to break the cycle. Only in so doing can we begin the process of setting up happier, more loving and more productive futures for ourselves.

The turning point in my life came when I attained a state of insight and understanding where I knew, without a doubt, that we, ourselves, are in control of everything, in both the short and long-term. This goes from what kind of life we lead to what state of happiness we reach to whether we have to come back here and do it all over again. Until we get it right. In short, if you think you're in Hell or going there, you need look no further than the mirror to find the architect of that hell and, more importantly, the gatekeeper that has the keys for you to leave.

For anyone that has such a perception, I can only tell you that in my own way, I placed myself in such situations in this lifetime and following the pathway outlined in this book have been freed of those bonds. Freed forever.

It says in the poem at the beginning of Chapter Seven, "I am the master of my fate, I am the captain of my soul." When you know that at the very depths of who you are, you will hold the key in your own hand to open the door to your eternal happiness and liberation from the cycles that force all of us to return here facing lifetime after lifetime of challenges, suffering, pain and, difficulty. And merely realizing that truth – when you can genuinely embrace it – will afford you such total and overwhelming peace that you will be propelled forward along your **own** journey beyond the strictures and illusions of this life. You will find yourself accelerating toward the magnificence of where we all come from and are destined to return to. It will happen so fast that you'll be back home before you know it. The only thing left in doubt is how much suffering you choose to take on before you get back home. And that too is a choice. Your choice.

In the end, it is our ego that essentially tells us that we can, indeed, make it back to Source if we want to; back to being our part of the "One-Source-God" if we must. But only over its (our egos) dead body so to speak. And oddly enough, that is the only thing that ego ever tells us that is exactly right. Because it is that precise surrender, the letting go of "self" that is the exchange that is required. That relinquishment – the abandonment of the obsession with the "I" – that offers in return absolute and forever peace and happiness. It only requires us to see this lifetime for what it is; barely the duration of a thunder clap in the grand scheme of the Universe.

What we believe we are will be gone from this earth in an instant. But we try so desperately to hold onto that flash that we call a life as opposed to investing in our long-term – as in, forever – existence that we miss the point completely. It's a choice that our ego directs us to make. Forces us into. And we allow it happen. Over and over. Lifetime after lifetime after lifetime. And we suffer lifetime after lifetime for it. Painfully. Cyclically. Needlessly.

You have to make the decision though; this life will be over before you know it and, you're not taking anything with you onward. Well, not anything except your actions, your learning and the outcomes of your intentions. You're going to deal head on with those without any room for equivocation before you know it. When the reality of *that* truth finally occurs to you; when you are able to actualize this essential reality into the life you are living now, you will begin to soar upward and, onward. Back toward your magnificent point of origin. It is the quintessential doosie of a first step. What lies beyond is more absolutely unconditional love, compassion and range of quintessential experiences than you could ever imagine. Or hope for.

Kalista wasn't joking when she said that there were no ATM's in the reality that comes after this one. Most of the things we exhaust ourselves working for and trying desperately to hold onto will be gone from our hands in the scheme of things faster than that bolt of lightening I just referred to. I spent the first forty years of my life listening to my ego trying to tell me that it's all worth it. That driving myself into exhaustion so that I could have more "things" – things that would be gone before I could think about it – was worthwhile. What an incredible waste. Because, until we accept – beyond the limits of just our brain – that we are far more than just flesh and some ideas walking around in a package for sixty or seventy years on this planet, we're destined to come back over again to sort out the mistakes and cycles that we, ourselves, initiate and perpetuate.

Until we realize that simple and essential truth, we will remain prisoners of our own delusion. Jailed within our own self-manufactured folly. One of the most incredible realities of all is that, people cry out desperately for the jailer to come down and release them. They adopt all manner of religious practices seeking redemption and salvation through others. The mistake we make is believing that others have locked us up here. That release must come from some outside "God." This reminds me of the guy who walks up to you asking if you've seen his glasses. Of course, they're right there; on top of his head. They were all the time he was looking for them. In the same way the jailer you're crying out for, is you. The keys to release you from your prison of suffering, emptiness and sadness, right there, within your own hands.

If you come away from this book with nothing else, know that you alone choose to learn or beat your head against the wall. All you have to do is learn without lashing out in anger or embracing retribution at the fact you are in school and, you will begin immediately to move onward. Finding the beauty and perfection in that reality is a tremendous step forward along the pathway toward true and lasting enlightenment. It is the unfortunate truth though that *resisting* that very reality – which one way or another equates to refusing to go to school – is the root cause of most of the pain and suffering that we endure in this world.

I've managed to finally not merely accept but moreover, weave into my daily life the truth that compassion, love and empathy are not, as I was so wrong about when I set out on my journey, destinations that we strive to reach. The reality of the Universe is that love, compassion and empathy are actually pathways that we learn to walk. In truth, the pathways of incredible perfection and beauty that we **must** walk in our daily course of living if we are to advance from here. And when we learn to do that with great consistency and proficiency, it's pretty much time for us to begin the serious part of our journey home. Make no mistake though, some part of the journey home begins and is nurtured right here. Much of what we have to learn in order to rekindle our spirit is based on work that we do here, in this world. There are, unfortunately, no shortcuts to circumvent that reality.

No matter how shattering and awe-inspiring the insights that have been passed on to me have been, the fact that I must accept is that I still live in this world, no matter how much I'd rather be in the reality that comes afterward. The truth that I have no choice but to accept is that I still have lessons to learn here. We all do, or we wouldn't be here. The key to all of it though is to learn the lessons we came here for without making the mistake of getting trapped in more endless cycles that we all start and then perpetuate. We become so involved in revenge, retribution and retaliation that we fail to see that those are the very instruments that construct the trap that keeps us coming back to work it all out.

The way past this is amazingly simple: first forgive and next, forgive yourself. It is not only okay to be human, it is your assignment in the Universe for right now. And being human means that you're going to make a certain amount of mistakes. Accept that. Beyond that, as Kalista said, our ability to break our cycles and not initiate any new ones comes almost naturally when we shift our intent at the basic level of the soul. When we start each day *intending* compassion, empathy and love after a while, you can't help but end the day doing the same thing. And before you know it, you've integrated it into your style. Your Resonance increases. Your perspective and outlook becomes so bright that you will barely remember the old you. Beyond that, I can only say that, it has worked for me and, worked so completely as to make the world and my existence in it unrecognizable from where I was only a few short years ago.

Still, life does tend to throw some amazingly difficult challenges into our path. But we need to understand and accept that those are the very lessons from which we are meant to learn and through which, by mastering those challenges, we can move onward. To a place where there is no anger, greed, war, hate, despair, sadness or suffering. No old age. And no death. No sickness. No pain. Back to where we originated. Where there is only perfection. And true boundless glory without end. And without measure.

All of that is so close to where you already "are" that if I was able to take you by the hand right now and show it to you, you'd be totally shocked that you didn't stumble upon it yourself. You walk past it several times a day. It's right there, just barely underneath the deafening noise that the world creates that distracts you from seeing it. Just past your numbing fear that what you think of as being "you" will die when your body expires. Only around the corner from the belief that, you're not welcome back in God's arms because you left in the first place, even though in the overall scheme of the Universe, that was barely a second ago. And barely across the street from the mistaken thought that we all tend to entertain that we've done things that make us unredeemable or worse, unlovable by the Source-God of all things.

There is no such thing.

All that you seek – everything, all of it; it is there for you to claim. I promise you. It lies... just beyond the broken gate that we somehow convince ourselves that we, as unredeemable souls that have erred, that have made a few mistakes, are. But the reality is, just behind the surface that defines our minor imperfections as human beings, you will find absolute, immeasurable and unending beauty, everlasting love and ceaseless compassion, that we derived from. Every one of us, no exceptions. It doesn't matter what you've done or not done, with your life thus far. Only what you choose to do going forward.

Such unconditional love derives and can only derive from the Source. The Original Center of All Things. The love that lasts eternally and can never be challenged or diminished or abated. Absolute empathy and understanding for who and what you are, have been and have done. Acceptance of anything you might think, do or might do, without condition. Love and acceptance beyond our ability to comprehend at this point in our existences.

To get there, you simply have to remember that, the pathway home begins by recollecting that Source is not something that is simply just inside of you but is, when all is said and done, what you are. When creation occurred, Source reached within to find the building blocks of individual souls, and everything else there is in heaven and earth. And everything else that is outside of heaven and earth left for us to discover and experience on future journeys. All that there is derives from pure Source. That includes you, me and anything else you can possibly imagine. Including whatever comprises the known, the unknown and, the unknowable.

To attain true peace and eternal happiness then, you need only recollect, recognize and begin the process of Resonance with that universal truth and, begin to adopt behavior toward others and, toward yourself that will raise your Individual True Resonance back in the direction of the Source.

From there, well, from there the rest just happens. You wouldn't think so but, it does. And once your effort has begun with earnest determination and purity of intent, a unique kind of spiritual momentum just takes over. It's like a homing beacon the leads you back to your point of origin. And the closer you get, the louder, more enchanting and more blissful the music is. That warm blanket feeling takes over and transports us to levels that can truly, only be experienced. They are that blissful. It's irresistible. And mesmerizing. And, most of all, familiar. It's like hearing your favorite song from when you were in high school only you have to multiply it by a factor that exceeds our ability to even understand. Even vaguely comprehend.

Like all other things in the Universe though, it's a choice. Your choice. And whether you make the choice to look and then to find that truth and point of Resonance within yourself or walk past it, believing there is nothing at all beyond the broken gate that you **think** you see in the mirror, is completely up to you. For the sake of all, I hope that you do find the courage to make that choice. To take that step. To begin your trip home.

In the end, the only victories of consequence are won in the soul.

My journey continues...

Permissions

The author and publisher gratefully acknowledge that the following quotes used in this book were used the with specific permissions granted as cited below.

Chapter Ten: Helen Keller, from *To Love This Life*, © 2000 by the American Foundation for the Blind, all rights reserved.

Chapter Twelve: Albert Einstein with the permission of The Albert Einstein Archives, Jewish National University Library, Hebrew University of Jerusalem, Jerusalem, Israel. The quote was used under the further permission from the publisher, Princeton University Press as extracted from *The Human Side* © 1979, by Albert Einstein, edited by Helen Dukas and Banesh Hoiffman.

The Journey Continues: Dennis Prager and Joseph Telushkin, with the permission of Simon & Schuster Adult Publishing Group as extracted from *Nine Questions People Ask About Judaism* by Dennis Prager and Joseph Telushkin, © 1981 by Dennis Prager and Joseph Telushkin.

All other material quoted within this book falls within the "fair use" standard and/or is already within the public domain. Nonetheless, the publisher and author gratefully acknowledge those quoted for their contribution to the effort through the expression of their ideas through the manifestation of their spirit.